Agon Culture:

Competition, Conflict and the Problem of Domination

Agon Culture:

Competition, Conflict and the Problem of Domination

Claudio Colaguori

de Sitter Publications
111 Bell Dr., Whitby, ON,
L1N 2T1, Canada

Library and Archives Canada Cataloguing in Publication

Colaguori, Claudio, 1964-
     Agon culture : competition, conflict and the problem of domination / written by Claudio Colaguori.

Includes bibliographical references and index.

ISBN 978-1-897160-63-3

1. Power (Social sciences). 2. Competition.3. Social conflict. I. Title.

HN49.P6C64 2011   303.3   C2011-905012-9

Cover design by David Moratto Book Designer

de Sitter Publications
111 Bell Dr., Whitby, ON,
L1N 2T1, Canada

deSitterPublications.com
289-987-0656
info@desitterpublications.com

Table of Contents

Preface vii

Chapter 1 1
Agon Culture: The Problem with Competition as the Organizing Principle of Social Life
Chapter 2 31
The Philosophy of Agonism

Chapter 3 77
The Agony of Domination

Chapter 4 97
Imposed Order as Insecure Order:
A Schema for Domination

Chapter 5 107
The Agon of War

Chapter 6 137
The Agonal Dialectic of History

Chapter 7 157
A Note on Violence, Instinct and the Question of Human Nature

Chapter 8 175
Agonized Consciousness and the Paradox of Self Preservation in a Competitive Culture
Chapter 9 217
Popular Agonism, the Mediagon and Competitive Sport

Chapter 10 247
Conclusion: The Agon – Life under Tension

Notes 253
Bibliography 267
Index 279

This book is dedicated to
Livio Anthony Visano
for his unending support.

Preface

> If, as it has been suggested, terminology is the properly poetic moment of thought, then terminological choices can never be neutral.
>
> ~Giorgio Agamben,
> *State of Exception*

This is a work of critical theory informed by the Frankfurt School tradition of social critique. It is based on the analytic model of Theodor W. Adorno in particular, and it proceeds on the premise that we are living in an age of organized domination – that the basic social problems of the early industrial age have not been resolved, and are in fact intensifying in their gravity and effect on human well-being. Thus, rather than being another commentary on the elaborate writings of Adorno, it takes him up seriously on a suggestion he makes for extensions/applications of the critical theory: In the dedication in *Minima Moralia* he says his thoughts intend "to furnish models for a future exertion of thought." This book does that by continuing the critique of how culture operates as a form of domination and by examining a particular manifestation of culture – which is, the cultural rationality of the *agon*. It is both a study of a type of reification and a new conceptualization of power based on the action orientation of "agonism." The study is premised on the idea that agonism – the cultural *ideology of conflict* – is materially related to the problem of domination; that the social, political and economic order that prevails in the world today is effectively maintained and normalized by a *dominant* rationality, an expression of *cultural* knowledge, one which is based on the philosophy of the *agon*. The agon is literally the arena of competition, the scene of contest, and the locus of adversarial conflict. The philosophy of *agonism* affirms the idea that transcendence, truth and growth are generated from the outcome of the contest. Thus the ideology of conflict is rooted in what is conventionally seen as the positive value inherent in agonistic contest and struggle – where agonism versus antagonism furnishes the ideal model of action that is believed to produce positive/productive results in virtually all aspects of life.

The concept of agonism is most often understood in this affirmative sense as the generative principle of economy, society and even natural ecology and personal growth. Cultural expressions of agonism have numerous manifestations, including economic competition, competitive sport, the military rationality of the state, the adversarial system in legal practice and the view that historical progress emerges from the dialectical unfolding of agonistic contradictions. This study argues that such a conception forms part of the mythology of power that underpins the project of domination operating in the world today. It does not conform to the Nietzschean and now neo-liberal tradition of thought that valorizes agonism as a primary element of political democratic struggle. Rather, this study sees the values of agonism as a form of cultural rationality that legitimates the reproduction of conflict, violence and destruction. As such, agonism is fundamental to the social institutions that reproduce political domination and other forms of human rights violations that continue to predominate in the post-9/11 global market society.

The ambivalent character of agonism is that it is often seen as a mode of transcendence, while its instrumental relation to the mode of destruction is rarely acknowledged. The ideology of agonism has been so prominent a cultural force in the *project of domination* that it has shaped power at the micro-social and macro-social levels. Agonistic forms of conflict underwrite global politics and the perpetual war economies of a globalizing capitalism, and agonism shapes the psychic structure of individual consciousness in the formation of the reified *agonal subject*. Reification is the process through which domination is exercised at the level of subject formation. Reification is discussed in this study as a form of self-incurred psychic defeat – a competition with oneself unto the point of self-defeat. Agonistic thinking, which believes that truth emerges from victory in the contest and from championship in battle, is itself a form of reified thinking, which conflates progress with destruction culminating in the cultural celebration of conflict and violence as instrumental forms of power.

The critique of agonism is thus a critique of competition and championship as an unquestioned value system that supports the order of domination in the current geo-political context. An agon culture is a winner-loser culture – it is both structurally and ideologically reproduced in the incessant celebration and institutional support of competition, sport and violence: a political order that engages in perpetual warfare as its forceful mode of hegemony is one that requires regularized consent in the support for war; and the economic order that is based on the corporate monopolization of resources and that results in scarcity, unemployment and poverty must be made to appear as natural aspects of society. These political and economic forms of domination are justified by an elaborate ideology of agonism – of an ideological order that pits all against all. Thus we see agonistic forms of thinking and practice expressed profusely throughout the spectrum of human culture and society.

The agon, which is the hyper-competitive society that produces domination, conflict and war, is celebrated in the media frenzy of competition programs from sports to "survivor" shows, to shows in which contestants compete for "love" to the odiousness of extreme fighting. Throughout our entire lives we have been infused with a discourse which claims the righteousness, the goodness, the benefit, the correctness of competition. From the competitive exercises inherent in childhood socialization to the ideological proliferation of agonistic clichés in language, to the practice of politics and education and consumption as competitive pursuits – we are constantly encouraged to compete for our own good. In the agon culture, those who question competition are looked upon with suspicion. This reactionary response is certainly a measure of the effectiveness of monumental indoctrination, and a historical blindness to the fact of co-operation has been the saviour of human anthropological ascent.

Agonism is the *primary organizing principle* of the global capitalist order – its most enduring force and most strongly defended cultural mythology – one that gives primacy to the ruling order of competition. Already I can hear the defenders of competition crying that most dangerous of defences, "*But competition and war is all very natural!*" And when pressed further, evidence of this "belief guarded against reflection" is quickly produced: "*In the animal kingdom...*" it starts. And just like that an entire century of sociology goes down the drain, and the naturalization of destruction finds yet another "champion" – all this despite the abundant social scientific evidence to the contrary.

Agonism is a form of power that is promoted by a particular type of dominant rationality arising out of the exaltation of instrumental force. It is the classic means-ends rationality writ large as a cultural mythology. When all reason fails, it is the strongest application of violent force that prevails – this is clear in the observation by von Clausewitz that "war is the continuation of politics by other means." At present, this agonal force, which includes the network of military, technological, ideological, cultural, libidinal, political and economic convergences, is unprecedented in human history. It underpins the continuing *dialectic of production and destruction* that threatens to wipe out the better part of life forms on earth.

The critique of agon culture contained in this analysis stretches from a consideration of the modern origins of agonism in the Western Enlightenment project of the domination of nature to contemporary modalities of agonistic power in popular media and political economy. In typical Adornian fashion, this analysis adheres to the analytic principle of social totality where the Universal is dialectical with the Particular, and thus the agonistic reification of individual consciousness is inseparable from the agonal order of power that drives the project of global domination and war.

****

This study began as a doctoral thesis in the late 1990s before the events of September 11, 2001 provoked a politico-military response that would consolidate agonistic tensions on an unprecedented global scale. A decade afterwards and we are still firmly facing the difficulties of a post-9/11 world. I chose to revive my interest in the issue of "agon culture" because its continuing relevance is proven daily in the intensifications of conflict that appear in the political, economic and cultural realms of society – and also because of the virtual absence of any substantial critique of competition as it relates to power and order in both the scholarly and political literature. What is offered here is a theory of power, one based on the modality of agonism – that is, on the connection between competition-conflict-combat and how this value couplet serves to perpetuate dominating power from the top and also works to interpellate human subjects into conscious conformity with the order of domination.

The need for an agonal critique of society is further warranted in the *extremification* of competitive/conflictual modes of action within numerous aspects of social life. The post-9/11 world order is characterized by intensifications of various forms of *agonistic* power: A reactionary neo-liberalism has intensified what Adorno and Horkheimer (1969) call "the economic mechanism of selection" that increases dispossession, immiseration, class polarization, open forms of corporate criminality and military "exceptionalism" that functions outside the established boundaries of legal conduct; new waves of human rights violations are emerging in the frenzy of fundamentalisms of thought and action; and civil backlashes, global resource pillage, and a growth in the scope and power of the not-yet-redundant military-industrial-complex all combine to form a new ontology of horror that can be named an "agonal order."

This study proposes an agonal model of analysis that can be used to identify agonism at both an ideological level (ideas, culture, entertainment, leisure and play, philosophies, operating rationalities and logics, motivational justifications) as well as the material level (war, state action, law, the labour process, sport, interpersonal difficulties and the litany of competitive activities that exist throughout society):

- An agonal analysis can be used to extend the critique of domination by examining the sociology of the practices of power where competition, conflict, and battle remain prominent features.
- Agonal critique can explain the ubiquity of violence. The use of violent force as a way of resolving difficulties – the so-called instrumentality of violence, the means justifying the ends way of thinking – is a direct rationalization that finds its philosophic basis in the logic of the agon.
- Agonal critique is based on the sociological axiom that we live in a socially constructed reality. It is the system of cultural ideas that shapes our institutions and our life-

worlds. The antagonistic nature of present-day human society is not the product of innate animal drives outwardly expressed. This is a growing and powerful discourse that has overshadowed sociological conceptions of the human condition with biological deterministic categories of analysis, in particular, evolutionary psychological and evolutionary biological ones. This is a dangerous and monumental Spencerian regression of social thought. It is the most classic example of the naturalization of human destruction that threatens to replace critical theory with a vulgar pseudo-Darwinistic Discovery Channel view of the world.

- An agonal analysis can be applied to numerous social antagonisms in gender, class and racialized relations where the competitive/conflictual mode of interaction prevails in the formation of social hierarchies based on competition and exclusion.

- An agonal analysis can be applied to the sociology of institutions in terms of studying how certain persons are able to achieve top positions of power within hierarchical institutions. This process is seen as the "competitive mechanism of selection," with the ideology being that if someone won the competition and made it to the top then they are deserving – regardless of tactics. The competitive nature of power processes within many hierarchical institutions has resulted in the election not of the most able and just to top positions of power, but often of the most power hungry and pathological.

- Agonal analysis can be applied to the reification of individual consciousness to develop a revived social psychology of subject formation in the context of a winner-loser culture where numerous forms of psychic defeat – from suicide to depression to aggressive displays of the self-as-warrior, bullying and narcissism – are subjective pathologies understandable through an agonistic cultural model of analysis.

- Agonal analysis can be used to inform an understanding of various institutional practices including some of the failings of the adversarial legal system where truth is based on the evidentiary contest between legal combatants rather than inquisitorial scientific cooperation in the search for justice as truth rather than justice as conviction. In such a system winning a conviction becomes the goal of the court contestants rather than finding out the truth.

- Agonism is rampant in the political and economic institutions of neo-liberal capitalism. It is the sublime ideology of global capitalist expansion. Critiques of the current imperialist expansion do not question the agonal order of war, sport and championship that helps to authorize the same order of economic domination.

- An agonal analysis of media content and other forms of cultural expression can reveal how the dominant ethic of championship and victory simultaneously perpetuate an order of domination and subjugation, where victimization in such an order can be more easily rationalized as the outcome of the contest as a fair form of social selection because of its presumed naturalness.

This text cannot possibly cover all of these fields of inquiry. It can only touch upon some of them. The main purpose is to introduce the critical concept of the agon into social scientific analysis. It is my hope that this study encourages others to employ an agonal critique of power in their own fields of study so that the resistance to domination can find new sociological grounding. What I also endeavour to accomplish here is the provision of a reconstructed conception of the *agon* that moves beyond its former deployment in studies of democracy and other conventional liberal contexts where the term has been depleted of its critical meaning. As my conception of agonism is informed by Adorno's critical theory, this analysis is a contemporary application of an Adornian critique of domination to the present geopolitical order of power. As such, *Agon Culture: Competition, Conflict and the Problem of Domination* offers a critical analysis of the culture of domination by examining how critiques of power that do not question the agonal order of competition and conflict fall short of being radical critiques of the social totality in their omission of the cultural realm of meaning that is necessary to support social violation, conflict and war.

****

This study is unlike most of the scholarship offered from "critical theory" practitioners (and by that term I mean Frankfurt School critical theory and not the entire gamut of scholarly analysis that claims the title of critical theory). It differs in so far as it does not perform its analysis entirely through the epistemological categories established in the canon of European philosophy. As is implied consistently throughout Adorno's work, social critique is also a critique of knowledge, and that certainly makes philosophical discourse ripe as a text to be analysed for its immanent shortcomings and its potential relation to domination; however, this critique also works through the forms of culture we find in contemporary capitalist consumer society, especially as they are informed by *agonistic rationality*, which is indeed a distinctive form of cultural knowledge. The agonistic cultural form certainly has Western cultural origins but is no longer only Western, since it has been exported almost world wide in the globalization of capitalism – and this takes many forms, including the global corporatization of sport to the liberalization of the corporate marketplace. This expansiveness is indicative of the totalizing thrust of the *project of domination* that so ignited Adorno's sociology of power and the critique of totalization.

Although I am relying on Adorno's critical model insofar is it operates through a critique of reification, and how the ideal of sacrifice gets mobilized subjectively within the project of domination, the writing style is not quite so dialectical as Adorno's (as if anyone could replicate that deliciously epiphantic prose!). Rather, the style is more like that of Herbert Marcuse, who as one French critic remarked, performs an analysis that is "sculpted like bricks," meaning it was too straightforward and blunt, perhaps even too vulgar. I would offer a different reading of such a blunt Marcusian style, however. When it comes to matters of life and death it is best to "speak concretely" (as Deleuze suggested) – critical prose sculpted like bricks will do just fine for me.

This analysis is not a fetishization of Adorno's thought or another short-sighted critique of his presumed pessimism or elitism, or of his impenetrable style, or of how Adorno is too Marxist/not Marxist enough, and so on. This analysis is an application of his conceptual model to one of the ways power manifests in the world today. Not *all* of Adorno's concepts and not *all* of power, of course, but a significant aspect of it, namely: a*gonistic power as a type of reification.* It comes as no surprise, to those who understand Adorno's analysis of power and society, that it is entirely prescient to the order of domination operating in the world today. So why repeat it? The critique of agon culture is not a repetition of Adorno. As Adorno (and Horkheimer) mentioned: "the core of truth is historical" so the critical theory should be adapted to changing socio-historical conditions. Nevertheless, one should not misread such a caveat as saying that social theory has a definite expiry date, as many scholars presume. Although historical conditions have certainly changed since the World War II era, the mode of power that was identified in classical Critical Theory around that time is still very much in operation today, albeit the new authoritarianisms have changing forms, intensities and localities. This study represents a new way of tying critical analytic categories up with current social realities and calling the "substance" of the present power-order "by name." As Adorno and others have remarked, analytic concepts name social realities that otherwise proceed undetected. So he too, like Marcuse, thought it was best to not mince words.

Gilles Deleuze reminded his readers that it is the business of philosophers to invent (and reconstruct) concepts to capture that essence of a social reality that evades mention and thus thwarts collective efforts at amending its problematicity. And as Orwell too reminded: The richness and detail of social reality is captured in the words we assign to name it, and thus social control depends in part on obfuscating perception of that reality. So, the critique of agonism is a type of *conceptual intervention into the problem of domination* – it seeks to name this reality of domination by entering a new term into the critical discourse. Yes, the term "agon" is not new – this reconstruction and application of it, however, seems to be. There is much merit in developing a conceptual analysis that challenges the positively blinding connotations associated with "competition," "contest," "championship," "winner-loser," "triumph," "heroism," "warriorism," "struggle for survival" and the many other celebrated virtues of agon culture. As you can imagine, the list of concepts within the agonal discourse is quite extensive, and many are familiar to us. How and why has such a unified discourse of power (a grand hegemonic narrative in the purest sense) evaded critical scrutiny? It must surely have something to do with the ideological effectiveness that the conceptual thematic of competition-contest-conflict has on the individual consciousness of the social theorist – that is, how effectively so many have been seduced into thinking that agonistic competition is dialectically profound and associated with transcendence or play, or democratic struggle, or just a simple fact of human nature, or even essential to all social orders and life itself. Interrogating these deeply rooted ideological justifications and "beliefs guarded against reflection" will form the basis of this critique.

The concept of the agon is thus the single most exacting way of uniting the expressions of power that contribute to the problem of domination in the world today. All social formations are justified and upheld by particular forms of knowledge, which are thus *ideological.* The principal ideology that upholds the order of domination is the one based on the positive meanings associated with conflict and its many variations: rivalry, contest, competition, championship, warriorism, conquest, and so on. All of these ideals work to justify and maintain the existing order of domination. From the violation of human rights to the perpetuation of war, misery, injustice, including the domination of nature and the destruction of the ecology, we are confronted with an operating rationality that is accompanied by a cultural logic that supports the order of domination. Both of these conflicted tendencies were identified in the seminal critique of domination, *The Dialectic of Enlightenment,* wherein Adorno and Horkheimer (1969) made the connection between the rational impulse towards human emancipation that became coterminous with the rational domination of nature. Their conception of domination includes considerations of human motivation such as the subjective identification with power and those individuals who hold power, and also the problems associated with the otherwise unproblematized cultural values such as "sacrifice" – which really means death, but in popular, religious and most other senses is somehow read as a positive thing, as a gift one gives, rather than an act of reified self-destruction. And that is precisely what agonism is all about – the valorization of the mode of destruction. This valorization takes place through the exaltation of the ideology of *competition*, which is arguably the dominant cultural value system in our society.

Competition is the primary ideology of neo-liberal capitalism. As an ideology it is a form of "false knowledge," meaning it is deceptive and does not produce the promised result of emancipation, economic, personal or otherwise. Competition for resources is no more natural than the equitable distribution of resources – both scenarios are social constructions – it is up to humans to choose which type of world to build. As an operating principle agonistic competition as an equitable selective mechanism is a mythic order. Free competition does not exist in corporate monopoly capitalism in which concentrations of economic power dominate the entire globalization project. "Freedom through competition" and "exaltation of the self through the manipulation/destruction of the other" – these imperatives inform the grand mythology of agon culture. And as Adorno and Horkheimer (1969) indicated, no society can resist being processed by its own mythology.

I want to emphasize a point made in this project, lest it be criticized for being too negative, not hopeful enough, for having a model of power that leaves no room for agency, and other such puerile reactions to the observations of critical theory: The point is that although violence is a formidable element in the strategy of domination it does not always triumph, and that life lives on and life prevails over death. Humans do indeed struggle against the totality of power and against their domination – this is proved every day in so many places around the world and is the real essence of *culture as preservation*. This does not mean that all is well in the end. The problem of domination still remains the central focus of social critique, and there are far too many sites of suffering and human rights violations that need to be brought into focus and ameliorated, and so critical analysis must continue.

The quality and experience of human life is necessarily transformed by the presence of domination and death, and by the manner in which people come to terms with these. Death, which is feared, is precisely that which gets exalted in the reified consciousness of agon culture. In agon culture there are multiple forms of reification. These arise from the primordial fear of death, which the reified consciousness reacts to by honouring it and exalting it in cultural forms from the cult of the warrior hero to vampire eroticism. The cultural condition of mass reification represents the celebration and hence the victory of death in life. This has consequences in the ways we live our lives and are able to make sense of things. Life against death is the ruling binarism that underpins all discourses of power – how this gets formulated culturally is the problem at hand. What at first seems an ontological problem must in the end be reformulated as a phenomenological one concerning the nature of human consciousness formulated in the midst of social domination. And if we are to uphold the preservative essence of culture against domination, then it makes no sense to honour conflict and death while trying to preserve life.

~Claudio Colaguori
Toronto
Summer, 2011

Chapter 1

Agon Culture: The Problem with Competition as the Organizing Principle of Social Life

[The social totality] produces and reproduces itself precisely from the interconnection of the antagonistic interests of its members.

~Theodor Adorno, *Minima Moralia*

The competitive individualism of "in-your-face" incivility... as an essential feature of "market culture" itself... in which the advance of the logic of the market competition insinuates new systems of social classification and evaluation into just about every workplace as well as into the biographies of just about every working citizen... [where] the classification of individuals as "winners" and "losers" [is] a process which... is at the core of the defensive/aggressive individualism which many young people exhibit in a "winner-loser culture."

~Ian Taylor, *Crime in Context: A Critical Criminology of Market Societies*

O urs is an *agonal* society. It is competitively tied to a global economy that is based on a totalizing dialectic of production and destruction – with all of the human horror and *agony* inherent in that order. The *agon* is the space where the adversarial contest is played out. It is the site of conflict and the scene of battle. This agonistic mode of competition forms the fundamental organizing principle of the society as a whole. The hyper-competitive dynamic – which in liberal discourse is celebrated as the motor force of social growth (both historical and personal) – does not arise from the innate constitution of the human psyche that gets outwardly manifested in social forms. It is *not* a function of instinctual, biological, libidinal or evolutionary forces (despite a recent resurgence of such vulgar explanations in the form of evolutionary social science); it is predominantly a *cultural* phenomenon. Hence (and as the title of this work indicates), *Agon Culture* explores how the combative/conflictual system of social organization is rooted in the very forms of cultural rationality that have shaped human history since the dawn of militarized patriarchy about five thousand years ago and has come to define the geopolitics of the current post-9/11 era. This agon culture, which is based on the ideal of contest and competition as productive/generative forms of action, is not an entirely new phenomenon – only its current level of intensification is without precedent. It finds its origins in philosophical elements of classical Greek philosophy, politics and culture, which to no small degree continues to shape the life-world of the present order of power. Although competitive agonism is an organizing principle clearly evident in politics and economics, I argue that both of these are informed by a dominant agonal *cultural* rationality, and thus (with Max Weber) I posit that political and economic structures are upheld at the deepest levels by forms of cultural meaning.

In the essay "Education after Auschwitz," Adorno remarks on the educational need to "change the state of consciousness" that maintains "the horror of our world" (1998: 195-196), a horror which continues to escalate and which, in a previous manifestation, allowed the atrocity of Auschwitz and more recent genocides to occur. And additionally, as I shall argue, this horror escalates through an agonal type of domination as the primary mode of destructive power operating in the world today. This agonal consciousness is tied to an "archaic tendency toward violence" that for Adorno forms part of the rationality of domination in the present – both the domination of nature and of humankind. In "Education after Auschwitz" he writes:

> One need only observe how, with a certain type of uneducated person, his language – above all when he feels faulted or reproached – becomes threatening, as if the linguistic gestures bespoke a physical violence barely kept under control. Here one must surely also study the role of sport, *which has been insufficiently investigated by a critical social psychology*. Sport is ambiguous. On the one hand, it can have an anti-barbaric and anti-sadistic effect by means of *fair play*, a spirit of chivalry, and consideration for the weak. On the other hand, in many of its varieties and practices it can *promote aggression, brutality and sadism*, above all in people who do not expose themselves to the exertion and discipline required by sports but instead merely watch: that is, those who regularly shout from the sidelines. Such an ambiguity should be analyzed systematically. To the extent that education can exert an influence, the results should be applied to the life of sport. (1998: 196-197, my italics)

Adorno is saying a number of things here: 1) sport can signify the virtue of social fairness *and* also promote violence; 2) sport-related violence is also a behaviour found in those who are the observers of sport, and thus the social meanings of cultural rituals extend beyond the immediate actors into the cultural milieu; and 3) the generalized violence of sport needs further critical study. No doubt much has been written on violence in sports and this study is only secondarily interested in the critique of sport per se, that is, only insofar as it is connected to the larger agon of power. The primary focus here is on the rationality that governs the mode of action within competitive sport, a rationality that happens to be the ruling dynamic of social action and also the *architectonic of domination* in the world today: I am speaking of the adversarial contest, the competitive battle, all of which are modes of action epitomized in the philosophy of the agon.

The agonistic mode of rationality of success through victory and championship over the "antagonistic" other is associated with many social and cultural practices, sport being it would seem an obvious and important one, but which nonetheless has evaded critical sociological scrutiny (except for analyses of violence in sport and the functionalist analyses of sport one finds in organizational sociology). I want to take Adorno's call for further study of the double and contradictory articulation in sport to a higher plane of analysis of how this rationality of the contest is inextricably tied to the consciousness that reproduces and maintains the "horrific" domination Adorno's sociological analysis consistently reveals. Furthermore, this analysis seeks to develop a critical reconstruction of the concept of the agon beyond its liberal invocation as the wellspring of democracy, and develop a usage more attuned to its original denotative meaning – which is that brutal competition of physical force is the mode of power through which political control gets established.

Agonal Society – Problematizing the Competitive Mechanism of Selection

Agonism is thus not only an ideology and a rationality that informs material practices, but also a characteristic of the lived nature of social experience and part of the phenomenology of subjectivity; these are all dialectically interrelated as elements of the totality of power. In agon culture, positive valorizations of social conflict such as that exemplified by agonistic conceptions of democracy function to ideologically legitimate the generation of conflict in other areas of social life – just as liberal conceptions of agonism serve as apologias for the order of domination. It is not being argued here, for example, that agonistic cultural rituals and their meanings are directly responsible for *all* forms of social domination in some reductionist and deterministic way, but that the positive philosophy of agonism performs an ideological function which is part of the complex network of dialectical determinations that shape the fabric of a social reality wherein domination and war continue to feature prominently. An agonistic text of meaning imbues social life with specific meanings that enable and encourage certain human actions and limit the possibilities of other actions. Agonistic cultural meanings operate as forms of knowledge that *cultivate* notions of violence and the victorious subjugation of others. As such, there is a thematic and ideological relationship between sports and warfare; between a winner-loser culture and global poverty; between consumerist notions of glamour, beauty and success and reified self-hatred.

Agonism, the philosophy that growth arises through conflict, is not only tied to an ancient mode of dialectical reasoning that is overwhelmingly understood as a positive philosophy in terms of seeing competition as the wellspring of all that is progressive in life, it also is culturally connected to domination. Agonism gets materialized in the winner-loser culture that produces human atrocities from poverty to war. Examining the positive philosophy of competition that agonism represents is a critical-theoretical way of understanding the new intensifications of competitive individualism that arise in relation to the increasing polarizations of economic and social class under neoliberal market societies.

The market logic of "healthy competition" is both at the root of economic domination and at the basis of social inequality and thus paradoxically is this society's grandest mythological contradiction. On television and in the movies the mayhem of social crises from crime to financial meltdown and environmental apocalypse all get depicted as a moral dilemma of good versus evil, and the problems of unequal social structure, corruption and social class disparity get mystified away in a world of cops, drug dealers and drug users, street criminals, and CNN newsreels about a few bad apples and conspiracy theories... and then the sports news comes on as if it is a matter of relevance in a world of crisis. Well, sports *is* important – it reminds the viewer that oh-so-necessary competition produces winners and losers and "that's just the way it is," so enjoy.

This generalized mode of competition manifests itself in the generation of social reality in various problematic ways: competition as the mode of organization produces social structures where individuals compete for status and control. In bureaucratic institutions people vie for power in their desire to move to the top of organizational hierarchies, and those who make it to the top and occupy "leadership positions" are not always the nicest human beings or the best qualified to make decisions involving the lives of others. In the political spectrum in terms of competitive democracy the same theme applies. In electoral competitions, those who gain power through competition are seen as having gained their positions through a legitimate vetting process, because rulership was attained through the competitive mechanism of selection. What is achieved through competition is somehow justified as fair and legitimate. Even if there is blatant underhandedness and corruption, the victory is justified because the tactics are further evidence of the prowess of the victor who, it is hoped, can mobilize their cunning in the service of the public interest. This rarely happens – instead they help themselves, and those who assisted in their minor Machiavellianism.

Agonal society is also manifest in the economic realm in terms of how those who hold (have competitively attained) economic power are justified in their position because they have achieved it through what is touted as "free competition" – the "economic mechanism of selection" that Adorno spoke of is in operation again. It is a mechanism that is celebrated as being a natural and equitable filter among contestants in the "game of life" – even if it operates on a cunning of reason which does not play by fair rules but nevertheless produces a victor. It is often assumed that competition is a fair and equitable mechanism of social selection and that the results of the contest can be trusted. This is a belief that persists despite overwhelming evidence that competitive systems are horribly corruptible – from steroids and payoffs in sports to espionage, dirty tricks and lobbying in politics, to unfair trade practices, rackets, cartels, corporate bullying and legal manoeuvring, bribery and collusion to achieve market dominance in the business realm. This agonistic warfare is more than simply "the antagonistic interest of social members seeking out their own self interest" – this is a system of corrupt hierarchical power co-ordination that emerges precisely through the mode of competition which then justifies it as ethically sound.

Culture and Domination

This study of agon culture is a critical analysis of contemporary culture and the problem of domination. "Culture" is not generally thought of as a form of domination. Rather, cultural knowledge and tradition is something that is coveted precisely as a defence against life difficulties, oppression and the hostile forces of domination. Culture is more often seen as having an "affirmative character"[1] to it and is conventionally understood as being a positive force, one that enables, sustains and informs the course of human life. Thus the traditional usage of the term "culture" denotes an ethic of preservation and care, as in "the tending of something" (Williams 1976: 87). The critique undertaken in this study extends beyond this traditional understanding of culture as self-preservation to look at how its function has become transformed into the opposite of affirmation – how culture, in the epochal shift towards a post-9/11 global order, has become reformulated to maintain the competitive military capitalist economic and political order, thus becoming the principal medium through which domination is exercised.

Culture, however, is certainly not only about the repressive mediation of power. In terms of understanding human life, it is the sacrosanct realm of being and experience. As such, human culture is the most remarkable expression of life on earth. This is important to consider in terms of the *reification of culture*, in terms of how the realm of preservation, which culture represents, gets subverted to serve an order of domination.

What is being referred to as "global culture" is today increasingly becoming an expression of the imperialism of the globalizing corporate capitalist project of power and order. This is a project out of which many contemporary forms of domination and destruction are generated, including "the destructiveness of the new globalization process" (Jameson and Miyoshi 1998: 64). Culture, in such a context, is integrally related to the forces of production and the forces of destruction. Thus, in the contemporary reformulation of culture into *agon culture*, as Theodor Adorno writes, "the mechanism for reproducing life, for dominating and destroying it, is exactly the same, and accordingly industry, state and advertising are amalgamated" (Adorno 1974: 53). Within agon culture competition and conflict are simultaneously the sublime sources of cultural meaning as well as the structural forces of domination and destruction.

The concept of *agon culture* – which is that our society is organized around competition and conflict and that these are primarily understood as unproblematic value orientations – is the main focus of this study. It is also the analytic theme around which the multiple manifestations of contemporary domination are identified in this study. As a preliminary definition, agon culture refers to the rationality of power and order where competition, conflict, violence and war form part of the dominant systems of meaning through which everyday life is organized and social interaction takes place. These values of agonism support both the entertainment pleasures of the consumerized public as well as the destructive horrors of the perpetual war economy. Competition is the prime value that runs through the organizational structure of agonal society and works to augment the antagonistic bases of the political, economic and cultural orders. Agonism, which is based on the value of competition and conflict, is further celebrated through the litany of popular cultural texts that present conflict, combat, predation and championship over the other as authentic techniques of transcendence. The value of agonism is also tied to struggle, victory, conquest and domination as the means for the generation of justice and truth.

Of specific interest to this study, therefore, is a set of values based on the cultural normalization of conflict that will be herein referred to as "agonistic values." These include:

- competition and conflict;
- adversarial contestation;
- championship as conquest;
- domination and subjugation; and
- violence and destruction.

These values lie at the generative foundation of agonal society as well as forming the basis of domination within the order of agon. Agonism as a process involves the competitive-conflictual orientation of social action as well as the subjective internalization of agonistic reasoning as the mode of thought that informs the inter-subjective engagement with others. More importantly, agonism, in terms of open competition, adversarialism and "healthy" rivalry, is the primary *organizing principle* within the contemporary political and economic order. We shall examine these more closely later in this text as elements which constitute the social totality.

The critique of agon culture is concerned with the extent to which domination, exploitation and suffering have become

normalized in the aggressive intensification of global consumerism and the political-military apparatus which accompanies
it. The central problem is that agon culture is increasing in its colonization of contemporary culture, and it is maintained as a functional strategy in the reproduction of a larger geopolitical order
of social and economic organization and control. In this agonal
system of order the ideologies of consumerism, liberalism and
capitalism are reinforced by the coercive power of techno-mili-
tarism and are significant dimensions in the operationalization
of power. The violence of agon culture, which is the ongoing violence of human history, has not been reduced in the sense implied
by the concept of the "progress" of society, but has in fact significantly intensified with the passage of time and is actually
what is affirmed and produced within agon culture. Agon culture
is also, therefore, the culture of violence. How can it be that the
same principle that is thought to produce dialectical growth, truth,
transcendence etc. is at the same time also the principle at the
basis of most forms of human-made destruction?

Such a mystification of power is possible because of the
allure of competition as the grand explanatory theorem that links
the patterns of human life to the life of micro-organisms and the
workings of the cosmos! Like the religious conception of God,
or the physical conception of ether, it is an idea that explains
everything and nothing; such teleologies are of no analytic value
for the empirical world. The ideal of the agon and the universal
order of competition it promotes is the great harmonizing mythos
where the politics of right and left come together, where human-
constructed capitalism finds it analogue in the natural order of
the "eat or be eaten" animal world (another myth as well). Such
an ideological unison is surely a sign that something is amiss, for
the major ideal type – that of liberalism and its promotion of freedom through competition – becomes the meeting point of an
almost universal consensus. Neitzsche's valorization of the agon
is more of the same tough talk that led to facile appropriation of
his ideas by the forces of doom – despite his many displays of
critical brilliance in life his thought succumbed to sexism and
vulgar racial categorizations of social groups. In Nietzsche too
the psychology of insecurity also attached itself to ideals of power
and authority in an effort to elevate itself – this form of associa-
tive mimicry is an element of reification – a topic we shall turn

to in more detail later in the text, and the major strategy of cultural domination in the agon.

****

Culture, in the context of the agonal order, has been thrust into the service of domination. Thus the expression of political power is dialectically related with the dominant "popular" cultural discourse as well. Therefore, *hegemonic* culture, which is the culture supportive of domination, contains three distinct institutional manifestations which Jacques Derrida (1994) lists and which are essential hermeneutic fields of interpretation in the critical theory of culture. Together they constitute the integration and intensification of the ideational forces of politics, economics and the culture industry within contemporary agon culture. Derrida explains this in three ways:

    a. There is first of all the culture called more or less properly political (the official discourses of parties and politicians in power in the world, virtually everywhere Western models prevail...)

    b. There is also what is rather confusedly qualified as mass-media culture: "communications" and interpretations, selective and hierarchized production of "information" through channels whose power has grown in absolutely unheard-of fashion...

    c. There is finally scholarly or academic culture, notably that of historians, sociologists and politologists, theoreticians of literature, anthropologists, philosophers, in particular political philosophers, whose discourse itself is relayed by the academic and commercial press, but also by the media in general...

These [cultural] apparatuses... communicate and cooperate at every moment toward producing the greatest force with which to assure the hegemony or the imperialism in question. (Derrida 1994a: 52-53)

Agon culture is not a distinctive expression of culture (or subculture) that exists on its own as if somehow separate from the dominant culture. Rather, agonism is the dominant cultural rationality and thus is located within the fields of culture Derrida identifies as well as the institutional structures that administer society. Agonism therefore forms part of the historical text of meaning within contemporary culture. It finds its most caricatured expression in the mass-media promoted culture industry – what I refer to later in this study as the *mediagon*, in which representations of competition and conflict constitute one of the largest themes within mass media entertainment.

Adorno and Horkheimer's original analysis of "the culture industry" as the instrument of mass deception and social control (1969) is vindicated every day in the perplexing display of television shows based on nonsense and "rubbish," with an ideological subtext that needs to be taken seriously for the way in which ideological power operates in the agon culture. It should be recounted that such a critique is not a moral one – it is based on content analysis and cultural effects. Whether we disapprove of *The Jerry Springer Show* or *The Bachelor*, or the *Ultimate Fighting Championship*, or *Iron Chef* or *Fear Factor* or any competitive sport for that matter… (the list is not exhaustive), the theme is consistent and blatant: the need for competition as the strategy for results, and conquest over the other as the mode of transcendence and as the mode of entertainment and ecstasy. No doubt the bulk of television is profoundly anti-social scientific. This is obvious even to those who glibly discount Adorno and Horkheimer's early observations that the culture industry within technological capitalism was quickly defining itself as anti-enlightenment. This critique of *agon* culture extends upon that initial critique of culture in a number of ways. Ultimately, agonistic forms of entertainment lapse into the celebration of death: They promote transcendence through battle, self growth through sacrifice, the promise personal exaltation through the destruction of the other, which often results in the destruction of self. All of these are the hallmark of reified consciousness.

Competitively themed elements of culture, especially organized sport, have been a standard in popular culture for ages. What is unique today is this hyper-agonistic formation where everything can be processed anew under the mode of competition. I see the intensification of agonstic forms of culture rising alongside intensifying political and economic antagonisms. The post-9/11 political condition we are currently in is a power formation, of which the nearest historical parallel is the European fascism preceding World War II. All the elements are in place – from a new authoritarianism coupled with increasing public despair and corresponding escalations of wealth, poverty and war. Nevertheless, the historical differences from the past are also worth noting. The present era lacks any unified class consciousness on a mass scale. And the social solidarity that should normally accompany a state of war and unite a nation is also mostly absent – "asymmetrical warfare" is accompanied by an asymmetrical group consciousness. The counter-hegemonic consciousness that *does* exist is to be found in the radicalized, disconnected and maligned anti-globalization protest groups who come in and out of focus during publicized political gatherings and then disappear into a void of media misrepresentation – even there it is doubtful if counter-hegemonic political consciousness is able to escape agonistic forms of rationality.

The present era magnifies the propaganda efforts used by adversaries in World War II and makes them seem puny in comparison to the technological-media-culture nexus. The latter has so formulated public consciousness that it now openly glorifies in death. From vampire eroticism to Goth culture to history-buff Nazi war fascination to the extremification of boxing that is now the gruesomeness of mixed martial arts – the *mediagon* incessantly celebrates the thrill of competition and the spectacle of death. There is no alter-ontology offered in the media spectacle of the culture industry, no new possibility or transformative impulse, nothing approaching what Adorno would call an "autonomous cultural aesthetic" that runs counter to the totalizing rationality of reifying control that was already apparent in the early outlines of the culture industry. Thus the mediagon is the ideological centre of agon culture at the level of popular consciousness.

The Culture Industry and Hegemony

Adorno and Horkheimer identified the culture industry as one dimension of domination within the larger project of the domination they associated with the trajectory of the Western social, philosophical and scientific Enlightenment. Adorno writes:

> The total effect of the culture industry is one of
> anti-enlightenment, in which enlightenment, that
> is the progressive technical domination of nature,
> becomes mass deception and is turned into a
> means for fettering consciousness. It impedes the
> development of autonomous individuals who
> judge and decide consciously for themselves.
> (Adorno 1991: 92)

Rather than producing affirmative forms of cultural knowledge, whereby individuals can develop the level of critical awareness necessary for an enlightened existence, the culture industry works towards the obfuscation of social and personal understanding. It co-opts the affirmative dimension of culture by offering the subject social integration, recognition, pleasure and leisure. These, as we shall explore below, are often thrust into the service of a regressive function and work against the self-realization of the individual.

The culture industry, "which intentionally integrates its consumers from above" (Adorno 1991: 85), also speaks of the eclipse of the diversity of human cultures by a synthetically produced form of culture that, contrary to cultural formation throughout history, does not emerge from the people in a self-conscious way as the expression of indigenous effort and knowledge oriented towards the preservation of life. Rather, it is produced via a top-down approach in which a consumerist world view has been inculcated into public consciousness.[2] This is contrary to the traditional idea of a mass culture as "something that arises spontaneously from the masses themselves" (Adorno 1991: 85).

The term "the culture industry," however, was originally employed as an ironic term, and is one which today has been institutionally appropriated and circulates at face value in reference to the business of producing pop culture. All that is produced by the culture industry, no matter how offensive or trivial, is justified in the name of business. Adorno and Horkheimer write, "movies and radio need no longer pretend to be art. The truth that they are just business is made into an ideology to justify the rubbish they deliberately produce" (1969: 121). The undeniable industrial and commercial interests that are behind the cornucopia of "cultural products" the public receives as items for popular consumption in the form of films, music, news, endless commodities, travel, and fashion items, among others, "it is claimed... [are] based in the first place on consumers' needs" (1969: 121); they exist because it is said they satisfy a genuine demand on the part of the consumer and have thus survived the "economic mechanism of selection" (1969: 122).

Adorno and Horkheimer were somewhat apologetic about their scholarly interest in the newly emerging consumer/entertainment culture of the mid-1940s. They had initially conceived their task of the critique of the Enlightenment as one to be conducted on the basis of exploring philosophical issues. That something as self-evidently trite as the commercialization of popular entertainment should merit critical consideration was based on the insight that the power of cultural representation was becoming the form of dominant power over *consciousness* – which was something fundamental to Enlightenment. Through the culture industry, "Enlightenment had regressed to ideology," one "which expends itself in the idolization of given existence and of the power which controls technology. In the treatment of this contradiction the culture industry is taken more seriously than it would implicitly require" (1969: xvi). What Adorno and Horkheimer were able to discern at a time when the culture industry and the media apparatus was still in its infancy (circa 1944) was the potential of this new mega-institution in its power to shape communication, culture and consciousness in a way that served the interests of both political economy and social domination against the interests of the individual.

What the term "the culture industry" was once intended to draw attention to by means of exaggeration has since become a reality – meaning that culture *is indeed* the product of corporate interests. Culture is no longer an indigenous formation but has become the product of industrial design, manufacture and sale. This transformation of culture is thus part of a historical trend identified as the commodification of culture (Marx). The process of the commodification of Western urban culture into capitalist consumer culture is thus a form of *social technology* that was made possible through the modern instrumental means of cultural production. As Raymond Williams noted that "the invention and development of the material means of cultural production is a remarkable chapter of human history" (1981: 87), one made possible through the power of modern technological communicative media. While the development of the technological media apparatus created the potential for new social freedoms (Benjamin 1969), it simultaneously became instrumental in the extension of social and political control into the populace at large.

The necessity of conflating culture with the realm of politics as a strategy of the power of domination was already evident in Karl Marx's notion of "mental production" (1964). Adorno and Horkheimer's idea of "the culture industry" developed from Marx's insight into knowledge as a form of power and further indicated how the mass dissemination of public information had regressed into ideology. While Adorno and Horkheimer went on to develop Marx's insight into the "centrality of "illusion" as one of the new forms by which reality is obscured in late capitalism," they departed from the problematic Marxian analytic dichotomies of base/superstructure and capitalism/socialism, and were able to formulate "the problem of ideological domination without any reference to class-consciousness, alienation, hegemony or legitimation" (Rose 1978: 140). In doing so, Adorno and Horkheimer established a new centrality for the social and political significance of culture and in particular for how culture was to become the new frontier of hegemonic power in late capitalism.

The critique of the power of ideology to promote illusion in the production of the hegemonized subject forms the basis of Adorno and Horkheimer's (1969) critique of "mass culture as mass deception." Exploring the problem of domination through the critique of representation has a substantial intellectual history to it, one pertaining to the problem of the relationship between illusion and reality, and stretches back at least to the philosophy of Plato, in particular to his allegory of the cave.[3] Through their conception of "the culture industry," Adorno and Horkheimer (1969) explored the modern manifestation of cultural representation precisely as a primary new form of cultural power over people, not one by and for them.

The contemporary culture industry is but one dimension of the larger *communicative order of control* (O'Neill 1991; Marcuse 1964) associated with the realization of mass society and the production of a mass consciousness that became increasingly possible through the development of new media technologies. Through the dissemination of images, discourses and public narratives, the new electronic communication apparatus was able to construct and maintain various cultural mythologies that served as the texts of meaning in a consumer-oriented popular culture. Today the corporately owned and controlled mass media continues as the most active agency for the dissemination of ideas in the regulation of perception for the augmentation of public conformity to order.

The idea of a "mass society" as a modern reinvention of the polity is emphasized in a number of traditions of thought, from classical sociology to contemporary communication studies (Mills 1956; Lasswell 1949; Adorno and Horkheimer 1969). If the tendency for social thought to be informed by a theory of power based on dominant cultural production has waned in recent times, it is not because of such a theory having been rendered historically invalid, but because of an overarching network of reactionary ideologies which have effectively altered the way people think about the communicative apparatus of contemporary consumer culture as an extension of the "freedom" of the individual. As established social theory continues to fall prey to the march of a "forward looking" intellectual production and to the indomitable idea that established social theory should be constantly replaced with new theory, it has become unfashionable to question the problematic authenticity of popular culture and its false consciousness. Cries about "the end of ideology" have more to do with the relation between dominant discourse and dominant social processes (that construct diachronic forms of truth to serve specific vested interests) than the elimination of political conflict: It is the absolute audacity of dominant ideology to claim that the world has now entered a post-ideological era. If the cultural-political sphere today seems to be less characterized by a division of opinion on matters of democracy and economy, this is not because dissent against the dominant order has ceased to exist, but rather this "consensus" speaks about the totalizing effectiveness with which the techno-cultural web of ideological control has attempted to monopolize public consciousness.

The theory of "mass society," as it has been named outside of critical theory, sees mass communicative cultural power as a most formidable type of social control. Through its discursive mechanisms, the new electronic technologies of mass media, a substantial portion of society is effectively socialized into behaving in ways that render them subservient in relation to the totalizing dictates of communicative power. This "mass society" view, which readily recognized the power relation between media and culture at the beginning of modern communication studies (Lippmann 1922; Innis 1991; Adorno in general), has been passed over in favour of the more "optimistic" view, the one that celebrates the fusion of culture and technology as part of the aestheticization of modern techno-power as well as the mode through which the liberation of the individual will be realized. Marshall McLuhan's (1964) theory of communication, for example, which entails the aestheticization of technology, represents an enduring example of this paradigmatic rivalry. In McLuhan, the popular ideal about information technology and its so-called democratizing potential is contained in his seductive concept of the "global village:" Through the creation of a vast electronic global-media sensorium, with an efficient messaging ability capable of transcending space and time, modern mass communications systems would prove to be the tie that binds disparate nations and peoples. This connective development in media technology would finalize the implosion of distance and time (considered to be the great barriers to human communication, trade and social progress), and make the world akin to an inclusive village with its community of instantaneous free exchange, social familiarity and harmonious self-regulation. The capacity to transcend cultural and geopolitical boundaries was to be achieved through the electronic sophistication of global communication systems and would result in a humanizing "retribalization" of the earth's variety of peoples. This innovation of cultural technology would supposedly mark an evolutionary development in the human species.[4] The harmonizing appeal of McLuhan's techno-anthropology served to rewrite the politics of communicative empire in the triumphal discourse of communicative freedom and global belonging. Raymond Williams' dismissal in the 1970s that "the particular rhetoric of McLuhan's theory of communication is unlikely to last long" (1974: 128) came too early to anticipate the zeal with which postmodernism and positivist strands of globalization theory would fully embrace formalist ideals of communication that obscure the workings of power and so would form the basis of a communicative imperialism within the globalization of culture.[5]

   The dominance of "optimistic technological determinism," which emphasizes the ideal of the "global village" over the

reality of increasing global domination, serves as part of the mystification of what is actually taking place within the project of
the globalization of consumer capitalism. O'Neill writes about
the communicative power to distort reality through the presentation of the consumer world of things and its obfuscation of the
underlying political and economic reality upon which consumerism depends. He writes: "*The specular function of things
– their symbolic proliferation, unbounded by space and time,
their instant and imaginary availability – is to make modern political economy impossible to understand*" (O'Neill 1991: 179). The
situation of the globalization of media and the power relations it
standardizes is part of the *specular* functioning of the media in
terms of the representation, transmission and hence the normalization of cultural mystification. The political economy underlying the situation of globalization and to which the euphemism
"global village" is applied at one level correctly refers to an intensification of global relations (via the expansion of the capitalist
marketplace), but not a global community that is decentralized,
non-hierarchical and village-like. Nor is the newly emerging
global formation of power one which is characterized by a net
improvement in the standards of living for the majority of peoples
on the globe. Rather, it is characterized by an increasing *globalization of exploitation;* by a new form of imperialist order that
maintains itself, through the order of consumerism, through the
discursive re-invention of the capitalist marketplace, and through
a new discourse based on consumer choice, democratic freedom
and military security. This international discourse of beneficial
dependencies is coupled with various inter-state arrangements
that serve in the neoliberal project of corporate globalization.
Tying this all together is the supra-agonistic apparatus of the military-industrial project of control – the unrelenting war machine
that underpins the project of cultural domination through the use
of destructive force. What is transpiring in the name of capitalist
globalization, therefore, is in effect, a new totalizing form of
"hegemony" (Gramsci 1971).

"Hegemony" is a concept that pertains to the consensual
normalization of control over the citizens in a given society, and
it is one of the forms of power operating within the order of domination identified in this study of agon culture. As "hegemony"
will be a consistent undercurrent in this book it shall be defined

provisionally as a process involving the ideological formation of political perceptions which serve the interests of ruling elites, those who stand to benefit from the political and economic order of society. Antonio Gramsci (1971) developed the concept of hegemony to refer to a form of ideological power that marked a historic transformation in the relation between ruler and the ruled. His thought is a continuation of the Italian tradition in political theory founded by Niccolo Machiavelli (1952) who saw the politics of rule as nothing less than muted warfare.[6] Theorizing on Machiavelli's distinction between political governance through the instilling of fear among the citizenry or alternatively through the cultivation of respect for the leaders, Gramsci indicated that respect, awe, admiration and the love of power and "leadership" were coming to define the character of twentieth century democratic-political control.[7] Machiavelli insisted that given the choice between the two, fear would prove to be the most effective strategy of control. But this measure grew incompatible with the "enlightened" character of the modern state which disguises its tyranny through the various mechanisms of coercive consent. This included "ideological hegemony" and other modes of legitimation wherein the citizen shares in the power of the state, as for example, through constitutional rights and guarantees. Although

> the term "ideological hegemony" derives from Gramsci, it describes an important aspect of capitalism to which Marx drew attention: the capacity of the dominant class to rule not only by its control over the means of production but by its control of *ideas*. (Lee and Newby 1983: 132).

According to Jere Surber, hegemony organizes

> an entire ensemble of cultural formations, including education, the organization of family life, associations in the workplace, religion, and popular culture, [which] work together to infiltrate the daily private lives of individual members of civil society, producing a texture of beliefs and relationships that guarantee the allegiance of the individual to the state. (Surber 1998: 86)

Gramsci was particularly disturbed about the rise of popular fascism in Europe in the 1930s: "He was struck by the resilience of the modern state in commanding the allegiance of its populace in the face of severe economic dislocations and crises" (Surber 1998: 86). However, hegemony, as a form of ideational power that dictates political opinion and social awareness, was for Gramsci not a problem in itself. From the standpoint of revolutionary politics the problem emerges with respect to those who possess that power and how they use it to govern. In the discourse of proletarian revolution, for example, when the subaltern classes take power they too are required to resort to hegemonic forms of governance. Securing popular hegemony is a requirement for the formation and control of a new social order. Thus in Gramsci's conception, hegemony forms a necessary part of the modern political organization of society. He describes the modern "State as force plus consent" (Showstack Sassoon in Bottomore 1991: 230). However, Gramsci did not problematize the concept of "hegemony" as a component of rule that is necessarily repressive, but referred to it as a functional instrument of political power and governance, as did Marx. This reasoning follows directly from the revolutionary ideal in Marx that called for the "the dictatorship of the proletariat" where the issue becomes that of who has possession over the power to rule, while the problem of the dictatorship itself is left unproblematized. Gramsci was concerned with hegemony as an instrument of revolutionary politics, and not explicitly concerned with the extent to which ideological hegemony would become the primary mode through which political power would disguise an ever-growing modern tyranny.

Although the political legitimacy of hegemony was not problematized as inherently repressive in classical Marxism, in this analysis the term "hegemony" is used to refer specifically to the *repressive functioning of ideological control* that is characteristic of the new totalizing aspect of agonal power, one that stretches into the very formation of culture. What is being identified here in terms of the contemporary project of domination is the scope of hegemony in contemporary agon culture: the extent to which people have been so thoroughly *hegemonized* that their allegiance to order is no longer merely a matter of a dull conformity to the status quo as such, but rather that ideological-hegemonic control has extended into the very formation of consciousness and towards the affirmation of subjectivity. Hegemony succeeds not by coercion but through consent. It can therefore be characterized as a form of "soft control" – in contrast to the forms of "hard control" (military and para-military forms of coercion) which nevertheless work in tandem with each other.

****

If there has ever been a strong relationship between culture and domination, it has been in the context of imperialism. The predominant way in which culture has been historically understood as a form of domination is through theories of imperial contact whereby traditional, indigenous culture is forcibly replaced by an imposed foreign culture. Cultural domination in the order of consumerism is related to this notion of imposition but takes another form – one that pertains to the simultaneous "loss of meaning" resulting from the atomization of social relations under industrialization and the subsequent fabrication of new meanings that worked to sustain a new consciousness of consumption.[8] The imperialism of culture today thus is not so much about colonial rule as it is about hegemonic rule. Hegemony involves political and cultural control by consent to dominant power and thus differs from colonial domination and its forcible imposition of otherness onto a people and the consequent destruction of indigenous culture. In the *hegemonic* order of contemporary agon culture, domination is normalized because it attaches onto (colonizes) the "affirmative character of culture" in ways that reinforce patriotism and consumerism as extensions of the subjective pursuit of self-interest.

It is precisely the hegemonic dimension of contemporary cultural power that ties cultural domination to a neo-imperializing process. Hegemony involves the "manufacture of consent"[9] as a form of rule – a process which works to produce political control through the "integration" of individuals into accepting and identifying with the authority of the state and its monopoly over power as a means of eliminating dissent. The project of the construction of consciousness in mass society through hegemonic mass communications is intended to augment predictable modes of behaviour and so to increase the level of conformity to modes of repressive governance. As Ralph Miliband writes,

> In many regimes the men who control the state have found it necessary to rely on the continuous and systematic repression of all or most manifestations of opposition for the maintenance of their power and for the preservation of the existing social order. (Miliband 1973: 161)

Although hegemony remains a part of imperialist control, it disguises its mechanisms in the form of culture. Hegemonic cultural power is realized in the ability to generate public consent to the dominant project of power – this is contemporary imperialism's[10] most insidious quality: that the mode of oppression by which contemporary empire operates is no longer something that is naked and visible, and which can thus be avoided by virtue of recognition of its exercise of power. Old empire was "less 'ideological,' in so far as it openly proclaimed the principle of domination that is [today] concealed" (Adorno 1974: 108). In the empires of the past, the state and the people remained separate entities, and the people feared the power of the state as it was often used against them in public display. The spectacles of public torture and hangings in the town squares served to remind the people that the power of governance was coterminous with the power over life and death. Today agonal states parade their military tanks and high-tech weaponry in the name of a National collective might.

Today the people, who have been reconstructed as the democratic citizenry have become increasingly integrated into the nation-state apparatus of power by virtue of public consent, and thus drawn into accordance with the dominant rationality of an empire which proclaims to have distanced itself from former historical barbarism and is now continuing its "civilizing mission." Citizens who have been successfully "hegemonized" firmly believe that the tyrannical nature of political governance has mostly disappeared. Instead of exercising control through overt tyranny, the contemporary nation-state-empire formation solicits consent through the creation of the illusion that individuals have a share in its power, where the belief is that to be one with the system is to be on the side of victory and strength – this bond forms the ideological basis of nationalism and patriotism.

Such forms of agonistic integration play on the false belonging that is part of national consciousness[11] and also speaks of the mimetic identification with mastery that is part of the master/slave dialectic of domination (Hegel 1931). In fact, citizens have been so effectively socialized to be in accordance with the dictates of empire that a new type of *agonal consciousness* has become the dominant cultural mode of belonging and being.

The process of the ideological construction of the subject which is made possible through the modern technologies of mass media pertain directly to what Adorno and Horkheimer (1969) referred to as the project of "mass deception," one of the primary features of how the present configuration of empire differs from previous empires. This ideological power inscribes itself into the cultural consciousness of individuals more so than ever before. Loyalty to domination is the strongest form of control – it is the hegemonic control over subjective desire. Through the intensification of values pertaining to allegiance, the love of power, and the correctness of technological and "civilizational" imperatives, social integration into forms of cultural domination is intensified through the massive power of contemporary communicative media (in particular the capitalist media). Such a media is not only an industry which earns huge profits in fulfilling its function as the new Orwellian "ministry of truth" but also serves as the dominant instrument and institution of cultural power in its capacity to define large swaths of the modern life-world. Culture has thus become the principal medium through which consent to domination is legitimated. Culture transmits and reflects the objective character of the larger societal project of power and order in which it is circumscribed, and we shall examine this in various ways in what follows.

Why Agonism? Seventeen Theses on Agon Culture

- *Agonism* is a concept firmly in tune with the geopolitical stakes of the present post-9/11 era. It is a concept that lends critical understanding to the contemporary order of domination and the multiplicities of conflict. Many critiques of the problem of human domination and global conflict stop just short of performing an agonal critique

– they recognize the problems of an exploitative political economy, the proliferation of war and violence, but see no problem with the dominant forms of cultural meaning that lend ideological and structural support to the realities of violence and war as a daily norm. The society of violence and war could not continue to exist unless it celebrated and affirmed conflict and war in numerous cultural forms. Contemporary agon culture accomplishes this precisely through the popular systems of meaning and value that are based on the virtues of competition and the instrumentality of conflict: the celebration of competition and predatorial elimination in media entertainment; the continuing political ideology that promotes the need for just wars; the ideas that inform philosophies of personal growth as something that is best achieved mainly through competition with oneself.

- Agonism is an ancient philosophical ideal derived from classical Western antiquity, and is now a globalizing ideal of power. Agonism forms part of the value system that works to intensify capitalist globalization and the international rivalries among political states and their corporate entities. The value of agonism is based on the idea that truth and justice can emerge from the outcome of the combative contest and out of situations of conflict. However, agonism, which is the ideology of productive destruction, produces neither truth nor justice but leads to a continual cycle of destruction, an *anti-dialectical historical momentum*, a situation of *life under tension*. This is stuck in-between dialectical movements means stuck in the crisis phase between thesis and antithesis, without any synthesis really taking shape. (Baudrillard called this process of perpetuating sameness metastasis – the cancerous growth of death). The destructiveness that takes many forms in the world today, from the violence, misery, abuse and atrocity of everyday life to the perpetuation of war – these are the lived effects of *life under agonistic tension* – agony. The society that celebrates competition, conflict, and violence in its cultural sphere is a society that produces the manifest forms of human domination in the material sphere; this represents the classic paradox of the reification of culture, that is, the values we develop to preserve life actually work towards the opposite effect. This paradox is the central problematic of agon culture. The ideology of conflict is seen as something productive, beneficial, natural, primordial and virtuous, and it is socially and culturally promoted while it upholds the very bases of social domination.

- The agonal society is in a constant process of organizing itself for war. The neo-Spartan agonal society maintains a disciplinary culture through numerous institutions such as the military, competitive sport, the militarization of science and a culture which has been trained to understand conflict as a generative principle rather than a destructive one. The majority of popular cultural forms support an orientation towards conflict, and this is readily achieved through the exalting of competition, conflict and combat in the cultural realm of sports and numerous entertainment programs. These produce what Herbert Marcuse termed "repressive satisfaction" in their fetishization of competition and violence.

- *Agonism is not a natural law* but a type of imposed cultural rationality. That is, agonism is a socially constructed and historically privileged value system, and not an eternal or inevitable condition mandated by the biological bases of human behaviour. The thesis of agon culture argues that the violence of agonism cannot be reduced to bio-evolutionary factors, but rather emerges out of specific cultural ways of thinking and doing that are deeply rooted in patriarchal, military-agonal historical traditions that continue to inform modern culture. These cultural modalities of agonism extend from certain values contained in religious beliefs systems to philosophical and scientific systems of thought, as in the Western Enlightenment project. Agonism also finds its most celebrated expression in the cultural rituals of competitive sport. The criminal treachery we see as a normal part of both business and political practice is thus an inevitable result of the almost universal acceptance of inter-human predation as a powerful, productive and legitimate expression of social action. Agonism is presented as fun in the entertainment offerings of the popular culture and media industries – what I have termed the mediagon – whose programs stridently invoke the idea that personal or national growth emerges from the competitive control or destruction of the other. In this dialectic of transcendence based on the destruction of the other we must acknowledge how agonism is also the celebration of death.

- The popularity and ubiquity of agonistic thinking is relational to its power in the economic and political functioning of the global capitalist order. Agonism is tied to the operation of dominant political power – to the power of an *imposed order*. Imposed order is the organization of society that emerges from the repressive power of the agonal state with its military and para-military forces of domination and control, and its market-based production of scarcity, unemployment and poverty as a constructed scenario that aims to mimic the predatory (and presumably "natural") world of the animal kingdom. To invoke Adorno's wonderful phrase, an "economic mechanism of selection" is erected in place to mimic a system of natural selection, but of course this "whole is false."

- The thesis of agonism is presented in this book by examining a number of critical themes. One of these themes is the Hegelian theory of history, of dialectical progress. In this critique of history I rely on Adorno's critique of Hegel's positive philosophy of history. Adorno emphasizes that the history of Western society neither progresses nor improves the lot of humankind but rather intensifies a particular trajectory of societal development that intensifies human suffering. History has become a type of perpetual crisis where no real dialectical synthesis is seen to take place – instead, there is the continual tension and crisis maintained by crisis managers, public relations firms, lobbyists and warriors. Another theme in this book characterizes the unfolding of history as *the dialectic of development and destruction* with no real substantial dialectical transformation actually taking place since the industrial revolution. We are still stuck in the raw industrial age with its pollution, class disparity and its crass consumerism; only its quantity has intensified, the basic qualities of the society remain essentially the same.

- The agonistic view of human history conceives of all history as the history of victory. This is a mythology of history that passes ideologically into the glorification of victory, to valorize and justify victory as a popular virtue – as the mechanism of growth and progress. To simply and reductively view all of human history as the events that happen through the outcome of conflict and conquest is to greatly mystify and silence everything else that happens that is not agonal and so is not counted as legitimate history. In agon culture, history and victory are thematically related; as Winston Churchill said, "History will be kind to us gentlemen for I intend to write it."

- The theoretical foundation of the project emerges from consideration of Adorno's critique of *reification*. Reification in Adorno's work is not specifically associated with agonism, although he mentions the trouble with agonism directly and indirectly in his writings and is certainly keen to the dynamic of conflict that underpins the social order. Adorno and Horkheimer recognized that the totality of liberal capitalist society is constituted on an antagonistic basis and that this certainly has concrete effects on the constitution of subjectivity and the formation of history. It is agonistic rationality which gets realized as the dominant social form.

- Reification is a concept which seems to have been neglected in much recent theorizing. Part of this neglect has to do with the fashionable rejection of Frankfurt School-type of analysis as being negative and pessimistic – so the theory which recognizes and identifies the dire conditions of human domination and social suffering is rejected, and attempts to understand the social and political bases of these same conditions is silenced. I have indicated in the extent to which the perpetuation of social domination has much to do with the standpoint and the institutional dominance of positivist thinking and the reaction against total critique. Nevertheless, agonistic thinking precisely exemplifies the type of reified consciousness and action that Adorno identified – one in which attempts at self preservation culminate in self destruction.

- In contrast to positivism, a major point of this book is to revive the critique of agonistic forms of reification for a radical consideration of how social domination in the present is related to the very cultural forms of knowledge that are regularly celebrated and cherished. Reification is characterized as a type of insidious and concealed domination because it "transmutes repression into satisfaction" – for example, the rituals of combat within competitive sport come to be seen as pleasurable, fun and healthy for individual character growth, rather than being seen as types of self-negating and destructive forms of behaviour. Competitive sport takes the military model of discipline and turns it into a pleasurable ethic of the self.

- The institution of sport has been virtually unrecognized by the sociology of power. It is a *major* institution in the constitution of society being tied to the state, education and childhood socialization, business, the family, personal pleasure, and international affairs. It is time to draw critical attention to the role played by sport and competitive thinking in their ideological support for the system of domination that exists in the world today. The ideology of competition which gets institutionalized in sport is (after patriarchy itself) the world's largest secular religion complete with an established set of values and beliefs, norms, rituals and even a vast administrative bureaucracy that organizes, corrupts and profits from sport. Families attend sports events and have their children inculcated into sports culture the same way they do in religious organizations – except sport is far more popular. Although sport is not based on superstition, it is based on a series of myths about transcendence, power, self growth, human nature and more.

- Agonistic reason is a type of reified reason. Reification also emerges as an ill-fated response to fear. Fear lies at the basis of all reification, the fear of self-loss, the fear of death, the fear of non-recognition by others – all of these drive the combative response against it. Reification is thus dialectical with the effort at self-preservation, but a reified response to the problem of fear ends up ensuring that fear prevails and self-preservation fails. Adorno writes, as "physical injury cripples the body, fear cripples the mind;" the reification of the subject is an expression of this failed attempt at coming to terms with fear because the method of transcendence utilized is a false one.

- Agonistic rationality is contradictory. Agonistic rationality presumes that violent force can be instrumental in efforts at preservation, that conflict can solve problems, that bigger and better bombs can stop war. The problem is not only with the contradiction inherent in such thinking, but with the manifold levels of personal rationalization that justify and mythologize conflict and conceal this contradiction allowing the destructiveness of reified agonal perception to continue.

- We cannot celebrate the championship and losership inherent in competitive sports and expect that the values of peace will come to predominate in the culture at large. Sports, the Olympics, hockey, soccer, mixed martial arts, and so on, and all the other competitive ecstasies, regardless of the pleasure they provide to players and onlookers, also function as forms of mass propaganda, which people, parents and children, the state, the media, schools, the left and the right, all actively participate. Sport is an acute cultural expression of agonism. It advertises hatred and condemnation of the other, the wish that the other be vanquished and defeated as the means through which the self can be elevated to higher levels of being based on the oppression of the other. This aspect of sport promotes destructive narcissism and is based on the inferiorization of the other and the heroization of the celebrity-victor-sports star.

- "The agon" is the society that emerges out of organized and institutionalized conflict. It is no surprise that in this context global poverty, crime, material depravation, murder, rape, self-abuse, suicide, self-cutting, depression, anxiety, psychosis, alcoholism, multiple hatreds including sexism, homophobia and racism, war and destruction, and all manner of human rights abuses are taking place. Beyond child soldiers and child prostitutes, now we have new horrors such as "corrective rape" where men in South Africa rape lesbian women to "correct" their sexuality. In Uganda and too many other places homosexuals can and are being executed, women are having their eyes splashed with acid and are left permanently damaged. Journalists are being imprisoned for reporting on abuse and minor atrocities, children are being sold into sexual slavery or stolen to be adopted in the West, or kidnapped to become organ donors in greater numbers across more nations as impoverishment and economic need continues to grow... the varieties of human rights horrors are beyond mention. The agon is indeed characterized by multiple forms of human agony and domination.

- If we are going to have an action-model (praxis) to deal with the numerous problems of domination outlined in this text in relation to agon culture, this action-model cannot be based on purely competitive conceptions of social or political action, but instead has to be based on modes of de-reified co-operative praxis (and corresponding values) that set out new social rituals based on peace and the affirmation of life. It should also be based on the unmasking of the contradictions that exist within agon culture, which is dialectical with the awareness of the role of conflict in the social fabric of daily life troubles and generalized domination and human strife. De-reification depends on the recognition of the irrationality of conflict, to be able to see through it, to "call its substance by name" as Adorno would put it.

- It is time to stop thinking about competition as a fixed law of life and to rethink it as an agonistic ideology of domination. That way we may be able to transcend it, to lay bare its systems of control, and re-affirm that aspect of primordial human history where an ethic of co-operation prevailed to shape human evolution and usher us into a better, more "enlightened" future that still remains possible.

Chapter 2

The Philosophy of Agonism

They want to annihilate one another... to enter the "agon," each the mortal enemy of each.

~Theodor Adorno, *Minima Moralia*

[The ideology is that] life can be reproduced only by virtue of conflict. And this has resulted in what might be termed the theodicy of conflict... because society has been essentially conflict-ridden down to this very day... the moment this realistic element is accepted it becomes an affirmation that simply reinforces the negative, destructive side of society.

~Theodor Adorno, *History and Freedom*

The "agon" is a spatial term that literally refers to the arena of combat. Agonism also refers to the individual agonized conflict of reified consciousness, where self-hatred and self-destruction emerge from the culturally induced competition with oneself, and collectively, to the global political-economic arena of competition and war. "Agon culture" is about the lived system of meaning, the social text of values, rituals and practices that are based on the myth that conflict and competition are forms of positive productivity necessary to generate human social progress. The *philosophy* of agonism is the way of thinking which promotes, valorizes and sets out in logic, the idea that conflict is not only a positive force but a universal principle of life itself.

"Agonism" refers to a type of knowledge and rationality that underpins the logic of domination emergent out of the Western tradition of thought which conceives of a transcendence based on victory within a universal order of opposition, including the domination of nature. Agonism is thus not only about the underlying structure of oppositions in social life but has been invoked as an ideology about the transformative power inherent in adversarialism and conflict.

One of the conventional uses of the term agonism refers to "both competition or rivalry and the conflicts of characters in tragic drama" (Gray 1996: 1). The *agon* in the strictest sense refers to the arena of combat and the site of violent conflict. Adorno invokes this meaning of agonism as the scene of the negation of the other when he refers to the space of "the *agon*, [where] each is the mortal enemy of each" (1974: 75). Its action-orientation is based on head-to-head conflict ranging from competition to battle where physical force over an opponent is a means to an end.

Agonism, the idea that superiority, truth and growth emerge out of contest, is one of the dominant philosophies that have a governing force over the constitution of the Western psyche and is part of the architectonic of meaning within Western culture, reason and history. *Agon* is a term derived from classical Greek philosophy. As Johan Huizinga writes:

> Jacob Burckhardt coined the world "agonal" and described the purport of it as one of the main characteristics of Hellenic culture… According to Burckhardt, the earliest type known to Greek history is the "heroic" man, who is followed by the "colonial" or "agonal" man… The "colonial" or "agonal" period is thus the 6th century BC – the age of Hellenic expansion and the national games. (Huizinga 1950: 71)

Agonism is thus an ancient philosophical ideal that reached its archetypal form in classical Greek (especially Spartan) society, where the Olympics was developed as training for war. This formation of cultural militarism originally emerged with the advent of patriarchal warrior societies approximately 5,000 years ago (Lerner 1986). The agonal ideal has been consistently upheld by enduring Western mythologies of imperial expansion associated with icons of classical antiquity such as Alexander the Great or the Roman Empire. Agonism is thus a famous historical ideal, yet one that survives into the social and political organization of the present order in a number of significant ways. The ideal of triumph contained in the philosophy of the agon is that the culture of the victor, the culture of the conqueror, is seen as a justifiable one – where mere strength of force prevails as the ultimate manifestation of power. Consequently it is through the cultural celebration of contest and victory that notions of the social and the political are based in agon culture. I shall discuss the cultural expressions of agonism in later chapters.

The agon also speaks about the general contest of adversarial forces played out in the field of the social, the generalized antagonism of capitalist social life and the everyday violence inherent in the social formations to which the cultural normalization of conflict gives rise. "Agonism" speaks of the ecstasy of competition and the very process of conflict as the mode by which social action is stimulated and life is affirmed. While also at the root of the contemporary competitive order, agonism is a governing rationality in the social production of meaning, pleasure and play. Many of these positively charged ideas are highly problematic as they manage to ignore the fact that agonism involves destructive forms of negation of the other.

The term "agon," around which this inquiry is centred, refers to a specific arrangement of power and order based on the instrumentality of conflict and the power of violent force. In the spatial scenario of the agon, conflict among rivals is seen as the positive means to produce a desired action or result. Agonism, at the physical level, speaks of the direct confrontation of opposing adversaries, and at a social level speaks of a generalized mode of opposition between individuals as the organizing principle of society. Agonism is, for example, the ideal contained in the ideology of social Darwinism, where the axiom of "the survival of the fittest" in a war of "all against all" is used to justify, valorize and promote a specific set of values pertaining to the strength of brutal force, and the power of destruction and elimination as the means of guaranteeing survival or achieving transcendence. In this manner Herbert Spencer's social theory and certain misappropriations of Darwinism give conflict, competition and agonistic struggle a hallowed role in the metaphysics of growth and in the idea of development and progressive change. The ideal that underlies social selection by brute strength is that of a predatory agonism. This predatory element is more a feature of human social orders than it is of animal orders. We shall discuss this particular aspect of agonistic ideology further in chapter 7. In human societies the ideology of agonism is also given religious justification in the credo that "good always conquers evil" – which aside from being a belief that seems to withstand abundant evidence to the contrary, gives sanctimonious legitimacy to the conqueror, the destroyer who emerges victorious.

Agonism is one form of power among many that circulate in the constitution of contemporary political and economic realities, but certainly a form of power that substantially informs contemporary instances of social domination and the problem of global conflict.[1] While agonism is the dominant organizing principle in the constitution of contemporary social order, this is not to imply that it is natural, metaphysical or ontological; rather, it is tied to the instrumental-rationalist configuration of the modern social world, the globalization of techno-military capitalism (Kellner and Best 2001) and the generalized turbulence of human domination that ensues from this conflict-ridden order.

Agonism is the philosophy of conflict. It is about the power of destructive force as a measure of strength, a power that consequently gets defined as the means to victory and championship, as productive power. Agon culture, which develops from the philosophy of the agon, involves the elaborate, constant and insidious normalization of the power of destruction, which in wartime also involves the "democratization" of destruction.

There are numerous *ideologies of conflict* in our agon culture. An ideology of conflict is a popular and taken for granted way of understanding conflict as a positive thing. For example the form of conflict we are all familiar with as competition is widely presented as something we need in order to build character, to develop strength, and to prevent stagnation and make the "world go round." In formal philosophy too there is an ideology of conflict – this is the philosophy of dialectics – where catastrophe is dialectically related to creation and the process of creative destruction is seen to underlie the mode of becoming and the trajectory of human progress. This dialectic of productive conflict within the agonal imaginary is seen as the matrix of transformation and growth that gets applied to virtually all natural forms. This conception of productive conflict, as we shall discuss later, forms a significant dimension of the Hegelian dialectic of self-consciousness and also informs the agonal dialectic of historical growth. It is therefore part of agonistic ideology to see transcendence as something that arises through the contest of power and force, and is ultimately realized in the triumph of victory in warfare.

The teleology of agonism is based on the cycle of victory and defeat. The agonistic cycle of force and *antagonistic* counterforce creates the cycle of perpetual violent action. It is a cycle of generation that underlies the belief that triumph takes place through the mode of destruction. It is supposed that through agonistic struggle, and both the victory and vanquish it entails, competition unto creation becomes the final arbiter in the constitution of reality.

What is initially attractive about agonism, at first glance, are the ideas of conflict resolution, progression/development, self-preservation, resistance, empowerment and transcendence that are seen to be inherent in it. This is the positive ideological articulation of agonism and forms a substantial part of the cultural mythology of conflict in agon culture (military-democratic/competitive-capitalistic/winner-loser societies). The agonistic social mythology depends on an almost sacred belief in the *instrumentality of conflict* and in the transcendental potential of the competitive contest. The primary ideology of agonism is that contradiction can be resolved through the contest of opposing forces, thus resolution through conflict. This view has a substantial history that informs thought surrounding conflict up to the present day, and will be addressed in what follows as part of the destructive dimension of agonism.

Within contemporary social theory, "agonism" has not yet been established as a primary concept around which questions of violence, conflict and domination may be explored. Rather, agonism has become a topic of renewed interest in social and political theory because of its discursive relation to the currently celebrated political paradigm of "democracy," which lies at the ideological basis of the alliance between liberalism and the so-called free-market expansion project of global consumerism. Agonism in its positive sense is seen as a form of political resistance, and is associated with the operation of democracy in its purest form (Arendt 1958, Villa 1999, Gray 1996). It is seen as the discursive mechanism by which dominant political power in a democracy is challenged and kept in check through the process of constant contestation and debate. The concept of agonism thus has been appropriated by the discourse of neo-liberalism as a cunning metaphor for "agonistic democracy," in which, as Jon Simons writes, "liberal freedoms are valued as the necessary conditions for the practice of strategic games of liberty" (Simons 1995: 22). Thus the concept has gained currency recently in terms of its positive connotations as a form of political empowerment. This analysis takes exception to such liberal usage. The term was never devised in the context of political liberalism but as an adjunct to the warrior society. Hence, this text develops a reconstructed notion of agonism against the liberal appropriation of the term.

Although the use of agonism has at least a clearly double-articulation to it, it is not generalizable to refer to all instances of conflict, contradiction and opposition. In contrast to Simons who writes, "agonism maybe as serious as political domination or as light as child's play" (Simons 1995: 85), this study will consider "agonism" beyond its typical liberal and uncritical usage within contemporary political theory. *"Agonism" is reconstructed here as a critical concept by emphasizing the negation and domination inherent in agonistic rationality instead of its connotations of positive productivity.* Agonism will be explored insofar as it informs the critique of the larger geopolitical order in which contemporary cultural domination is manifest. The agonistic principle is thus identified as the *architechtonic of domination and the primary archetype of organized human violence.* Both of these operate within contemporary global order and the project of economic and military domination that supports it. In the new global agonal order *the instrumentality of conflict* has become the fundamental stance of an insecure political reason; where triumph takes place through destruction, war has become a normal practice of politics, and imperialism is concealed as order maintenance and security. The celebration of conquest, conflict, conquest and victory become the principles upon which social and political structures are constructed and cultural meaning is generated. And hence we have the formation of multiple social systems which uphold and perpetuate the ideals of agonism.

The "agon of culture" will be conceptualized here in terms of providing an analysis of the aesthetics of violence that is supportive of this adversarial arrangement of social life. The ideology of agon culture is based on the valorization of conflict. In agon culture competitive modes of seeing get reproduced and serve to reinforce repressive *arrangements of power and order.* Within such an order the individual values of aggression, cunning and one-upmanship are seen as virtues that one must possess in order to be defensively equipped to survive.

As a critical concept the "agon" reveals the negation that takes place in the generalized arena of combat that has become neoliberal society. The battlefield of war and the hostile confrontation of forces inherent in the action orientation of competition come to construct the conflict scenarios of everyday life. Thus the critique of agonism serves as a theoretical model for inquiry into the production of contemporary forms of domination that emerge from relations based on the celebration of conflict. It is important to emphasize again that agonism is not to be understood as a natural law. Nor is the ubiquity of conflict within agon culture an expression of an underlying antagonistic human nature – these are ideological myths. Agonism is primarily a type of cultural, political and economic rationality, one based on the ideal of power as an expression of violent force.

Agonism as a Form of Social Power

This study questions the validity of arguments pertaining to the naturalness of agonistic ontologies and is more interested in how *agonistic reason* works towards the development of a corresponding *agonistic social order,* that is, how agonism and its products – the glorification of competition and conflict in society, from sports to war, including their ideologies and their agonies – have become normalized, resulting in the destructive intensification of conflict as a primary feature of contemporary society. This study offers a critique of the current world paradigm of domination, which will be argued here is based primarily on an agonistic type of domination and as such can be understood through a critique of the concept of agonism. Agonism relates the productive-destructive dialectic of contemporary social power and serves, at the economic, political and cultural level, as its fundamental organizing principle.

In the functionalist conception of society, which remains purely agonistic, social order is maintained by various forms of conflict that are seen to occur at different levels within the social totality. Within contemporary capitalist society for example, and as has already been noted, *the social "totality produces and reproduces itself precisely from the interconnection of the antagonistic interests its members"* (Adorno 1974: 17, italics in original). This principle generates both its productive and destructive tendencies. It is problematic however to draw on parallels between the scientific conception of the natural order and its positivistic laws, and how the social order is materially, politically and historically constituted. This is the basis for the dominant mythology of conflict, one that seeks to shape social order in a way that confirms the normality and naturalness of conflict as something other than the product of human will and action.

Agonistic Social Order as the False Simulacrum of the Natural Order

The agonism of the human social world gets reinforced by the dominant institutions of the life-world which operate on the basis of agonistic principles, from economics to politics to sports; agonistic competition is presented as the natural way of the world. The agonal order bases its legitimacy on an effort to model itself after the supposedly hostile and predatory "natural order" of the animal kingdom – not on the actual complex, interdependent, symbiotic, self-regenerating and life-sustaining order of nature, but on the Western agonistic view of nature – that which is based on the belief in a "violent state of nature:" This is a view upon which the predatorial law of "survival of the fittest" is premised. In the Western Enlightenment imaginary, the forces of nature are hostile and need to be subdued. Nature is viewed as an agon of life versus death, subjugating everything under its purview to operate under the iron law of "eat or be eaten," where the kingdom of flora and fauna is condemned to a brief existence of competition and inevitable predation.

It is axiomatic for positivist science that the order that underwrites the life dynamic of flora and fauna is reducible to deterministic natural laws; however, death or predation in nature is not agonistic. Agonism is a form of social rationality and not a law of nature. Agon culture is designed on the mimetic similarity to this scientistic and presumably universally hostile "natural order" in which life survives on death. The agonal order of agon culture promotes the objectivity of this hostile order and then mimics its "nasty and brutish" character in the name of living up to the authenticity of agonal nature. The agonal social order and the natural Darwinian order invented by the Western scientific gaze, which often misunderstands nature, is identical to the predatory natural world of animals only in mimesis; and since the natural world is mythologized as brutal, it remains a mimesis of what is not real. In attempting to resemble the truth of nature, it erects a false simulacra of nature in human society, much more violent than the natural animal world itself.

In the economic sphere, for example, "free market" capitalism ideologically reproduces the "survival conditions" of a "nasty and predatorial" natural order in the commercial production of scarcity and the economic climate of brutal competition. The agonal playing field of economic order is thus based on a socio-cultural mimesis of the presumed "violent state of nature" (Hobbes), on the reproduction of a "survival of the fittest" (Spencer) type of human environment. "Predatory capitalism" gets naturalized and legitimated as the most authentic economic type of order – the more competition and hierarchy gets institutionalized, the stronger the ideological justification for its continuance becomes. It is in this context that capitalist monopolization and corporate greed, violation and criminality are excused as justifiable attributes of competitive economic strength. *The justifiers of agon culture call the natural world of animals predatory and violent ("it's a jungle out there"), valorize the ideals of mythic competitive struggle for survival, and then plan a human society modeled on this order as a means of living up to its natural objectivity and presumed ethical neutrality.*

Agonism as a mode of organizational rationality comprises a functional system of values in that it normalizes the competition and conflict that is necessary for the generation of the order of domination: The litany of competitive cultural spectacles, the rivalry of economic competition, the triumphalism of force and the personal conflict inherent in the ideological domination of popular consciousness are all dimensions of agonistic forms of domination. The agon is not only about conflict and struggle as a form of transcendental growth, but extends conceptually to refer to the forms of domination generated in the lived sphere of human experience such as exploitation, suffering, tyranny, violence including psychic violation, and the *agony* inherent in these. The agonistic nature of the social order is thus significantly related to the eroded quality of human experience and the character of human suffering it produces in the current geopolitical crisis of the post-9/11 world.

Mythologizing Agonism

If the philosophy of agonism also has a mythical character to it, this is because it is also falsely conflated with a naturalistic and metaphysical theory about the unity of opposites. Walter J. Ong (1981) has written extensively on the theme of agonism precisely in this light. Ong's treatment of agonism is one that mystifies opposition as something metaphysical. It serves as an indication of how agonism has been conceptualized as the mere tension between opposites divorced from any conception of sociological power. Such a conception does not develop the problematic of domination contained in the critique of agon culture. As such, Ong's position is not without serious problems. In *Fighting for Life: Contest, Sexuality, and Consciousness*, Ong writes that "Contest is a part of human life everywhere that human life is found. In war and in games, in work and in play, physically, intellectually, and morally, human beings match themselves with or against one another" (1981: 15). With the unctuous tone of a naturalist revealing the evident order of that which he surveys, Ong sees contest as a unifying principle of human life in which war is equated unproblematically with play. This sort of totalizing analysis of the ubiquity of contest takes the cultural order of agonism as if it were the natural order of everything – this is pure mystification. If play and war have something in common, this is because they are ideologically connected under agon culture, and not because contest is a universal drive force that shapes human reality.

The mystification continues… Ong further identifies what he terms as the "adversativeness" between opposing elements, as a universal binary paradigm that informs numerous historical and intellectual traditions. The antagonistic interrelationship seen to exist between binary polarities or dialectical duos is the source of insight into the agonistic "nature of things" rather than a false conflation of socially constructed and disparate phenomena. For Ong "adversatives" are ubiquitous to human understanding: "Various kinds of adversativeness have been exploited to deal intellectually with the world and with being itself from as far back as we can trace human thought up to the living present" (Ong 1981: 16). He states,

> We find adversatives in all but the ubiquitous Mother Earth and Father Sky, the Chinese *li* and *ch'i*, yin and yang, Empedoclean attraction and repulsion, the Platonic dialectic, matter and form, Abelard's *sic et non*, essence and existence, Hegelian dialectic, and countless other binary modes of analysis. These modes proceed by taking one or another sort of adversativeness as an ultimate given and reducing or otherwise referring everything in one way or another to it, thereby satisfying the appetite for understanding, or part of the appetite. Empedocles used adversatives to construct a cosmology, Hobbes to construct a kind of sociology, Hegel to construct a metaphysic of historical change, Charles Darwin and Herbert Spencer to construct a biodynamics of "struggle" for life. (Ong 1981: 16)

Another significant example of agonistic hermeneutics includes the work of Richard Dawkins (1976) in the field of evolutionary biology – a field that is quickly establishing itself as the dominant discourse in the human sciences, and problematically so.[2] Dawkins has identified what he terms the "selfish gene," which operates egoistically at the micro-cellular level of human DNA. The theory proposes that bio-molecular processes operate on a "tit for tat" basis and thus represents a form of natural logic based on agonistic competition. Dawkins' study of the "biology of selfishness" has been used to extrapolate about the natural order of individual selfishness whereby human beings are understood as "survival machines." Dawkins argues that evolutionary forces do not operate at the level of the species, as is commonly understood about evolution, but at the level of the self-seeking individual. He posits his theory of an innate agonistic egoism to debunk illusions about the inherent altruism of humans. These are highly problematic assertions when they become the basis for extrapolation to social phenomena, as human consciousness is not tied to an innate evolutionary drive which determines conscious behaviour.

Although there may very well be natural manifestations of oppositional forces that operate in bio-mechanical systems, including processes at the level of microbiology, it is a mistake to conflate these processes in the nature of living matter with general laws concerning all living phenomena, and certainly dangerous to draw general principles from these conclusions and apply them to social systems. This is merely nineteenth century instinctual theory repackaged in the discourse of evolutionary biology.

New theories from modern quantum science and chaos theory have cast many former scientific assumptions about the orderly nature of matter and intricate process into serious doubt. Contemporary chaos theory,[2] for example, seriously problematizes the thesis that there is a logical rule-bound underlying order in bio-chemical, physical processes and in the nature of light, energy and matter. Nevertheless the allure that agonistic first principles offer in terms of explanatory logic is quite seductive. For all the explanatory power that identifying agonistic adversatives serves in terms of identifying certain patterns in systems, understanding agonism as a metaphysic of ultimate reality works towards an essentialization of conflict in the fabric of all reality and throughout all aspects of life. This sort of thinking falls into a prescription for agonistic conflict as the natural mode of existence – pure grand mythology.

The idea that conflict forms the basis and nature of all reality, including social being, is a highly problematic ontological first principle, and is negatively consequential for an understanding of human social systems as the product of dominant determinant rationalities. The tendency within various systems of thought to locate agonistic conflict everywhere within the substance of reality has contributed towards a functionalist description of conflict in reality, so that where conflict is identified, so it is seen to naturally occur. The belief in the naturalism and essentialism of agonistic conflict contributes to a dominant agonistic form of reason where social agonism is no longer seen as that which has been cultivated politically and historically. Agonistic reason thus, is based on the view that conflict is normal, inevitable and socially functional, and that conflict is "healthy" and mediates the basic dynamic of society.

Ong explores the structure of agonism as a universal hermeneutic based on oppositional structures as naturally occurring phenomena. In support of this position he courts positivism by relying on the notoriously problematic sociobiology of E.O. Wilson to ground his observations concerning the ubiquity of agonism in natural systems. In doing so he risks naturalizing agonistic conflict within the social realm, and yet does not develop his analysis of agonism into a critique of social rationality and the constructed nature of agonism occurring within the social order. The danger in such an approach is that the identification of agonism in bio-mechanical processes may lead to the assumptive leap that locates agonism naturally in the structure of human consciousness. This seems like an inviting deduction; since human society is so thoroughly overrun with conflict, explaining it away through recourse to the presumed naturalness of an innate agonistic consciousness seems like a logical explanation to account for the vast scope of conflict and violence in social life. However, the search for structural correspondences between the nature of the human psyche and the underlying order of society involves an error in principle, one that represents a gross misunderstanding of the primacy of human culture in the determination of social being. (The question of agonism, violence and human nature is an important one and will be addressed in chapter 6). Ong's is therefore not a sociology of agonism as such but a mythology of agonism that identifies a valorized notion of agonistic adversarialism as a universal occurrence in all facets of life.

Although Ong does not engage in an explicit critique of conflict in society, he relates a set of concepts that pertain to the proliferation of conflict in everyday life. He identifies "aggression, contest, combat, struggle, conflict, competition, and agony" (1981: 41-44) as concepts related to agonism (the Greek *agonia*).

That these are collected together gives us direction in developing an understanding of the varieties and scope of conflict that occur within the social order. To this list, however, must be added the important concept of "violence." Violence is a significant product of agonism and a basic component of agon culture. As violence and agonism are dialectically interrelated phenomena, they will also be discussed at length later in this text.

Agonism as Grand Mythology

The process of social conflict has always held an ambivalent status in the history of social thought. It is seen as natural, historic, equalizing, simultaneously productive and destructive. This multivariate conception of conflict has affected sociology's (in)ability to adequately develop an adequate critique of conflict. Even though the discipline of sociology was birthed in the concern with the problematic of modern social organization, social order and social control, the issue of conflict only became the specific theoretical terrain of Marxist theory. The latter, however, never adequately formulated a sociology of conflict, but rather focused on theorizing social contradictions that emerge under the political economy of capitalism. Within the context of traditional sociology, the understanding of conflict lapsed into a functionalism that was supported by the dominant economic conception of social order.

The most pervasive discourse on conflict remains the cultural mythology of conflict. Conflict in the agon of human interaction gets mythologized in a number of ways. In each case the mythology functions to prevent further inquiry into the nature of conflict. The reasons for not inquiring into conflict include seeing it as over-determined, as either too complex and primordial to ponder, or simply as transhistorical, fateful and inevitable, as if conflict was the mode of genesis in all of life and human history, and not just part of the history of human domination, as Walter Benjamin saw it.[3] The empirical fact of violence as the primordial motor-force of history gets reinvented into anything other than the absolute irrationality that it is – for agonistic reason is fundamentally irrational since it conflates means and ends to culminate in destruction.

In agon culture the ubiquity of conflict takes many forms including competition, antagonism, aggressive force, power, and violence. These are tied together to form a total system of meaning that exalts conflict as the primary generator of change and the mode of transformation and growth. Perhaps the primary mythology of conflict is that "conflict produces truth" – that truth is revealed through the contest of adversarial processes and hence that truth is equated with victory. This idea is supported by the religious edict that "good always conquers evil." This is especially the case in the ancient biblical mythology of conflict where "might is right," where the aggressive force which is deemed victorious is validated as "the good" simply on the basis of having vanquished the other through superior strength of force. It is proposed that good conquers evil, not by refusing to enter the contest, or by allowing evil to self-destruct of its own accord, but by mimicking the character and strategy of evil and conquering it through a greater, more destructive expression of force. This is a form of flawed reasoning that automatically labels the victor as the good, and is consequently a violation of the notion of goodness.

The agonism of the ancient biblical code, contained in the Old Testament Mosaic Law, which includes the threat of "an eye for an eye," is equivalent to the "tit for tat" type of logic that epitomizes agonistic tautological reasoning. The sacralization of the ancient agonistic code, which lives on to this day, is part of the justification of the persistent *mythology of agonism* that valorizes the strength of victorious force.

Mythology, however, is a problematic form of knowledge. Simon Jarvis writes that myth is "a kind of rationality, a way of ordering, classifying and controlling the world" (Jarvis 1998: 23). The range of phenomena that are connected to agonism are rendered meaningful in such a way that the social constructedness of human conflict is not adequately addressed: Their naturalization as social categories serve to mystify conflict in human behaviour within social systems. Human conflict gets explained by resort to the presumed inevitability of conflict and is further justified by its productive results. This functions ideologically to obscure the fact of negation inherent in all forms of conflict, since for every victory there is a vanquished.

The sense of awe and respect that forms part of the mythologization of power imbues it with an explanatory magic, a sort of "false clarity" that is endemic to social and historical mythology. "False clarity," Adorno and Horkheimer observed, "is only another name for myth; and myth has always been obscure and enlightening at one and the same time: always using the devices of familiarity and straightforward dismissal to avoid the labour of conceptualization" (1969: xiv). This is particularly relevant to the popular positivist thinking that naturalizes conflict. The positive thinking – conformist thinking which is the antinomy of critical conceptualization, and which is part of the dominant ideology and mythology within agon culture – automatically interprets strength and victory (mostly achieved through the use of destructive force) as just and transcendental based on the presumed validity and productivity of its aims; this view is preferred over the insight that gives primacy to the negativity of violence that is inherent in agonistic power. The culture of the victor is perceived as a justifiable one, regardless of the brutality and destruction inherent in attaining victory. As such, the spoils of victory get rationalized as the price of progress, and as it is expressed in the cliché of agonistic victory, "the spoils go to the victor."

Mythology thus serves as an attempt to impose a particular order of perception on the world as a means of securing control over it through the attempt to define its activities. The consequence of this processing of understanding by myth is that the culture pays homage to the very entity that represents its primary characteristic in negation; its taboo becomes the icon of its rule.[4] The power of that which negates life is feared and subsequently is deified and revered as that which controls and thus affords life. This scenario of mythical (and religious) belief systems repeats the paradox of reification and thus becomes the unintended celebration of the power of death.[5] Fear and respect have always been associated with a mythology that seeks to contain fear. The rituals of rule to which this control of fear gives rise often take the form of sacrificial behaviours. The act of sacrifice, which was once performed on living things, including the Son of the Almighty Father, gets symbolized in the sacrificial acts of religious devotion. Sacrifice symbolizes the deification of death and its power over life.[6] Psychic entanglement with the mythology of primordial domination, represented by the power of death, is at once a form of appeasement and submission based on a recognition of the loss of control. Self-preservation is thus dialectically related to the fear of self-loss, self-destruction, or death. Adorno and Horkheimer write,

> Man imagines himself free from fear when there is no longer anything unknown. That determines the course of demythologization [to seek to know truth]… Enlightenment is mythic fear turned radical. The pure immanence of positivism, its ultimate product, is no more than a so to speak universal taboo. Nothing at all may remain outside, because the mere idea of outsideness is the very source of fear. (1969: 16)

to know it
is to control it

Knowledge driven by fear seeks control over the world in the desire to extract its "truth." It is the horror of death, and the desire to control the power that wills it, that makes the mythology of force and destruction so compelling to the agonistic imagination. The mythic representation of pure evil is mistaken for the success of understanding it, seeing through it, and thus overcoming it. The culture industry exploits this theme ad nauseam: The extent to which people have become psychologically immersed in the agonistic offerings of contemporary consumer culture is a measure of its mastery over social consciousness. The agonism of everyday life with its death ecstasies and competitive pleasures ranging from the eroticization of killing and the popular lust for war is indeed a most disturbing concern and lies at the basis of the problem of agonistic domination and its mythical reinforcement. The relation between religious systems whose power develops on the basis of malevolent deities, death and sacrifice and the present celebration of death and violence in agon culture is an unconscious expression of fear related to the conscious suffering and despair experienced in people's lives. As Bernstein writes, "That despair manifests itself in aggression and violence, a violence now represented, exploited and celebrated in the media" (Bernstein 1991: 22).

The mythology of good and evil, life and death, within the dominant discourse of the Abrahamic religions, gets transplanted in the secular order to the authority of the sovereign. This sovereign, be it king or state, Foucault argues, exercises its power over subjects on the basis of a force on the body. Since for Foucault power acts on the body, as such the mythology of agonistic power gets realized in the power/right "to take life or let live" or "to foster life or disallow it to the point of death" (1978: 138). It is therefore both sacred and secular values that serve to reinforce the persistent mythology of agonism and its relation to power.

The mythology of agonism continues to sanction brutality in terms of war. One can hardly problematize agonism without condemning war: The ideology of militarism and war is the highest societal expression of agonism – its most destructive manifestation: the organized killing of human beings through the technologically intensified production of death. Agonal society is the totalitarian order of war culture replete with its propagandistic notions of conflict, such as the mass production of hatred that forms part of the construction of the other as enemy and the agonistic belief that complex difficulties are resolved through the resort to the instrumentality of violent force. We will examine the agonism of war in greater detail below, in terms of how the positive mythology of conflict serves in the cultural normalization of war.

The project of domination identified in this analysis as the globalization of agon culture cannot be simplistically reduced to agonism as its only operating principle at the exclusion of other systems of value. There are other types of domination that are not necessarily based on the agon. There are also other systems of value which do not form part of the totality of domination and are in fact an implicit critique of domination, such as the anti-globalization awareness that is developing as an intellectual and a popular culture of protest in favour of human rights. We should also not neglect the oppositional forces that exist which do not take institutional/organizational form: the social detachment from the culture of the mediagon and its decadence, the numerous small groups and collectives who insist on developing a critical awareness to domination by making the pursuit of social enlightenment a part of their everyday lives and their social relations. We shall examine this politics of counter-hegemony in greater detail in the conclusion. Nevertheless, in our concern with the character of domination, it is important to identify the power of agonism, since it forms a substantial part of the character of contemporary domination – its system of values, philosophies, forces and orders that underpin the project of power in its complex totality.

Agonism and Enlightenment

1) Transcendence and Domination

The period in Western history known as the Enlightenment, roughly from the 1600s to the 1800s, is consistently identified as a pivotal point of transformation in the history of Western civilization. Its categories of knowledge have provided the conceptual precursors for the neoliberal world order of today. Enlightenment is associated with the epochal shift from religious authority to rational, secular-scientific authority, a shift that helped give rise to the new character of power in the West. Enlightenment sought to redefine the categories of human freedom. In setting itself out a task no less than the emancipation of "mankind," the Enlightenment exalted the pursuit of freedom and progress as its highest aim. Enlightenment conceived of itself as a form of "demythologization" (Adorno and Horkheimer 1969). It sought to sever the development of "mankind" from the repressive foolishness of antiquated systems of meaning and perception which perpetuated both ignorance and want and human servitude. Jere Surber writes:

> Enlightenment thought emerged as a critical reaction, a protest on behalf of reason against what were regarded as the prevailing superstitions, prejudices, and outright falsehoods inherited from the medieval period, which was considered a "dark age"... (Surber 1998: 8)

The Enlightenment developed its momentum on the belief that freedom, or the "sovereignty of man lieth hidden in knowledge" (Francis Bacon quoted in Adorno and Horkheimer 1969: 3). Consequently new forms of knowledge were the primary products of Enlightenment.

> A great number of ideas are typically associated with the Enlightenment – the ascendance of the secular over the sacred, the rise of modern science, the belief in unlimited progress, and the modern conception of democracy, to name some of the most often cited... (Surber 1998: 8)

Along with the development of modern science and technology, the Enlightenment gave rise to new set of liberal social, economic and political categories that have come to characterize the ideology of modern society. These include values such as liberty, the capitalist free market, individualism, privacy and self-interest, reason, and the discourse of universal rights. Adorno and Horkheimer among others, however, charge that the knowledge and categories of thought developed in the Enlightenment, the power of its "encompassing principles" (Held 1980: 148), and its forms of rationality, were mobilized on the basis of an actual increase in the efficiency of calculation and control, and thus an increase in the potential for human domination. The values of Enlightenment were based on a mathematical, procedural, machine-like logic, which served to intensify the hegemonic power of the modern totality. Hence Enlightenment became the occasion for the intensification of domination and not the horizon of new freedoms. As Surber writes:

> The liberal humanism of the Enlightenment had emphasized the liberty and rights of the individual against the domination of religious dogma and aristocratic excess, but a high price had been paid for this. In place of the former structure of domination emerged an even more insidious complex of structures: the alienation of human beings from nature, which now appeared merely as a field for technological manipulation and control; the blind mechanism of the capitalist market, which while potentially satisfying individual human desires, resulted in the division of society into competing and mutually hostile classes based on human exploitation; and the bureaucratic administration of the social system, replacing any sense of human community or solidarity with its own impersonal and purely formal procedures. (Surber 1998: 135)

Adorno and Horkheimer argue that the control element of Enlightenment rationality was what came to predominate in the realization of modern society and was an expression of the "indefatigable self-destructiveness of enlightenment" (1969: xi).

"Still, they agreed with the Enlightenment's affirmation that reason, suitably redefined and applied, was the privileged, indeed the only vehicle through which the genuine enlightenment and liberation of humanity could be accomplished" (Surber 1998: 16). Adorno and Horkheimer write, "we are wholly convinced – and therein lies our *petitio principii* – that social freedom is inseparable from enlightened thought" (1969: xiii).

The Enlightenment presented a new view of the universe and of social life as rationally ordered and thus made reality amenable to scientific inquiry and rational control. The increase in the efficiency of control, however, gave rise to a type of society instrumentally ordered, one that served to intensify various forms of domination that existed in older, pre-Enlightenment society, as well as produced radically new forms of rationalized domination. As David Theo Goldberg writes,

> Subjugation perhaps properly defines the order of the Enlightenment: subjugation of nature by human intellect, colonial control through physical and cultural domination, and economic superiority through mastery of the laws of the market. The confidence with which the culture of the West approached the world to appropriate it is reflected in the constructs of science, industry, and empire that principally represents the wealth of the period. (Goldberg 1993: 29)

In the attempt to transcend the repressive ways of the past the Enlightenment promised the triumph of freedom but paradoxically, it unleashed unforeseen powers of transformation and destruction. Among these were the new forms of totalitarianism and the scientific powers of technological destruction that reached their peak at times of war, an event which too was becoming a more normalized occurrence. Ultimately Enlightenment failed to deliver on its promise of transcendence, and as we shall explore more fully below, prepared the way for the most brutal and destructive span of time in the history of humanity: As Adorno and Horkheimer claim "the fully enlightened earth radiates disaster triumphant" (1969: 3).

Adorno and Horkheimer wrote over fifty years ago about how the project of the Enlightenment so thoroughly changed the character of the modern life-world; the changes since then have been exponential, and many cannot be accounted for in this book. The concern with Enlightenment here is its fundamental association with the problem of *modern domination as being agonistic in character* – in particular how the rise of "instrumental reason" (Weber, Marcuse, Adorno and Horkheimer), a primary product of the Enlightenment, corresponds with the intensification of agonistic rationality.

Agonism is informed by the profound changes that arose through the foundation of the new Enlightenment world view and the subsequent establishment of modernity. Enlightenment values worked to substantially transform the nature of life and society: the fundamental transformation in the relation between the individual and nature, and also the individual's relation to others. The following are among the important changes created by the Enlightenment and its relation to modern domination:

- The shift from religious authority to the secular authority of the "liberal humanist" state;
- The development of a multi-disciplinary discourse of liberal humanism based on the values of Individualism, Liberty, Equality, and Utility;
- The break with nature through the rise to dominance of "instrumental rationality" and its cultural products: science, technology and bureaucracy; and
- The pragmatic application of the edict of the domination of nature as the mode through which "enlightened" transcendence would be attained.

The categories of the Enlightenment are antinomical constructions since the ideal of freedom of which they partake occurs through formidable manifestations of agonistic rationality – where transcendence is dialectical with domination. Nevertheless, the ideal of agonism significantly predates the Enlightenment era. Agonism is a historical mode of reasoning that has been firmly entrenched in the Western socio-political imaginary. Although agonism is historically associated with early Greek thought,[7] it is more profoundly entwined with the destructive character of the present age. Its expression has only intensified with the rise of modern instrumental reason (Weber, Marcuse) and the new technologies of power, and has since crystallized to become the dominant rationality of power in the West. Agonism represents the continuation of Platonic metaphysics that has become intensified today because it fits so well with the modern mechanistic/Cartesian/Newtonian world view that prevails in the present techno-scientific and military ordering of reality.

Agonistic rationality lies firmly at the basis of modern science, one heavily informed by militaristic interests and which has resulted in the coupling of science and destruction (Nelson 1987; Nandy 1988; Krakauer 1998). Agonism, whose power is based on force, is therefore a principle which has been substantially extended by Enlightenment rationality. Consequently, agonism has become a major dimension of the meaning and structure of "reason" in history.

2) The Element of Technological Control

In order to understand the transformation of the meaning of reason in history initiated by the Enlightenment knowledge project, we must begin with the Enlightenment's relationship to nature. The European Enlightenment project lies at the basis of what Morris Berman writes is a "scientific worldview that is *integral* to modernity, mass society" and the situation of modern alienation. The Enlightenment forms part of "the new mental framework of capitalism, and the new definition of reality based on the scientific mode of experimentation, quantification and technical mastery" (Berman 1981: 22). Adorno and Horkheimer write that "the program of the Enlightenment was the disenchantment of the world" (1969: 3). The Enlightenment instituted a new relationship between the humanity and nature, one, Berman argues, which represents a shift from what he terms a "participatory consciousness," where the human bond with nature was holistic, animistic, and enchanted, to one which externalized nature as a threatening, hostile, objective entity which needed to be mastered and controlled. In the Enlightenment, knowledge was seen as that which would deliver pragmatic results in terms of dealing with "the problem of nature" – how to conquer it and how to profit from it. "If nature is dead," Berman writes, "then there are no restraints on exploiting it for profit" (1981: 126). Enlightenment therefore finalized the epochal break with nature that was begun with the rise of the new world view based on science and secularization. Berman writes:

> For more than 99 percent of human history, the world
> was enchanted and man saw himself as an integral
> part of it. The complete reversal of this perception in
> a mere four hundred years or so has destroyed the
> continuity of the human experience and the integrity
> of the human psyche. It has very nearly wrecked the
> planet as well. (Berman 1981: 23)

The Enlightenment mythology of nature was significant to the formation of a perception which objectified the natural world and the ecological order as well as the nature of what it is to be human; it therefore also transformed the human body itself into an objective externality of self. The body conceived of as object/other is most clearly revealed in Descartes' problematic mind/body dualism, which lies at the basis of modern disenchanted consciousness and alienated being.

In the mythology of the Enlightenment nature is constructed as a hostile entity. Nature represents domination and is seen as the origin of violence. The Enlightenment upheld the belief that there is a "violent state of nature," that nature controls the possibility of life and death for humans and therefore that nature itself must be controlled. The power of nature, as revealed in floods, hurricanes, famine and other natural disasters gave it a whimsical power over life and death, one which Enlightenment wisdom could no longer accept as divinely ordained. The oppressive power of nature needed to be confronted, to be brought under control. Similarly the problem of the scarcity of essential survival resources was primarily seen as a problem of nature, one that could be overcome through technological intervention and intensification of the control over natural resources. This utilitarian mastery over nature would later culminate in the technological development of the means of mass production to give rise to the abundance of modern consumer society.

Enlightenment knowledge set this goal of mastery over nature as its primary task. As Rene Descartes writes, "knowledge must move from pursuing speculation to establishing utility" and thus work "to make ourselves masters and possessors of nature" (quoted in Berman 1981: 25). Francis Bacon, often seen as

Descartes' co-conspirator, writes in a similar vein, "we govern nature in opinions, but we are thrall unto her in necessity: but if we would be led by her in invention, we should command her by action" (quoted in Adorno and Horkheimer 1969: 4). The internalization of this belief system was at the basis of Enlightenment's transcendental philosophy based on the edict of the *domination of nature* (Leiss 1972) – the belief that the control and subjugation of nature is the means through which emancipatory self-determination and human progress could be made possible. Thus it became an edict of Enlightenment that the human species constitutes itself precisely in its self-assertion against nature.

The domination of nature was seen as a means of mastering the problem of human survival, hardship and toil. The transcendentalism of Enlightenment posited that countering the presumed hostility of nature with calculated mastery, subjugation and control would realize a form of emancipation from nature's hostile and violent subjugation over humankind. "Violent nature" therefore must be overcome by greater force of violent/instrumental control. It is this efficiency of instrumental/technological control over nature and over the natural resources of the planet that forms the basis of the agonistic counter-response in Enlightenment thinking; one which gets realized in the rationalist, positivistic, scientific, mathematical and rule-bound forms of knowledge, as well as in technology, which is the physical/material manifestation or the instrument of the domination of nature.

The thesis that nature is violent and threatening and that human survival requires mastery over it is one which was uncritically accepted by Enlightenment philosophy and is consistently reproduced in the rationality of contemporary agon culture. Despite the growing mass of contemporary evidence which warns against pursuing this confrontational trajectory against nature, it is a belief system that continues to dominate Western consciousness because it allows for the continuing depletion and destruction that is endemic to the political economy of global capitalism.

There are a number of indigenous cultural and Eastern traditions of thought that are not based on a hostile view of nature. These are discredited as naïve or "unscientific" in that they do not lend material legitimacy to the hostility of the agonistic order. A recent theory of natural order that is not agonistic is the Gaia hypothesis (Lovelock 1979), which is scientifically based and proposes the theory of a "living earth" system. Gaia proposes that life on earth is the result of a vast complex of processes based on symbiotic interaction between creatures and the environment, between organic and inorganic matter, which indicate that life is the cardinal principal of the natural order, and that the principles of regeneration and the persistence of life are the cardinal principles of natural order on earth. This is in contrast to the agonistic rationality of Enlightenment, which favours the thesis that nature is based on the struggle between life and death, where survival of the fittest is the cardinal principle and primal law of Being. In this agonistic view, the power of death is given priority over the primacy of life, and the edict of "eat or be eaten" gets formulated into an ideology that promotes the legitimacy of aggression and predation as primary natural values.

The fundamental problem of the Enlightenment credo of domination as the mode of transcendence is that you cannot dominate nature without simultaneously dominating human beings in turn (Adorno and Horkheimer 1969). The attempt to dominate nature as a means to advance human interests therefore contains a basic contradiction, since as Marcuse indicates, "the scientific conquest of nature [equates with] the scientific conquest of man" (1964: xiv). Adorno and Horkheimer repeat the same idea when they write, "domination in the conceptual sphere, is raised up on the basis of actual domination" (1969: 14).

One of the primary legacies of the Enlightenment therefore was the edict of the domination of nature. This edict lies at the basis of the control element in Enlightenment knowledge and gives rise to Modern Western positivist science and its methods of predictability and control, its dispassionate objectivity, which is related to its complicity with destruction and the coercive instrumentality of its technology. The modern technological imperative therefore emerged historically from Western society's agonistic relation to nature. This is the type of reasoning that gave rise to the *technology of the agon*, one that Marcuse identifies as "technological rationality." Technological rationality, Marcuse indicates, is equated with "the logic of domination" (1964); that is, technological logic is rule-bound and inflexible. It is based on the logic of the machine, where the machine is developed as an intrusive, aggressive mechanism of intervention into the natural world. Technological rationality shapes the dominant mode of social and administrative perception into a procedure-bound form of reasoning, thus "technological rationality has become political rationality" (Marcuse 1964: xvi).

Similarly, Adorno and Horkheimer write that "a technological rationale is the rationale of domination itself" (1969: 121). Such claims stand in direct contrast to the litany of positive "ideologies of technology" (Bender and Druckrey 1994) which primarily associate technology with progress; for example the idea of the liberation of human labour through such things as automation and machine assistance, or that medical advances will stave off disease and save lives. The ideas of technological benevolence and progress go hand in hand. "The main ideology of modern technologies" Stanley Aronowitz writes, "is that *virtually* all of our problems – ethical, economic, political – are subject to technical solutions" (1994: 15). This level of ideological legitimation of technology is necessary to maintain the continuing onslaught by technology over human lives. Technological intervention into the human life-world has reached unprecedented levels. Timothy Druckrey writes,

> Technology forms the core of the cultural transformations that are generating startling changes in virtually every cultural and political activity… never before has there been such an integrated transformation of culture… Technology pervades the present not simply as a mode of participation but as an operative principle. (Bender and Druckrey 1994: 1-3)

The progressive ideology of technology contains an injunction against castigating technology as something negative. There is the implicit suggestion in the ideology of technology, which claims that it has no intrinsic value or character to it – that technology is purely functional and thus the primary question of technology should focus on its utility. Furthermore, the argument goes, technology's capacity for progress or destruction depends on the specific use to which it is put, and debates over whether or not it is a positive or a negative thing should not prevent the continued development of science and technology and impede its scope of influence.

Technology does not develop in a vacuum. It has a specific developmental trajectory to it. Therefore the nature of technology cannot be separated from the history of its inception and development. To do so proposes an artificial separation between the objectives of utility and design. Technology always develops in relation to an instrumental need. Thus there can be no neutral technology – no objective or pure technology to speak of. As technology is used to intervene in social processes it fundamentally transforms them according to the dominating logic that it establishes. Technology does not only transform in terms of intensifying the degree of efficiency in the various procedures in which it is utilized, it also changes things at the level of human value. Although "efficiency is a technological value, a machine characteristic" (Nelson 1987: 14), the primary efficiency of technology is based on bringing things under greater instrumental control.

The efficiency of technology is also about speed. Technology, as Harold Innis (1991) observed, works to compress the realms of space and time. This transforms everything from the nature of human communication to human geography. While the benefits of communication and transportation technology may seem obvious and form part of the wonder of the modern age, these benefits have largely been incorporated into the efficient functioning and administration of global capitalism. The conduct of business is made more efficient and hence more profitable, but this does not translate into more time savings for the worker or the businessperson – it gets realized in a far greater number of tasks and technological commands to which one must attend in the intensified compression of the workday. The efficiency of technology is supposed to be based on time-saving but actually works to intensify the hectic pace of life by speeding it up and consequently robs us of time by allowing more tasks to be "efficiently" inserted into a given frame of time. The technological pacing of time took hold with the monitoring of labour through the time-clock. The clock is a formidable piece of technology in this regard; it was intended to move people out of the natural rhythms and into the industrial pace of life, into the order of production (Thompson 1967). Technology thus has a substantial reality-ordering dimension to it, and this forms the basis of its dominating character.

Martin Heidegger (1977) theorized on the transformative capacity of technology through the idea that technology "enframes" and thus transforms reality. This transformation occurs in such a way that technology is not merely an addition to a given reality, but that something altogether new emerges out of the conflation with technology. Whenever technology is inserted into the social realm a certain change takes place – this is part of the ontology of technology. The effect of this ontological trans-formation, this re-shaping of reality by technological enframing, is so immense in scope and quality that it alters the nature of real-ity at a fundamental level of lived reality. Technological enfram-ing also suggests profound changes in the relation between the human subject and its relation to nature. As the relation between the individual and the external world gets mediated technologi-cally, the more the pace and experience of reality gets subordi-nated to the patterning of technology, to its technical, procedural mode of functioning, which is akin to the dominating logic of the machine; for Druckrey "technology subsumes experience" (1994: 3). Andrew Feenberg similarly writes, "technological develop-ment transforms what it is to be human" (1999: 2).

The autocratic nature of the functioning of technology therefore has the effect of automatizing the humans who engage with it. "We ourselves are incorporated into the mechanism, mobilized as objects of technique" (Feenberg 1999: 183). Druck-rey similarly writes, "technology is assimilated into popular cul-ture in ways that reinforce its authority but mask the tactic of domination" (1994: 5). The operator of technology must conform to the procedural functioning of technology in order for it to func-tion as it was designed. Using technology involves interfacing with it. This is a form of technological enframing that involves the technological shaping of consciousness to facilitate compli-ance to the techno-capitalist order of things in agon culture.

Technology, although mobilized for democracy, is not democratic. This is indicated in the claim that attempts to conceal this fact, the claim of technology to be "user friendly." Insofar as technology enables, it also constrains. Thus technology, in its dominating order of control, has a totalitarian dimension to it. Technology develops into an apparatus of societal functioning and control in the manner by which it is inserted into nearly every aspect of modern existence.

Technology was not always so alien to the human. Technology was not always super-advanced electro-scientific technology – basic tools are also forms of technology. As *homo habilus* (the tool maker), humans needed tools as technology which positively allowed for basic existence. Today the machine is wholly other and it has engulfed us, both in the immensity of its scope and in the mystification of its inner workings. Tools cannot serve if they escape the user's basic understanding of their workings; in that case they take on a dominating logic all their own. Derrida (1997) writes:

> Never in the history of humanity, it would seem, has the disproportion between scientific incompetence and manipulatory competence been as serious. It can no longer even be measured with respect to machines that are used every day, with a mastery that is taken for granted and whose proximity is ever closer, more interior, more domestic. To be sure, in the recent past every soldier did not *know* how his firearm functioned although he *knew* very well how to use it. (Derrida 1997: 335)

The increasing power of machines to mystify their users (the evolution of the machine over the human, perhaps), is part of their magical spell over those who love them. For, in agon culture, the totalitarian character of technology is ideologically supplanted by the cultural love of machines. Some of the most prized commodities within consumer culture are machines of one sort or another, from stylish automobiles to household gadgets, technological devices are purported to service human needs – they are dreamed as the servant-robots of science fantasy. Machines are deemed liberating, magical, intelligent, empowering, modernizing, life-saving; this ideology works to mystify the extent to which the increasing mechanization of life is thrust upon people as a benefit to life rather than as forms of imposed technical co-ordination. Most individuals in agon culture welcome more and more technology. Those who do not want it have little choice in the matter in any case. Social integration involves technological integration. To reject modern technology, therefore, is to risk social exclusion, not only by being out of the communicative loop but in being deemed an enemy of progress, for technology is discursively related to the concept of progress.

Technological development has consistently served as a measure of human civilizational progress. The phases of human history are measured precisely on the basis of what are termed "technological revolutions:" from the "stone age" to the "iron age," the "bronze age," the "steam age," the "electric age," the "atomic age," the "computer age" – we measure human progress not on the basis of the integrity of the human condition, but by the level of sophistication of our machines. This ideology works to conceal the fact that in our time technological innovation has consistently served the interests of both militarism and capitalism (Harris 1977: 262). Technological development is often touted as liberating and democratizing, yet it is "one that facilitates the rule of capital over wider spheres of social existence" (quoted in Nelson 1987: 14).

This technological measure of progress is also expressed in the vision of the future based on the ecstatic merger of human and machine – the cyborg dream (Haraway 1990). The cyborg dream is not just the hybridization of human and machine, but includes the aspiration of the agonal body to become a machine. This is the aspiration of technological efficiency in the agonal body as a "sport body," as a winner body, as an instrument body, a warrior body (O'Neill 1985). For Deleuze and Guattari (1977), the capitalist-schizophrenic body marks the disembodiment of the individual into a machine-like body as parts.

The aspiration of the agonal body to become machine-like is paralleled in the program of the agonal state that seeks technological solutions to many of its problems – including the problem of preparing for the future – which it uses as an ideology to mystify the poverty of the present. The dream of futurism is based on the achievements of science and technology, which are hailed as markers of the "greatness" of a "great civilization" – proof that everything else the state, in its partnership with corporate science does, is necessarily worldly, legitimate and based on maximizing the lot of humankind through the pursuit of its highest intellectual achievements – how far these "achievements" are from the original humanizing promises of technological enlightenment, such as the removal of humans from conditions of toil, scarcity and disease. Corporate capitalism intervened in this humanizing dream to profit from disease through pharmaceutical monopolization, to construct scarcity through market management and to cheapen the value of labour through various forms of economic slavery. The benefits of technology have largely gone into making more efficient the machinery of production and the apparatus of power, and not necessarily into improving the daily lives of people. The dream of technological progress (Romanyshyn 1989) continues to persist nonetheless, in the arrogance that we in the technologically advanced West have ushered in achievements which are "firsts" for humanity.

Examples of the presumed benevolent progress of techno-science is indicated in the vast cultural, financial and engineering efforts that support ventures like the vast co-ordinated and costly efforts of space programs, and the nuclear, medical and pharmaceutical science projects that are required to maintain the continuing advance of civilization and the "race to the future" (Heilbroner 1995). The building of space stations and the pouring of billions of dollars into the possibility of colonizing Mars come to be seen as civilizational achievements of which "we can all be proud." They are presented as the self-evident testaments of the collective progress of humanity as a species, and not seen as the extension of the power of the state techno-military project of control.

The coercive instrumentality of technology reaches its highest expression in the destructive power of military technology. Military science has created the means for the destruction of virtually all life on earth. This is the absolute antinomy of science's claims to enlightened "objectivity." The destructive element in techno-military science was already prefigured in the Cartesian/Baconian conception that the "sovereignty of knowledge" lies in the principle of the domination of nature. Domination, therefore, is a theme which is present in the very origins of Western science. The capacity for domination and control is in fact what epitomizes the character of agonal knowledge and technique. Vandana Shiva writes: "The nexus between modern science and violence is obvious from the fact that eighty percent of all scientific research is devoted to the war industry and is frankly aimed at large-scale violence" (Shiva 1998: 232). Modern Western science and technology is therefore fundamentally about the research, design and construction of machinery and weaponry whose primary aim is the destruction of human life. The fact of its destructive power and intent is sanitized in the new identity discourse of advanced weaponry which names the instruments of destruction as "smart bombs" and "patriot" missiles. Bombs and guns too form part of the "happy family" of intelligent, efficient postmodern technology (Gray 1997; Kellner and Best 2001). What is euphemistically called "the arms industry" is actually the largest industry in the world (in terms of financial figures), one upon which an entire "permanent war economy" (Nelson 1987) and a set of geopolitical relations known as the "military-industrial complex" (Melman 1970) is generated. The war machine, Manuel DeLanda (1991) argues, is not just about the increasing sophistication of the military as an institution on its own; the war machine represents a profound shift in the relation of human beings to the world of machines and information. Not only is the war machine progressing through the use of weaponry with "predatory capabilities," it is based on the wholesale deployment of society, its knowledge institutions and fundamental social and political structures, for the service of war (De Landa 1991:1). Melman observed that this trend was already apparent after World War II, when war had become integrated with the normal operation of society through "societal logistics" and "battle management systems" (1970: 34). On the same point, O'Neill writes:

> The "unnecessary" size and power of the world war industry; the pre-eminence of the military establishment in every society, whether open or concealed; the exemption of military or paramilitary institutions from the accepted social and legal standards of behaviour required elsewhere in the society; the successful operation of the armed forces and the armaments producers entirely outside the framework of each nation's economic ground rules: these and other ambiguities closely associated with the relationship of war to society are easily clarified, once the priority of war-making potential as the principal structuring force in society is accepted. Economic systems, political philosophies, and *corpora jures* serve and extend the war system, not *vice versa*. (O'Neill 1972: 43)

The society of the agon is the "monstrosity" of absolute war production; the giant "tele-technoscientific machine, this enemy of life in the service of life" (Derrida 1997: 327) that integrates all of its elements and subjects into an agonal whole. If we are to understand the relation between agon culture and technology beyond the obvious agonism of the war machine, which will be examined further below, it is necessary to point out the other significant manifestation of technology operating in the service of agon culture, that is, the technology of the mediated image, which is significant for the mass dissemination of the textual discourses of agon culture.

The technology of the mediated image in agon culture constitutes a form of semiotic domination. This semiotic domination includes the mass aesthetics of violence: An entire aesthetics of violence has emerged in the last century. The two principal images of this aesthetic are Picasso's *Guernica* and the infamous haunting image of the exploding atomic bomb (Nelson 1987). Both of these iconic images embody the dominant aesthetic of the twentieth century – that is, the aesthetic of destruction – which in *Guernica* is both a lament over modern mechanized destruction and its canonization as art form. It is interesting to note also in this regard that the iconic images of the burning and then collapsing Twin Towers of the World Trade Center in New York City on September 11, 2001 have become an aesthetic signature that defines the post-9/11 era. The technological aesthetic of violence and destruction is a substantial part of the sublime of agon culture, and yet one which has lost the capacity to frighten. It seeks to dominate fear itself and has passed into the realm of mere normalcy. In the agonal aesthetic, technological might and power is presented as awesome and beautiful. It is part of what Nelson (paraphrasing J. Robert Oppenheimer) refers to as "technological sweetness" (1987), which is akin to the "caress of steel" – and like the technological aesthetic revealed in Leonard Cohen's line "the beauty of our weapons" – it is an ideology of beauty based on the aesthetic design of the weapons of high tech, such as "state of the art" jet-fighter planes, and the many popular discourses which celebrate such an aesthetic.

The aesthetics of technological destruction capture something in the cultural unconscious of fear. Media technology and its power over the realm of cultural representation is part of what Druckrey identifies as the "technological unconscious," where "the ideology of form" gets reproduced "in the illusions of artificiality, simulation, immateriality, and the virtually real." This has the "staggering effects" for a "culture encompassed by representations legitimized by the discourses of capital, science, media, photography, and computers" (1994: 6). Among these effects is the pleasure of "capturing destruction" as an image, which functions to service the illusion of control. This forms the basis of much popular agonistic entertainment.

The vast of scope of the technological communicative apparatus has become such a formidable dimension of contemporary reality that, in Jean Baudrillard's (1983) terms, it has supplanted reality in the form of a simulated hyperreality; the order of simulation then as the highest stage of social technology, where the mechanically reproduced image no longer merely refers to reality but has become it.

We cannot underestimate the power of the image in the context of systems of power. The ancient religious injunction against images was a recognition of the power of the image and thus forbade it. Joyce Nelson writes that "the image is a pathway to our deepest psychic levels and is thereby an incredibly powerful thing to be used wisely, even ritualistically, because of its potent resonance with the unconscious" (1987: 22). The communicative apparatus of corporate capitalism fully exploits the power of the image in the remanufacturing of the cultural and mental environment of agonistic consumerism. We now live in a society where social relations themselves are "mediated by images" (Debord 1995: 12). (Guy Debord wrote about "the society of the spectacle" before Baudrillard had fully developed his theory of "simulation.") John O'Neill also has explored the relation between reality and representation through the phenomenon of the "specular functioning" of media power. Communication technology is a formidable type of social technology, one whose capacity to transform and supplant reality and thus function as a mechanism of cultural domination cannot be overestimated. As Druckrey writes, "technology concentrates power as it deconcentrates the individual" (1994: 3).

This study began by alluding to the importance of the communicative order of control to the functioning of agon culture and it will examine this theme further in the concluding sections. This study has also already indicated the importance of the individual subject as the ultimate "target" of power in agon culture, and it is to this matter of the individual to which we shall now return – to the history of the subjectivity of self-interest which also forms part of the core changes in the definition of reason developed in the Enlightenment.

3) Individual Self-Interest

The transformation in the meaning of reason in history is a development that Horkheimer identifies in the *Eclipse of Reason* (1974) as fundamental to the modern conception of the individual as a rational being in the pursuit of self-determination. "According to the basic assumptions of bourgeois [liberal] social philosophy and economics, each individual socially maintains his life by rationally pursuing his own, clearly understood interests" (Habermas 1984: 388). Such a conception of the individual corresponded directly with the value system of modern reason. Yet prior to the modern "eclipse of reason," Horkheimer writes, "Great philosophical systems, such as those of Plato and Aristotle, scholasticism, and German idealism were founded on an objective theory of reason" (1974: 4). In them Reason was based on the individual's "harmony with the totality"[8] and served in the "task of passing judgment on human action and ways of life;" thus it was oriented towards the affirmative character of culture. With the advent of modernity this changed to a notion of reason based on the "subject's interest in relation to self-preservation" and "subjective gain or advantage." Reason had become identical with instrumental rationality and thus marks the "eclipse of reason" by a new set of competitive values came to that define the modern concept of the liberal individual. This emerging category of the individual and its conception of self came to be known as the "sovereign individual."[9]

　　I have discussed two of the contemporary manifestations of self-serving and yet fatally agonistic forms of individualism earlier in this text as the political subjectivity of the citizen, and the economic conception of the consumer – both of which are based on the *subjectivity of self-interest*. Classical Individualism is a conception that "glorifies the individual in general and not

the self in particular" (Abercrombie et al., 1986: 12). Consequently the values and ideals of Enlightenment would work
towards formulating the individual as the "fundamental category
of bourgeois society," its ultimate category and monadic expression (Adorno 1974). Marx rejected this conception of the transcendental individual "on the grounds that 'economic man' was
not a universal statement of the human essence, but on the contrary a specific, time-bound commentary on free-market capitalism" (Abercrombie et al., 1986: 8). Nevertheless it is precisely
this conception of the individual that persisted and was tied to
the growth of consumer capitalism as the ultimate system of freedom. With the rise of consumerism, this conception of self would
eventually culminate in a form of subjectivity that C.B. Macpherson (1962) identifies as "possessive individualism." Emerging
from a mere concept of the Enlightenment, today entire discourses and industries are erected in the name of the individual.
Freedom and power are conceived in relation to it: "personal freedom" and "self-empowerment" are two terms which capture this
monumentality of the individual that is part of the ideology of
self pursuit in agonal modernity.

The discourse on the subjectivity of self-interest was
simultaneously a discourse on the ethical viability of selfishness
and the sovereign right of profit making. This is a theme which
runs through Enlightenment philosophy and which eventually
capitulates to the categories of economics and culminates in the
vulgarity of Ayn Rand's "objectivism," where the "philosophy of
selfishness"[10] is tied directly to the legitimation and exaltation of
agonistic capitalism and brutal egoism.[11] This conception of self,
which today is identified primarily with the supposed sovereignty
of the consumer-subject and the expansion of free-market capitalism, is fundamentally supported by Enlightenment reason,[12]
where self-enlightenment was equated with the pursuit of rational
self-interest. Horkheimer states:

> However naïve or superficial this definition of
> reason may seem, it is an important symptom of
> a profound change of outlook that has taken place
> in Western thinking in the course of the last cen-
> turies. (1974: 4)

Egoistic self-interest had become the "reasonable" mode of
enlightened self-determination – a notion which also included a

definition of self-interest in terms of a self-assertion against nature. "Utility becomes, as Hegel noted, the ethic of enlightenment" (Held 1980: 153). The ethical rationality of the Enlightenment was superseded by both economic rationality and by scientific rationality, both of which have been shaped in support of agonism. The modernist, capitalist and agonistic notion of reason that informs this conception of subjectivity, as *homo economicus*, is congruent both with the ideology of classical economic thought as well as with the instrumental domination over nature that lies at the basis of modern scientific reason.

While the Enlightenment raised up its system of values in the name of the "sovereignty of the individual," it was actually a revised conception of the sovereignty of the state that was being formed. O'Neill writes:

> The truth of the Enlightenment is utilitarianism, which judges everything by its utility to humankind; but utilitarianism is unable to solve the dilemma of one individual's utility to other people, which raises the problem of exploitation, insoluble within the utilitarian tradition... Hence the attempt to base the social and political order on the postulate of the natural identity of interests fails once and for all. (O'Neill 1995: 75-76)

That the utilitarian mode of order continues in full force today has to do with its ideological ability to overcome the contradictions O'Neill identifies. Utilitarianism as a state directive functions in terms of its utility to the state's own existence and perpetuation, and thus in relation to legitimating its imposition of order. The problem of the exploitation of the individual has been solved through the magical power of the commodity relation and the reification of the life-world, which has reduced the scope of utility to an arrangement among objects, and given its function new meaning. The insoluble contradiction has thus passed into reality and the problem of exploitation gets buried in a new form of agonistic kinship among people; but the contradiction remains nonetheless.

The rational and forcible pursuit of self-interest remains an enduring ideology because it corresponds directly to modern rationality of the self-serving agonal state.[13] If Enlightenment means transcendence through a rationality of self-care, then the empire-defensiveness that has come to embody the character of agonal state power can be seen as legitimate developments which are reasonable in their being based on active forms of self-preservation. It is not unusual, therefore, that the modern agonal state should equip itself for security and defence if it conceives of its own sovereignty on the basis of a rational self-interest in relation to others pursuing the same ends, and which are thus in competition with each other. These imperatives have given rise to the intensive "security measures" of states that result in the maintenance of vast armies and the resort to various forms of mental and physical coercion to maintain power. The paradox is that in the defence of freedom it is the power of defence that prevails – the right to life becomes entangled with the power of death. State agonism is thus about the political economy of death. This defensive momentum of the state speaks of its perpetual insecurity and the consequent formation of an insecure social and political order. Insecure systems, as with insecure individuals, are inherently aggressive in that they take a defensive posturing as their normal mode of being. Thus in the modern context the agonistic rationality of the sovereign self equates with the agonistic rationality of the agonal state. If the imperatives of states and individuals are guided by the rational pursuit of self-preservation, then war is a logical and rational outcome of this line of reasoning. It is not surprising then that the destructive conflicts of the past century have been rationalized in terms of their necessity and utility to the progress against tyranny.

Horkheimer noted also that this instrumental "formalization of reason leads to a paradoxical cultural situation," one that has given rise to "the destructive antagonism of self and nature, an antagonism epitomizing the history of our civilization, [and] reaches its peak in this era" (1974: 163). Horkheimer wrote this in the late 1940s, and the situation of which he spoke has only intensified further in our times.

****

The modern egoistic conception of sovereignty, the new economic conception of society and the new mission of enlightenment knowledge as the rational domination of nature, were all primary features of the Modern Western European Enlightenment, which was identified by Adorno and Horkheimer as the historical dialectic of rationalized destruction. The enlightenment project that sought to pursue social freedom precisely through enlightened knowledge has become subordinated to the overwhelming power of domination and has resulted in a grand "reversal" that is "universally apparent today," in the ubiquity of domination that prevails at various levels of social life. This "recidivism" of Enlightenment, which sought to transcend the barbarism of a social order erected on the basis of repressive mythology, is not the result of a failure in will, but according to Adorno and Horkheimer is due to a logical flaw in the very rationality underlying enlightenment knowledge. As freedom cannot emerge from a logic based on domination, Enlightenment through the domination of nature results in the domination of nature and of humankind (1969). "For Enlightenment is as totalitarian as any system" (Adorno and Horkheimer 1969: 24). Kellner and Best summarize Adorno and Horkheimer as follows,

> In their conception, Enlightenment turns into its opposite when instruments of liberation become the means of domination, and when a mode of objectifying thought that was intended to dominate nature also becomes a framework for objectifying and subjugating human beings. (Kellner and Best 2001: 68)

For the most part Adorno and Horkheimer's critique of domination is conducted mainly through a critique of philosophy, its concepts and categories of representation, and does not specifically address the particulars of political economy except insofar as the philosophy-knowledge-culture nexus operates as an extension of the political and economic order. This has led one of Adorno's earlier critics to charge that he proceeds with an "unsatisfactory theory of the development of capitalism and without an4adequate theory of the state,"[15] although this claim is unfair in its expectation that Adorno should be asked to write on everything that pertains to power and order within society. Adorno's critique of ideological domination through culture is an immanent critique of the commodity form as the basic unit of social analysis and therefore presupposes an entire theory of political economy inherited from Marx based on the idea that domination is located in the principle of commodity exchange. That it should be incumbent upon Adorno alone to furnish an all-encompassing theory of society represents a misunderstanding of the intellectual milieu in which he worked, namely, the Frankfurt School, which was comprised of numerous other scholars working in diverse and related fields (Held 1980; Jay 1973; Wiggerhaus 1995; Friedman 1981). For instance, it was Frederick Pollock's work on state capitalism[15] that served generally as a model of the state that informed Adorno's analysis (and that of the Frankfurt School in general), while Adorno's specific analytic object was the problem of domination in history.

Adorno's work is by no means unproblematic, however. If there are any aporias in his analysis, they lie in his neglecting to extend the critique of the destructive dimension of the European Enlightenment and its world-historical momentum as the foundational basis for global empire.[16] Adorno's analysis, despite his invocation of the "world-historical" momentum of power, never leaves Europe and its new-world progeny, the United States of America, and hence does not extend the problem of domination explicitly to Euro-American empire and its enslavement and colonization of others. His notion of *domination as barbarism* extends from the atrocity of the Nazi extermination camps, and not from the colonial atrocity perpetrated by the Euro-American imperial states against colonized peoples in numerous countries.

Adorno, however, does not delimit the actuality of modern atrocity to the particular historical events of Nazism. And it is a mistake to confine or periodize Critical Theory to being purely a theoretical response to the totalitarian horrors of World War II, as the detractors of Critical Theory are wont to point out. The radicalism of the Frankfurt School, and I am thinking particularly of Adorno, Horkheimer and Marcuse, is to be located in the manner by which they linked the historical atrocity of the extermination camps to the normal operation of power in the modern Western state form, its casual fascism, and the extent to which the normalization of domination extended into the everyday life of modern societies through the tyrannical actions of the state. Fascism is thus not seen by the Frankfurt School as an anomaly of European history that occurred in the World War II period, but instead they locate the autocracy that was character-

istic of fascism firmly within the history and thus the normal
character of the modern European state form. Nor does the operation of democracy, as it is presently manifested within media-
democracies (where votes are generated through promotion and
advertising), contradict the claim that the normal order of government is an autocratic one. One of Marcuse's theses is that
given the extreme level of social control that is exercised in *One-
Dimensional* society (1964), it would not be unlikely that a country today could go fascist by the vote – that authoritarian
populism is alive and well in one-dimensional societies like the
present-day United States of America. The disturbing trends that
are being witnessed across the world today – the increase of
authoritarian governments around the world and their repressive
policies, which have eroded basic social institutions, squashed
public dissent, increased incarceration and detention, and
destroyed basic civil rights, freedoms and protections under their
charters – are clearly developing in a totalitarian direction and
confirming Marcuse's worst suspicions. The capacity for this
mal-development of state rationality has always been there in the
monopoly of the state on the use of violent force, which is also
combined with other perhaps more benign forms of what Max
Weber (1968) termed forms of "legitimate domination."[17]

The modern state that emerged out of the Enlightenment
was merely a more philosophically developed and juridically
reinforced conception of the Imperial state of former times,
replete with its self-arrogance and fear of the other it constitutes
as enemy. This point leads us again into considering the European
Enlightenment in terms of the extent to which it did not radically
depart from historic barbarism and thus continued to sanction
various forms of domination and atrocity. Arguably, the Enlightenment preceded one of the worst periods of colonization in
human history. This was possible in part because the philosophy
of the Enlightenment contained a racist imaginary of the other,
which prevented it from achieving the ethical ideal of the true
humanism it aspired to. This is one of its primary antinomical
contradictions.

While European philosophers were busy defining the
conceptual ideals of Enlightenment freedom based on the categories of individualism, liberalism, sovereignty, which are all
concepts taken to be committed to equality and humanity, Euro-

pean and American states were busy competing over the colonization of foreign lands, plundering their riches and destroying their peoples; this is what Ashis Nandy calls the "high-noon of imperialism" (1995: 82). This process was carried forth, presumably, by the civilizing imperative of Enlightenment knowledge, and guided in particular by a gross distortion of Immanuel Kant's "categorical imperative."[18] The conceptual dehumanization of the other, as part of the philosophic-knowledge system that informed state empire practices, lent moral justification to the marauding, ethnocide, and genocide that was endemic to colonization. David Theo Goldberg reminds us that "liberalism has become the defining doctrine of self and society for modernity" (1993: 4). Its panoply of "socio-conceptual conditions" including the "self-destructiveness" of enlightenment, its flawed ethics (and the antinomical character of its primary social concepts), penetrated into the very materialization of these concepts as social practices. In this regard it is important to consider "race [as] one of the central conceptual inventions of modernity" (1993: 3). Goldberg writes:

> By working itself into the threads of Liberalism's cloth just as that cloth was being woven, race and the various exclusions it licensed became naturalized in the Eurocentered vision of itself and its self-defined others, in its sense of Reason and rational direction. Racial divisions and racist dominations came to be normalized in the Western sociophilosophical tradition. (Goldberg 1993: 10)

Even though Adorno never extended his critique of Enlightenment into a detailed consideration of its inherent racism, it is quite probable that Adorno would have had no illusions about these issues. His work on anti-Semitism is an implicit critique of racism. Racism is a form of domination that is undoubtedly related to the trajectory of imperialist atrocity in history. The "indefatigable self-destructiveness of enlightenment" (1969: xi) that Adorno and Horkheimer identified as part of its internal logic is today directly connected to the contemporary globalization of empire, and thus the critique of the Enlightenment, primarily as a type of dominant and dominating rationality, furnishes a conceptual model worthy of extension to the present situation of empire domination.

It is in partial response to these concerns with the omis-
sions in Adorno's critique that this analysis will extend upon and
redirect Adorno (and Horkheimer's) critique of culture by investigating the relation between *culture, political economy* and
empire through a discussion of the dominant rationality of agonism which they share; for agonism is part of the dialectical operation and interrelation of these spheres in contemporary society
and is also inextricably linked to the contemporary formation of
consumer society and its reified categories. For example, liberal
democracy and consumer culture (which represent the institutional spheres political economy and culture respectively), are
based on the ideal categories of Individualism, sovereignty, utility, liberty. All of these converge in the legitimation of society as
a particular social order, that of "consumer-democracy" and the
production of the universal consumer, which is part of "agon culture" and the larger "agonal order" of the world today. The ideological basis of this order depends on legitimating agonistic
ideals, such as the instrumentality of force in the name of good,
as part of a power/order which sees violence as an instrument of
transformation. Thus "agonism" has become valorized in the production of meaning in a number of different *cultural* ways that
reinforce the *political economy of values* that are necessary for
the maintenance of order and the rationalization of domination
as the mode of normalcy.

The racism of Enlightenment follows in the same tradition of dominant values that are part of the efficient functioning
of the market order, values that pertain to competition, aggression, success as winning, the ethical defensibility of strategic
advantage, and the possession of power as transcendental. The
agonal thinking that encourages and affirms competition and
conflict as a social value with positively productive consequences
is not unrelated to that philosophy which justifies atrocity and
violation as natural elements in the course of human history; for
the present socio-political and cultural order must be understood
as a particular historical configuration, one which reveals a
process at work within history operating through an internal logic
that ultimately expresses itself in a particular formation of social
order and a corresponding formation of individual cultural consciousness. In this sense, individual empowerment and state
rationality merge: Agon culture is based on the idea that the cul-

ture of the victor is a justifiable one. It is an agonal logic which claims that to halt destruction you must be more destructive – yet to do so without questioning the "rules of the contest." Agonistic rationality has been so deeply engrained in the system of values within agon culture that it is difficult for those who have been successfully socialized into agon culture to conceive of greatness and the sublime outside of the text of agonistic meaning. Agonistic logic is based on the supposed virtues of agonism and it serves as the basis for the legitimation of power in the defiantly named "new world order" of economic imperialism.

The critique of Agon culture is simultaneous with the critique of empire and with the dehumanization inherent in imperialism and the forms of power by which it exercises control. The project of cultural formation, in the case of global consumerism, is coterminous with the political project of domination that corresponds to the realization of American-centric economic empire. Agon culture is primarily about the utilization of conflict as a means of social and political transformation and the subsequent deification of conflict as a cultural value. Agonism is thus one of the prominent ruling ideologies serving the advance of economic empire today.

Agonism is the privileged object of critique here, insofar as it invokes the objective character of contemporary domination, its unquestioned celebration of conflict, techno-military escalation and war. The agonistic organization of culture forms part of the rationality of economic and political rule, and this is dialectically related to the empirical reality of human misery as it is also related to the inability of organized human society to realize the dreams of human emancipation conceived of in Western Enlightenment philosophy.

Chapter 3

The Agony of Domination

> ... never before, in absolute figures, never have so
> many men, women, and children been subjugated,
> starved, or exterminated on the earth...
>
> ~Jacques Derrida, *Specters of Marx*

Today we are living in the midst of a global project of economic and military empire formation whose far reaching effects are to be understood as a measure of the effectiveness with which, in the words of Jacques Derrida, "neo-capitalism and neo-liberalism are attempting to install a new world disorder" (1994: 37). Dominant discourses within both politics and the academy are calling this expansion project the advent of progress and democratic freedom (Fukuyama 1992, for example). Yet the human atrocities that flow out of the empire-political imperatives of the dominant nation-states aggressively seeking to universally establish this order, are events that call upon us to reflect on just how little "progress" has been made with regards to the "perpetuation of peace" and human well-being as a matter of international human interest. Rather, what we are witnessing at present is the continuation of multiple forms of the domination of peoples throughout the world. The agon, in the conceptualization offered here, is precisely this global arena of conflict maintained by an economic and political arrangement of power that produces human domination by its very nature and operating rationality. Thus, "agonistic rationality" serves both as the organizing principle of political and economic practice as well as *the architectonic of domination* underlying social and cultural formation. At present this dominant and dominating arrangement of power, this network of economic, political, technological and militaristic convergences is unprecedented in human history. The imperialist atrocities of the former colonial European states and the American enslavement of African peoples stand as a horrific historical prelude to the sanitized order of domination that is occurring in the world today. The concentration of power represented by the capitalist alliance of the dominant nation-states is the new global empire order of the present: In this sense all domination descends from patriarchal-imperialist-agonal domination – that is, on a form of power based on the hierarchical organization of social systems where the mode of competition becomes the basis by which certain dominant actors gain a place at the top of the pyramid of society.

There are multiple strategies of domination in operation – ideological, technological, libidinal, racial, and religious, which are intensified through the autocracy of this new world dis-order. Yet this *dominant* and *dominating* (Derrida 1994) order defends itself as the highest form of society, and indeed names itself the pinnacle of history, in the competitive mania that is exporting corporate consumerism on a global basis.

This is the time of intensified domination: an order of domination emergent from the agonal system of social organization. What could this entail? It suggests a theory of history that is named by what is most auspicious about it, about what is dominant: dominant discourses, dominant systems, dominated peoples. Do not such notions lay bare and uncontested the fact of domination? Domination, then, as the definitive characteristic of the era, what Adorno would have called the "historical objectivity" of the age. However one may choose to characterize the present era in terms of a particular historical trajectory – progressing, evolving, expanding, differentiating, regressing, metastasizing, globalizing – in each case it is a *telos* of history understood here in relation to the rise of the domination of peoples, where despite the real forms of progress that have been made, is nevertheless marked by a net increase in exploitation, suffering and death. Jacques Derrida referred to this condition as the "macroscopic fact" of the age. He writes the inequality of techno-scientific military, and economic development maintain an effective inequality as monstrous as that which prevails today, to a greater extent than ever before in the history of humanity. For it must be cried out, at a time when some have the audacity to neo-evangelize in the name of the ideal of a liberal democracy that has finally realized itself as the ideal of human history: never have violence, inequality, exclusion, famine, and thus economic oppression affected as many human beings in the history of the earth and of humanity… let us never neglect this obvious macroscopic fact, made up of innumerable singular sites of suffering: no degree of progress allows one to ignore that never before, in absolute figures, never have so many men, women, and children been subjugated, starved, or exterminated on the earth. (Derrida 1994: 85, my italics)

This "macroscopic fact" of global domination is directly relational to the nature of the agonistic social and political structures through which conflict is multiplied and which today centres on the re-generation of a "perpetual war economy" at a number of determinant levels, from the coercion of public consciousness into accepting war as an everyday way of life to the actual atrocity of mass killing that war necessarily entails. War in everyday life, therefore, does not only refer to the devastating effects of guns and bombs on the immediate areas where people live to the fields of battle (the "avant garde" of the agon), but also extends to the public acceptance of "civilian casualties" as part of the costs of modern warfare. The destructive power of the perpetual war order extends from the propaganda that rages in the battle over people's minds to the cultural domination of consciousness required for individual compliance that legitimates the agonistic order of domination. This is among the most significant components of the ideological fabric of agon culture: the celebration of conflict, revenge and war as a nationalist credo and primary popular cultural theme. When a society has been nurtured or "cultivated" in such a context, into the ecstatic acceptance of war and conflict as a way of life, then the public consent for war is more easily

achieved. This form of the ideological domination of consciousness has been evident across many sectors of many populations
in the post-9/11 era in the rallying call for a "war on terror."

This "conflict machinery," both the military-industrial
complex and the ideological *mediagon* which incessantly promotes war, warriorism and predatory forms of competition as the
ontology of life, is the new motor of history. Virtually all of the
other forms of social and political domination descend from its
epicentre of agonistic turbulence. The new war machine, which
is comprised of the partnership between the "advanced" industrial
nation-states who together subjugate the peripheral nations within
the global capitalist system, simultaneously produces dire forms
of poverty alongside the production of vast forms of "wealth,"
capitalistically defined. This is a wealth that mostly comes in the
form of increasing the flows of capital into the hands of those
who already monopolize the economic mechanisms of its concentration.

No military conflict in modernity, whether it be civil war
or religious war or territorial war, can be separated from the eco-
nomic-empire order of the world today and within which all such
wars are circumscribed. The expansion (penetration) of the
market, the production of wealth and the perpetual war economy
are thus dialectical unities in the agonal order of world-historical
momentum today.

The realization of a global market society depends on the
developmental agenda of economic growth measured in financial
output, capital expenditure and "gross national product." This
means that the costs of waging war, of corporate environmental
disaster cleanups, the state-sponsored building of more prisons,
all of the vast sums spent on aiding the sick and the dying (mostly
made so by economically rationalized famine and by the various
forms of corporate pollution and nutritive degeneration done to
people's bodies), all of these costs are seen in the logic of economic growth as "positive," as adding to the "creation of wealth"
as an abstract numerical index of capital value. Gross national
product, which is the capital measure of the economic abstraction
of wealth, is therefore a highly distorted and invalid measure of
prosperity. A high GNP, at whatever cost and for whatever reason,
is supported by the capitalist ideology which states that "what is
good for the economy is good for everyone." This is a highly mis-

leading slogan, one which leads to the insidious economization of every aspect of life in the name of social advancement. The individual, who identifies their own private interest with that of the economic collective, is seduced into cheering for the prosperity of the economy, where victory in the pursuit of profit becomes a national-collective obsession and a matter of deep personal concern. Not that people do not have real economic concerns that are tied to the national economy – they most certainly do, as every individual in need of money can attest. But this economic connection to the national economy also functions as a form of mastery; personal participation in the political economy of capitalism is driven by an emotional fervour which gives rise to a competitive culture based on what Deleuze and Guattari refer to as "a generalized athleticism: the agon" (1994: 4) – a culture where the competitive pursuit of economic gain reconfigures interpersonal associations into instrumental "deal making," personal "empire-building," a culture of "winners and losers." "Winning" becomes the aspirational ethic in agonal business culture, one which produces personal emptiness and grief. Consequently, meaning is searched for in "personal power" techniques and "strategies for success" literature and "seminars," or in "martial arts" rituals that are supposed to equip the individual with the qualifications of the victorious combatant.

The desire for winning in the game of capitalism and the exaltation of the economy as the generator of wealth is inherently related to the agony of everyday life and the social and political formation of the loser. The society of despair masks its ugly "underside" with endless images of consumer prosperity. The lifestyle advertising dominating the cityscape above the streets seeks to deny the life of poverty inflicted on them. The semiotic colonization of the urban life-world through lifestyle advertising works to conceal the normalization of agony in everyday life, veiled by the promise of the commodity dream. In consumer society it is the "sovereignty of the commodity" that prevails and not the sovereignty of the consumer – "the customer is not king, as the culture industry would have us believe, not its subject but its object" (Adorno 1991: 85).

The planned obsolescence of commodities that are seasonally replaced according to the cycles of consumerism continually produce vast waste and the unrelenting depletion of natural resources. (The term "consumption" also means wasting away and decay.) The promise of victory and success is an ideological appendage to the American Dream, which is based not only on acquisition but also on a technique of acquisition: namely, competing with others for wealth. In this context victory is always dialectically related to losership, and consumerism has propelled this process into a societal model and an emergent global dynamic with dire consequences for terrestrial ecology that are already well known.

Agonistic consumerism is thus based on death-profit, and constitutes the new mode of depletion in the general economy of death in history and from which modern economic rationality in its tautological reasoning has not distanced itself. The economic logic of progress is the logic of continual expansion above all other imperatives, and thus it seems to have no end beyond its own *self-fetishization* as a totalizing process. Economic globalization, in its current manifestation as agonistic consumerism seeking to advance its frontiers in a global totality, is the *dialectic of development and destruction* on a mass scale. John O'Neill illuminates the point further:

> Once humankind no longer has an end beyond itself, nothing stops it in the relentless exploitation of the world and itself. In this project the vocabularies of liberal individualism and progress provide motivational supports for the private appropriation of world resources and the unthinking pollution of alternative human environments. It is no longer possible within this ideological framework to separate the processes of production and destruction. (O'Neill 1995: 86)

Production based on destruction – destruction as productive; this is the agonal imaginary, which normalizes destruction and valorizes it as a natural part of the universal project of expansion: *the dialectic of development and destruction.*

The advancements and achievements of Western civilization and its rationalities at this new horizon of millennial history have not been able to halt this sinister trend which has been mistaken (and mythologized) as the dialectic of progress in human history. The idea of "progress," perhaps one of the most discursive of concepts within the discourse of modern development, always implies however a process at work within history which operates through a particular logic that finds expression in both the organization of the social world and in the structure of human consciousness. As Adorno and Horkheimer write:

> The fallen nature of modern man cannot be separated from social progress. On the one hand the growth of economic productivity furnishes the conditions for a world of greater justice; on the other hand it allows the technical apparatus and the social groups which administer it a disproportionate superiority to the rest of the population. The individual is wholly devalued in relation to the economic powers, which at the same time press the control of society over nature to hitherto unsuspected heights. (1969: xiv)

Adorno and Horkheimer speak of the paradox of progress, which is another fundamental antinomy of Enlightenment modernity: that is, how developments have come to pass that initiate certain potentially liberating tendencies alongside increasing forms of repression. This paradoxical uncertainty continues to impinge on the shape of the future. Marcuse similarly asked, and the question remains valid today:

> What precisely has gone wrong in Western civilization, that at the very height of technical progress we see the negation of human progress: dehumanization, brutalization, revival of torture as a "normal" means of interrogation, the destructive development of nuclear energy, the poisoning of the biosphere, and so on? How has this happened? (Marcuse in Magee 1978: 51)

If critical theory has a disappointed tone to it, Marcuse continues, it is a

> disappointment that the incredible social wealth that had been assembled in Western civilization, mainly as the achievement of Capitalism, was increasingly used for preventing rather than constructing a more decent and humane society. (Marcuse in Magee 1978: 52)

Marcuse sees the problem of contemporary domination as emergent from "the conflict between our ever-increasing social wealth
and its destructive use," which seems unable to be

> resolved within the framework of Capitalism;
> when the poisoning of the life environment were
> to be eliminated; when capital could expand in a
> peaceful way; when the gap between rich and
> poor were being continuously reduced; when
> technical progress were to be made to serve the
> growth of human freedom – and all this, I repeat,
> within the framework of Capitalism. (Marcuse in
> Magee 1978: 53-54)

Economic domination is therefore fundamental to the character
of modern progress and its attendant forms of destruction.

The competitive principle in the capitalist marketplace
has not been able to create an even playing field among
financial players. Capitalism cannot even uphold its own
principle of free competition and regularly reinforces its
corporate monopolization powers among all of the major
sectors of the global economy. Nor does the capitalist
economy have the flexibility to be able to accommodate
all workers or forms of entrepreneurial activity. It is no
surprise that under such conditions the global black
market or underground economy has emerged – a symptom that the regular economy cannot accommodate the
economic needs of people globally. This has given rise to
forms of criminal destruction, such as illegal shark fish-
ing (there is even a shark fin mafia!), which is destroying
the life balance of the world's oceans, Nigerian baby mills
for babies for sale from young enslaved girls forced to
give birth, enslaved labourers and prostitutes, organ thiev-
ery, identity theft and internet crimes of all sorts. These
are some of the forms of "collateral damage" emergent
from gross economic inequality and the horrific depths
of predation that certain humans will resort to in the economic agon where the destruction of other life becomes
the means of one's own economic preservation.

****

If there is a new awareness emerging to account for the antinomies of progress, a "repressive progress" we may call it, it has to
do with the growing public unease with techno-growth, with a
lapsing into disrepute of the utopian civilizational dream of the
technological future (Heilbroner 1995; Romanyshyn 1989). It is
said that we are living in the most transformative period of human
history; it is one where the apocalyptic anxiety of the new mil-
lennium merges uneasily with the promise of a utopian techno-
future. The paradoxical character of the age is realized in the
uneasy conflation of panopticon and panacea, which is the hallmark of postmodern delirium (Conner 1997; Kroker and Cook
1986), a paradox that needs to be tempered by the clear recognition of continuing systemic domination.

In the present age all of the destructive tendencies of the
past persist – the phallocentric order of power,[1] tyrannical government, war, and all the forms of human cataclysm: "terror,
oppression, repression, extermination, genocide" (Derrida 1994:
57) – all exist alongside the numerous forms of social suffering
(Bourdieu et al. 1999). These include the increasing violation of
children culturally, emotionally, sexually, as workers, as consumers; the continuing violation of women, including the largely
under-theorized deformation of consciousness under corporate
consumerism into forms of reified femininity and masculinity;
the continuing vilification of the poor as the "dangerous classes"
of society; and the increase of a highly divisive racism that threatens exclude peoples through wars of enemy Otherness based on
a *prosthesis of identity*: Identities are prosthetic when they so
conceal and define the self that in their insecurity they prevent
people from recognizing the humanity of others (Fanon 1952).
The scope of exploitation extends at the political-economic level
to the official administration of crippling forms of social disad-
vantage, including part of the new political economy of domination that goes along with the restructuring of capital, the
privatization of various institutions into capitalist enterprises, and
the erosion of the welfare state, which includes but is not limited
to the loss of essential social and governmental services.

At the level of culture we are seeing the loss of language,[2]
both the disappearance of ancient languages and the world views

they contain, and the re-making of everyday language into a discourse that reflects agonistic and consumerist forms of consciousness. The loss of language is the death of culture. This re-formulation of culture also includes the ethnocidal elimination of indigenous cultural particularity and their knowledges which may offer last refuge of wisdom and a vision of alterity and harmony with nature that presents an option against total political integration and economic rationalization. This transformation of culture into conformity with the dominant order forms part of what, in critical globalization theory (Jameson and Miyoshi 1998), is referred to as the "homogenization" of culture. In such a context whoever speaks of homogenization speaks of destruction.

Beyond the destruction of the immediate human environment of the cultural life-world, is the destruction of the natural environment, the ecological catastrophe that continues unabated and mostly ignored by those decision makers in political positions of power. These all combine to form part of the scale of destruction that is the regression of modern progress. These realities of human exploitation are collected together in the present age and intensified by modern technological forces to develop the capacity for a wholesale impoverishment of human life, to realize what Adorno called "the inhumanity of progress" (1974: 36). In terms of the history of "progress," a condition of crisis has not been the exception in the human condition but has in fact become the permanent state of affairs – a dialectical ever-presence of crisis referred to earlier as "life under tension."

The question central to the critique of agon culture concerns the normalization of war; both the proliferation and development of actual war as an ideologically justified "fact of life" as well as the public acceptance of war – the normalization of war as an aspect of individual consciousness. The perpetuation of the war society and the war mentality is the single most abhorrent antinomy of the present age, and the clearest mark of the "barbarism of progress." (As such, we will examine the normalization of war and violence in chapter 4, below.) Thus, the question raised by Adorno and Horkheimer (1969) in the *Dialectic of Enlightenment*, of "why mankind, instead of entering into a truly human condition, is sinking into a new kind of barbarism" (1969: xi), still remains the fundamental question of our age.

Edgar Morin, in his essay "Approaches to Nothingness," writes in response to the "tragic context" of "destruction, waste, disorder," that it is the "ontology of the occident;" one that for Morin parallels the metaphor of a "primordial detonation of an exploding universe." For Morin, "Nothingness is a keen desire to liberate oneself in this world from the suffering caused by the world… in the detachment from the egocentrism of self and from subjectivity" (1989: 82). He offers:

> We must elaborate a moral of lost beings, an ethic of agony that adheres to the strict sense of this ancient word: in Agon there is struggle, terrible pain, and we do not know whether it comes from growing up or from death. We are living in an agonistic time, we are members of an "agonic" species. This ethic of agony is one of the will and thinking that certainly does not know whether it is heading for annihilation; perhaps not the annihilation of all humanity and everything that exists, but well perhaps the destruction of what we have heretofore considered to be the foundation of beauty and good, the destruction of culture, which also contains barbarism. Such an ethic of agony is at once an ethic of the end of the world and of the return as the new beginning of a world. This ethic requires an awareness of the end of the world, an awareness that, in all its immensity, is also moral consciousness, yes, conscience. (Morin 1989: 95)

Ethics and Domination

Surprisingly enough the branch of philosophy known as "ethics" has offered very little in terms of a critique of domination. The most radical critique comes from epistemology – in particular its treatment of power as emergent from the problem of representation, the truth versus illusion dichotomy, the mystification of reality, and the problem of how political power is embodied in the construction of social perception and thus serves to legitimate forms of political domination. This problem of the "centrality of illusion" by which reality is obscured in "late capitalism" is essential in the process that produces reified consciousness. Epistemological concerns form the fundamental field of power/knowledge relations within which social domination exercises its repressive effects on subjectivity. Ethical critique is merely a legitimating discourse. It looks at certain publicly controversial issues that institutions face in their continued functioning. Contemporary examples in the West include abortion, stem cell research and cloning. Only more recently have such issues become framed as human rights issues with the potential of taking the critique further. Ethics does not perform a critique of the ethical contradictions of various forms of systemic domination under corporate capitalism. Ethics does not undertake a totalizing critique of domination. It is issue based, in particular it is jurisprudential – civil society issue based. Even in the field of jurisprudence and human rights ethics does not get radical, in the sense of total critique, and thereby expose the unethical basis of the entire agonal order. As such it ignores the countless faults associated with this order, with the antinomical character of the system, such as the contemporary example of the post-9/11 era dilemma whereby liberty is sacrificed in the name of security. In virtually every nation on earth security legislation has become the dominant form of state power beyond the engrained mission of maintaining capitalism. In doing so, the cartel of dominant nations give each other the green light for the liberalization of war tactics. Nor does ethics contribute to a critique of criminogenic capitalism, which has intensified an increasing poverty, human rights violations and unequal distribution of health and welfare. The economic events (aptly named a "meltdown") of 2008 revealed in brutal and naked form the hegemonic role that economic crisis itself plays in maintaining corporate capitalism, rather than the opposite effect – which is that boom and bust cycles are supposed to be evidence of the inherent untenability of capitalism (its "destructive seed"). Economic bust events operate very much like the destruction inherent in war: they produce displacement, racialized forms of scapegoating, homelessness, death, vulnerability, exclusion and often dependence on the forces of domination. And contrary to the myth that recessions are bad for capitalist wealth, the opposite is true. The wreckage left in the wake of economic recessions allows those with enormous wealth to reap the rewards of good deals in the form of lower stocks, cheaper development land, and business buyout opportunities; all of these operate very much as does the legalized pillage known as the "spoils of war" where to the victor go the spoils – except that spoils is the wrong term since it is usually things of value that are taken. Are spoils allowed victorious combatants in "just wars?" Do war ethics change depending on the pretext for a given war?

Ethics is impotent in restraining the unethical nature of agonal capitalism. Under the totalizing power of capitalism ethics has been subordinated so that it confirms the functioning of capital systems. In this manner the categories of ethical value get translated into economic values. Ethics has become entwined with the myth of virtue contained in the ideology of enlightened self-interest. Ethics cannot distance itself enough from the workings of capitalism to wage a radical critique of the corruption, abuse and criminality of agonal capitalism. It generally approves of what agonal capitalism does: It prides itself on taking a strong stance on cloning research but it allows capitalist medicine to entrench itself in the pharmaceutical poisoning of populations. Ethics refuses to criminalize the state/corporate partnership of power which defrauds the public, violates workers, destroys and pillages the environment, and criminalizes harmless happy marijuana while allowing for thousands of pharmaceutically induced drug deaths each year – this, among so much more, happens with the blessing of ethics and law in agon culture. Ethics fails as a critique of domination because of its culpability in irresponsibility. The impotent discourse of ethics leads to such things as *ethical war* and the ethical validity of capital punishment. Philosophical ethics serves the ruse of capitalist freedom and thereby furnishes one of its fundamental mythologies. As O'Neill writes, the "logic of ethical development [is] the fundamental myth of political life" (1995: 127) and serves to underpin the grand myth of a dialectical progress of history (which we shall examine further in chapter 5).

Although philosophical ethics does not contribute to the critique of domination offered by critical theory, this does not by any means imply that critical theory ignores ethical questions. Ethics therefore forms part of what Horkheimer (1972) refers to as "traditional theory" (as opposed to "critical theory"). Traditional theory is "establishment thought." As Jean-Francois Lyotard writes:

> "Traditional" theory is always in danger of being incorporated into the programming of the social whole as a simple tool for the optimization of its performance; this is because its desire for a unitary and totalizing truth lends itself to the unitary and totalizing practice of the system's managers. "Critical" theory, based on a principle of dualism and wary of syntheses and reconciliations, should be in a position to avoid this fate. (Lyotard 1984: 12)

Critical theory, in contrast to traditional theory, "has society itself for its object" (1972: 206). Consequently the question is: "How is this society possible?" (O'Neill 1995: 177) becomes rephrased as "Why is this an impossible society?" The interest of a critical theory of society is the extent to which modern social forces develop freedom or impede it and thus foster conditions of repression and domination. And alternatively, how it may generate the conditions for freedom, and hence the emancipation from conditions of imposed domination. With this fundamental concern always in mind, Adorno, Horkheimer and Marcuse's critical theory proceeds specifically on the basis that social and philosophical thought should always take the form of social critique. As Adorno and Horkheimer write, "social freedom is inseparable from enlightened thought" (1969: xiii). However, it is Adorno in particular who emphasizes that the pursuit of social truth be dialectical with the human condition – and in particular with the fact of human suffering. He writes:

> The need to lend a voice to suffering is a condition of all truth. For suffering is objectivity that weighs upon the subject; its most subjective experience, its expression, is objectively conveyed. (Adorno 1973: 17-18)

What is objectively true for Adorno therefore is the fact of human suffering and misery. Alleviation of preventable human horror is the main concern of any social science that calls itself critical. Derrida repeated this *ethic* of care in his "macroscopic fact" that was noted above. We can go even further: not just critical social science but indeed all human endeavour should be secondary to the alleviation of this dire state of affairs, or otherwise it may serve to perpetuate it. Eric L. Krakauer (1998), for example, in his study of Adorno's dialectic of technology and its relation to "the current world paradigm of oppression" (1998: 12) indicates that Adorno writes in "response to atrocity," to the "technological mass killing of the twentieth century, to its massive, preventable and often overlooked suffering" (1998: 12-13).

****

This critique of domination, as with all other critiques of the negative condition of repression and imposed order, should not be understood as a lament over the loss of some blissful past or the "lost authenticity" of a once pristine human culture. Critical theory is concerned with alleviating the conditions of social domination in the present by drawing attention to them as emergent from the socially constructed present. The central task of critical social thought today is the one concerning the contradiction of power and its legitimation – specifically its claim of liberation and its reality of oppression. In the present, we, in the capitalist West especially, esteem ourselves "enlightened," but fail to organize and conduct our human affairs on an enlightened basis. In fact, to re-state a line from Adorno and Horkheimer that is familiar to those acquainted with critical theory and which seems more relevant now than when it was written near half a century ago: "The fully enlightened earth radiates disaster triumphant" (1969: 3). It is the reign of destructive irrationality within the human possibility of the rational emancipatory organization of human life. As humankind "progresses" in a way that is capitalistically defined, disaster is the result. This is now more evident than ever. Beyond the well documented forms of human rights violations and atrocities we now face the return of nature. As the Enlightenment sought to dominate nature as a precursor to human salvation, now the excremental waste of human technology has come back to haunt us in the form of a global climate disruption that fuels hurricanes, tornadoes, and sinking cities. Nuclear disasters, lost atomic weapons, radioactive desert dust, species depletion, oceanic dead zones and the litany of other postmodern niceties are things we can add to the list of the human-induced disaster that reigns today.

The irony of culture (or perhaps simply the contradiction of culture) is that humans can do so much better. There exists today incredibly innovative technologies and capacities of human ingenuity spanning all area of human endeavour from technology and science to artful forms of awareness and communication and various forms of indigenous knowledge about healing plants, all of which represent incredible manifestations of human cultural creative intelligence. This has not been part of what gets cultivated under agonal capitalism. Those with the power to orchestrate the control and political selection of this vast wealth of human ability have not chosen to eliminate human suffering and domination. Above all else the sanctity of human and other life forms is not the prime directive of our "fully enlightened" age. For example, the power of human creativity, innovation, resources and labour and the huge capital costs that are spent on the pursuit of the technological directives of the war machine outranks all other societal imperatives, including the elimination of poverty, disease and suffering on earth. This contradiction is the most fundamental of all legitimation crises facing human civilization at present. Quite simply, enlightenment can begin only when poverty and war have been abolished on earth. That the survival of the state and the intensification of its power maintains priority over other, more immediate human concerns speaks about the prevailing agonistic rationality of the state which is also part of its insecurity and its totalitarianism. The focus of this critique therefore is on the extent to which this agonal logic of the social order is related to the dire state of the human condition and results from a particular form of dominant and governing rationality that have supplanted the essence of affirmative culture and which continue to determine the organization of society and the consequent poverty of human experience.

Nor is the point of this critique whether or not conflict, domination and tyranny have been an inevitable part of human societies past and present, and that this belief that human conflict and strife is eternal and inevitable should therefore absolve us of the responsibility of further inquiry into it in the present. The cultural critique of domination depends upon the principle that the domination of humans by humans is not an essential or inevitable characteristic of human societies. It is the effect of a socially constructed, imposed order and is therefore a form of preventable domination. More importantly, the existence of such widespread conditions of domination stand in direct contrast to the dominant ideology of progress that legitimates the political tendencies and intensifications of the present age, such as the continued existence in the numbers of authoritarian governments, the erosion of state responsibility to the citizenry, and the expansion of capitalist empire and its various forms of economic oppression and social exclusion. The miserable conditions under which so many people on earth live today exists as an ordered response to a given set of historical circumstances. They are the outcome of cultural meanings and political rationalizations of aggressive force as a form of instrumental response in the perpetuation of order. The problematic of contemporary culture, the culture that calls itself "advanced," "civilized" and "the free world," is that it has not transcended the barbarism of history from which it seeks to distinguish itself. What is tragic in all of this is that humans today are denied the possibility of a better life, as Adorno remarked, "one more worthy of human beings" (15:1974).

If we accept with Marx that "men make their own history" (although certainly not all men – or women for that matter, only those who orchestrate power from the top of various social hierarchies), then social suffering must be understood as human-made domination, and thus it remains a historically avoidable form of domination. Furthermore this trajectory of social domination and destruction has an identifiable history and a distinct rationality to it. It is the task of social critique to examine this rationality and reveal its antinomical character, despite the urge to "accentuate the positives of progress" as a quick-minded defence of this order.

Lament and Ignorance

There is a widespread belief that if one smiles in the face of danger then one is being hopeful and that some good may come – that to acknowledge the negativity of the said danger is to give in to it, as if the recognition of danger was a form of capitulation to it. The charge that one should "be positive" calls for a subjective position that remains poorly thought out. It seems to be based on a fear of inquiring further into the hypothetical problematic condition, and on a hope that positive force or happy feelings, as in some child's nightmare, will make it go away or empower one to endure it. Perhaps this thinking arises out of too much social psychology; I mean the type that says we need to learn to better cope with stress, rather than eliminate the stressor.

The desire to "be positive" in the context of objective negation is itself an agonistic-reified response – one bent on remediation through confronting the negative with the positive. It presumes that positivity can compete with negativity and misunderstands the complicity with domination inherent in positivism – both the positivism of the social sciences and the naïve optimism of a deluded positive spirit. Remaining oblivious to domination by looking the other way, by rejection through non-recognition, does not solve the problem of entanglement with domination but only makes it more likely that domination will continue. It is a clear case of the falsification of consciousness. Simon Jarvis paraphrases Adorno and Horkheimer's point on this as follows: "the point that if rationality remains oblivious to the domination with which it is entangled, a real end to domination is less rather than more likely" (Jarvis 1998: 34). This was a point Habermas retained from his teachers when he was still a critical theorist, that "knowledge of states of affairs is structurally related to the possibility of intervention in the world" (1984: 387). Emancipatory struggles and critical thought are inseparable from one another (Schroyer 1973: 34). Critical theory engages with negativity in order to move beyond it. Transcendence, and not lament, remains its fundamental desire.

In studies that take domination as the main topic of focus, there is a tendency to look upon such studies as being cries of negativity, or melancholy forms of lament. Such attempts at performing psychological diagnosis of the authors of such texts that deliver "dire prognoses" of the state of the human condition is also a form of their facile ad hominem dismissal. It is also a misunderstanding of the negative tone of critical discourse misunderstood purely as pessimism and cynicism, which might be a reasonable misunderstanding, from the point of view of the layperson, but which seems odd from an intelligentsia versed in the critical discourse of the social and philosophical sciences. Adorno, who has consistently been charged with succumbing to lament and "resignation," specifically addressed the problem of resignation as a response which culminates in the ultimate capitulation to the very power of oppression that gives cause to social critique, and in doing so ultimately fails in its task. Adorno writes:

> Subjective reflection, even if critically alerted to itself, has something sentimental and anachronistic about it: something of a lament over the course of the world, a lament to be rejected not for its good faith, but because the lamenting subject threatens to become arrested in its condition and so to fulfil in its turn the law of the world's course. (1974: 16)

Lament is usually tied to loss, to the loss of something cherished and sacred. The critical theory of culture does not seek to restore lost tradition or the "good old days" – this is a vulgar reading of it, although critical theory building upon the "spiritual heritage" (Horkheimer 1972: ix) of affirmative culture seeks to establish something radically other to the escalating regression which presently exists – an other to the order of domination in the form of a culture that does not remain tied to the inhumanity of instrumental reason and the authority of illusion, or to agonistic delusion.

While lament is a symptom of the resignation to power, critical awareness is positive praxis. Negative social critique is not lament; it is the "negation of the conditions of negation" and is thus ultimately a positive gesture in terms of *affirming* life through the critique of forces that are inimical to it. The democratizers of knowledge today who claim that you need to mix positive and negative to be balanced, and who grossly mistake this practice as a form of critical dialectics, are the first to make the charge that misrecognizes negative critique as "gloomy," hopeless and despairing and in doing so help to maintain the order of optimism that pains itself greatly to see the negative state of real social conditions for what they truly are. In the conditions of objective domination it is a form of positive praxis to negate these very same conditions and "call their substance by name." To look upon social suffering and not see it as the workings of a repressive system of power is a form of perceptual delusion, one which is not unrelated to the forms of mass deception that have taken hold of cultural awareness within the contemporary project of domination and replaced it with positive cultural acceptance.

It is in the act of affirming life that antinomical critique must necessarily tarry with the negative – the negation of being through domination is its main concern and its primary analytic object. Thus, the "negative" – the "anti" in antinomical critique offered by critical theory – is not to be confused with the negative stance of pessimism, cynicism, futility, or resignation. It is "anti" the order of domination, anti that which is antagonistic to being and thus an affirmation of life. Negative critique is therefore ultimately a positive gesture of praxis in its active desire to reveal the conditions of negation for what they are, so that they may then be dealt with and transcended.

Chapter 4

Imposed Order as Insecure Order:
A Schema for Domination

One of the main features of the analysis of Western society offered by critical theory is that it identified the trajectory of Western thought and social progress as a *project of domination*. This was emphasized in *Dialectic of Enlightenment* (Adorno and Horkheimer 1969) where the authors critiqued the Enlightenment principle that human emancipation emerges out of the control of nature. They argued that the progressive domination of nature that culminated in the industrial control of natural resources became a system of domination over humans. In the socio-philosophical discourse which describes the process of the "dialectic between progress and domination," society is spoken of as a "system." And the power process which drives it is spoken of as a "project." While there is no doubt that such a discourse risks reifying the very object which it seeks to comprehend, namely human social relations, such a discourse allows the critic to identify trends, programs, strategies, and historical patterns that need to be identified if a critical, emancipatory social science is to be maintained. For the purposes of further clarifying the general analytic of power in this study, it is necessary to remark on some characteristics of the contemporary agonal formation of social order and the particular character of its hegemonic power.

> Hegemony is not simply something which happens as a mere superstructural derivative of economic and social predominance. It is in very large

> part, the result of a permanent and pervasive *effort*,
> conducted through a multitude of agencies…
> (Miliband 1973: 163)

Hegemony, therefore, constitutes part of the social mechanism enlisted in the *imposition of order*. Agonal order must be understood as a form of *imposed* order (Adorno 1973), in contrast to a social order which is truly democratic, that is, one which is designed "by and for the people" and which represents the authentic interests of the public. Imposed order is a coercive order, both because of the defensiveness and brutishness with which it establishes itself, as well as the pseudo-democratic[1] manner by which so-called "legitimate" systems of political domination are erected into power. As an imposed order, the system recognizes that its hegemony is not by any means secure, and therefore it remains uncertain about the ability of its power to achieve totalization and thus responds or reacts as if under threat. Imposed order is thus also a form of *insecure* order. *Agonism, as a form of competitive, repressive, reactionary power is an expression of the insecurity of the agonal state.* Insecure orders are political systems that objectively operate to maintain structures of privilege based on domination and thus whose power, inequality and illegitimacy need to be disguised and/or concealed. The concentration of hegemony is proportionally related to the insecurity of order and the need to retain security through the imposition of order. Insecure systems respond to felt threats to their security through the intensification of such imposition.

Adorno referred to the inherent insecurity of systems of power that exercise authority through domination by identifying the "antinomical character of systems" (1973: 26). Systems of power are "antinomical" in that they must contain the contradiction of their inherent illegitimate monopolization of power. Antinomical systems of power and order seek security and strive to preserve themselves – "they must constantly expand, progress, advance frontiers, not respect any limit, not remain the same" (Adorno 1973: 26).

The need to publicly justify the vast social inequity which exists alongside vast wealth has been the singular most important problem of ideological containment in late capitalism: it is a form of "legitimation crisis" (O'Neill 1991; Weber 1968; Miliband

1973). The concealment of social contradiction and the simultaneous presentation of the possibility of prosperity is a fundamental theme which affects the content and the meaning of what the media regularly disseminates. The media functions as part of the strategy of state power, to "manufacture consent" for civil rule mostly by way of news, entertainment and political opinion (Herman and Chomsky 1988, 1989; Parenti 1993; Postman 1985). Louis Althusser (1971) has indicated how the capitalist media functions as an "ideological state apparatus" (ISA) to compliment hegemonic state order.

Total hegemony is what the insecure order of the state, in its condition of perpetual threat, strives for as a mode of compensatory social regulation. This coercive regulation accounts for a part of the genesis of the state-form in history and will be discussed further below. Nevertheless it is important to point out that political states are born in violence, and the uncertainty of conditions with which they come into being continue to dominate the character of the institutions to which they give rise and maintain themselves.

The state, Deleuze and Guattari write, "is defined by the perpetuation or concentration of organs of power" (1986: 11). The modern state is "process" as well as "system." As system it engages in various forms of regulation, order and domination. This occurs mostly through formal bureaucratic and institutional means, such as the jurisprudential system and through the fiduciary and disciplinary relation between citizen and state. As process the state seeks to impose a regime of discipline on its citizenry and thus it seeks to produce "docile subjects" (Foucault 1979). Therefore, imposed order is also a form of *disciplinary order* (Foucault 1979; Weber 1946). The state jurisprudential and penal bureaucracies, which together comprise the institutions of "law and order," produce a form of juridical-disciplinary power that constrains people to fit into the prescribed order of social regulation and control. By codifying the parameters of socially and legally acceptable behaviour, people are disciplined into thinking and behaving in ways that are expected of them, in consensus-guided orientations. And when people do not behave according to the dictates of power, they do so under the threat of punishment – when self-regulation (conformity) fails, the agonistic power of the state enforces compliance through punishment. Punishment in agon culture ranges from social exclusion to incarceration to death, and represents the highest use of repressive force that operates within the disciplinary society to ensure compliance to order. The disciplinary mechanisms of the repressive state are thus prime manifestations of the insecurity of imposed order. It should be noted, however, that repressive control is not confined only to the penal/jurisprudential forms of discipline. It ranges from state-military and para-military domination to the cultural colonization of consciousness through the process of *reification* (Lukács, Adorno) which involves the objectification of the individual, or the subjective internalization of domination.

The coercive imposition of order is a characteristic of agonistic social systems generally. Imposed order is also organized and maintained through institutional means; these include the formal "civil" institutions of the state, from education and social services (the therapeutic state), to organized politics and the financial/corporate institutions. Order is also organized and maintained through the realms of culture and language, which form part of the regime of representation and perceptual control. The insecurity of order marks its effects on each and every one of these systemic elements.

The state's ultimate response to insecurity in the macro-social context of global politics is realized in the manufacture of war. Towards this aim the rivalry which exists among competing global nation-states produces political and economic alliances that give rise to a formidable military–industrial complex (Melman 1970), which is the contemporary manifestation of the archaic "war machine" that Deleuze and Guattari (1986) have identified, and which will be examined later in this study as a fundamental component of agon culture.

Imposed order seeks to maintain and even expand its power. It must do so by means of dealing with legitimation crises or social contradictions, something which it does not deal with particularly well. Its failure to do so leads to greater social strain and increased social suffering. Nevertheless, in order to sustain the process of regulation, security and control, an insecure order will "utilize all means available – including imperialist expansion and war" (Held 1980: 42).

Finally, the *insecure order* of agon culture produces ideational characteristics which get expressed socially in the construction of the *insecure subject* – which is that form of reified subject that has been successfully integrated into and thus identifies with the power dynamic that drives the order of domination, and is thus intimately subject to its inherent imbalances and consequent distortions of consciousness. The insecure/defensive order of the agonal state is structurally related to the production of social subjects who are themselves socialized to reproduce an insecure/reified type of identity; therefore, insecure order is dialectically related to the production of insecure subjectivity. While psychoanalytic theory posits that human beings are born with an innate predisposition for ego-insecurity – referred to by Freud as "primary narcissism," which this furnishes the basis for the repressive regulation of desire by the realm of objective necessity, such as the basic survival needs for food, shelter and social cohesion and recognition – a critical analysis of culture is more concerned with how *individuals have been socially, politically, and economically as well as culturally and ideationally constructed to behave in ways that culminate in self-negation.* The "consumer subject" as "insecure subject" is socialized into feeling inadequate and attempts to redeem self-esteem through the acts of possession and consumption. This is the motivational basis that drives the subjective "dialectic of desire and recognition" (O'Neill 1996). The production of insecurity becomes the motivational basis for consumption that is connected to the larger system of political and economic values necessary for the perpetuation of the order of consumerism. It is the system of values that creates a culture where insecurity is reproduced and multiplied within agon culture and not the inverse, where cultural meaning is seen as the outward expression of an innately insecure psyche.

The Rationalization of Society as a Form of Social Control

That there has been a historical process at work for at least a century involving the commodification of culture into consumerism is undeniable. This process is a significant dimension of the project of domination that exists as part of the establishment of the global agonal order. This globalization process manifests itself in the macrocosm of a politically co-ordinated international order and in the microcosm, at the level of individual consciousness –

thus completing the dialectic of domination between culture and populations. The project of the ideological construction of consciousness (Marx and Engels 1964; Althusser 1971), which is a vital dimension to the larger project of power in a globalizing consumerism, is the paramount manifestation of cultural domination and is tied to the more obviously tyrannical forms of social control exercised by the authoritarian state in its monopolization of the use of violent force in the maintenance of social order. This is a violence that the agonal state uses against others it violates in foreign lands, through war and by other means of exploitation that involve the oppressive transformation of life-spaces, and also includes the paramilitary violence it enacts on its own citizens when ideological hegemony alone remains insufficient as a means of control. In agon culture, the force of violence is the fundamental stance of political reasoning. Compliance to the dominant orders of control is guaranteed by both this coercive force as well as through the construction of perception through the successful internalization of the political economy of values that pertain to the perceived correctness of the authority of the repressive state. The use of coercive force is rationalized, that is, legitimated both culturally and through the rational ordering of society, through the institutionalization of dominant rationalities.

Domination and control, as central features of agonism, are thus related to the forms of *rationalization* that predominate within the order of agon culture. These rationalities include:

- technological/instrumental;
- mathematical/calculative;
- economic/utilitarian;
- possessive/individualist; and
- competitive/agonistic.

These are forms of the normalization of control and they pertain to the character of the modern agonal state, which through bureaucracy and technology maintains its organization and control over society. O'Neill writes, "Legal order, bureaucracy, compulsory jurisdiction over a territory and the monopolization of the legitimate use of force are the essential characteristics of the modern state" (1995: 45). These are elements that function fundamentally as rationalizations of social control. As such, rationalization is an *order-producing* orientation. Rationality should not be understood in the positive sense, or in relation to the popular usage of the term "rational" meaning "sensible" or ethically correct. Rationality is primarily a form of logic unto itself and not "objectively" or universally logical and reasonable: it is logical insofar as it conforms to the premises established by its own mode of reasoning, as in the logic of mathematics. Rationalization, as it was described by Weber, is about efficiency of control. As Weber conceived it, rationalization "defines the process in which abstract, calculable, and depersonalized modes of interaction replace those founded on personal relationships and traditional authority and beliefs. Instrumental rationality elevates means to the status of ends" (Benjamin 1988: 185).

The dominant rationalities of the disciplinary society exercise particular types of order on the social world. In doing so they function as structural-organizational containers that fundamentally channel and delimit the possible forms that social life can take. They subordinate independent social action and cultural change into routinized patterns of instrumental action and thus inhibit the cultural competence of the life-world.

Rationalization therefore relates both to rational administration and the functional determination of all aspects of organized life. Rationalization reinforces institutionalized forms of social integration and compels people to locate themselves productively, as objects of social processes, and in a manner which removes people from a life-world which is "in harmony with the totality" (Adorno 1974) of nature and of other individuals, and thus constitutes alienation as the primary social experience of rationalized disenchantment.

Rationalization supplants traditional and indigenous life-worlds, including knowledge that determines the use and control of land and other local resources, with a bureaucratic, instrumental organization designed for efficiency of human control (Marcuse, Weber). This has the effect of subordinating community social action, for example to external centralized administrative control over official political decision making and forestalling action through bureaucratic deliberation. Autonomous community interdependency is thereby destroyed and replaced with a new type of social bond that ties the individual to the administrative apparatus of society to create an order based on centralized social regulation and control. Through the rational organization of society, the principle of "the domination of nature [is maintained and becomes] an interest of the whole economic system" (Held 1980: 154). Thus, rationalization translates into forms of the rationalization of power and control and works to transform society into a bureaucratic/administrative and disciplinary apparatus (Foucault, O'Neill).[2]

Disciplinary rationalization is an expression of agonistic insecurity insofar as it is based on military order. Weber identified how the organizational rationality of society is modeled after military discipline. He writes, "the discipline of the army gives birth to all discipline" (1946: 261). This military model works to intensify the agonistic order of society as a form of rational discipline, where the command–obedience couplet serves as the model for social order and control. Later in this text we will examine how the rationalization of disciplinary order culminates in the cultural normalization of violence as a technique of political control.

Agonism finds its expression throughout the entire constitution of contemporary social and political life, where, to borrow Adorno's wording, the social "*totality produces and reproduces itself precisely from the interconnection of the antagonistic interests of its members*" (1974: 17, emphasis in original). This is a cardinal principle that lies at the basis of the contemporary social order. The antagonistic interrelation refers to the type of instrumental association among individuals, which also shapes the character of the institutional constitution of society. Agonism thus extends beyond the realm of individual action and finds its ultimate societal expression in the conflict of war and the practice of "power politics" that maintains the international order of war.

Agonistic interrelations generate the social totality across all the major spheres of what is referred to here as the *institutionalized life-world*, which includes the *political, economic, technological and cultural* realms of society, all of which are upheld on the basis of various forms of agonism:

- The *political order* is fundamentally agonistic insofar as it is based on the ideal of democracy which openly calls itself "agonistic democracy" (Arendt 1958; Villa 1999; Gray 1996). Such a conception of democracy is based on the valorized practice of political contestation and adversarial debate. Political freedom is said to depend on the contestation of leadership and on adversarial debate as the guarantee of self-determination in political democracy. Also, and more significantly, the ultimate basis of political power is the power of agonistic force – political rule ultimately is rule by the sword (Weber 1946; Benjamin 1978; Brown 2000).

- The *economic order* of capitalism is firmly based on the mode of competition as its primary generative element. The economic order of capitalism depends on the value of competition as the mode through which freedom is said to emerge. The importance of competition as a value of capitalist economics is an ideal consistently emphasized in both classical and contemporary economic theory (Friedman 1982). The agonistic ideal in economic social theory gets translated into the belief that "each pursuing his/her own economic self-interest" gives rise to a sort of economic social harmony. And while it does produce, at one level, a distinct type of orchestrated social conflict, this order does not come about without serious transformations in the nature of human interaction: This is a change revealed in the economic instrumentalization of the social bond – the creation of a "deal making" culture. Joseph Schumpeter (1975) reveals the logic underlying the edict of competition within capitalism when he calls capitalist development a form of "creative destruction."

- *Technology* is agonistic insofar as it originates in the Enlightenment ethic based on the "domination of nature." Also, modern technology developed in and continues to develop in the context of war. Technology has thus given rise to the most destructive, conflictual-agonistic instruments known to humanity. The agonism of technology extends to the capacity for catastrophic intensification of those forms of power already existing in the social order.

- Contemporary *media culture* is agonistic insofar as it functions to disseminate, legitimate and ideologically reproduce the destructive values of agonism. From the ecstatic celebration of competition to the eroticisation and heroization of warriorism and death, contemporary media culture is based on a number of agonistic genres of entertainment spectacle. We shall examine this phenomenon later in this text as the *mediagon*.

The modern *social totality* and its systemic power is therefore controlled on an agonistic basis, agonism is what holds it together: the totality of society is an agon – an arena of generative conflict. Willem Van Reijen (1992) interprets Adorno's philosophical program as one which "attempts to explain the form of new relations among the elements of an existing order." Such an analysis

> shows us that an interpretation of society must be performed in terms of conflicting interests. Conflicting interests indicate that the whole in which they originate and develop is not a true whole. As long as this is true everything must be understood in terms of conflict, which means in regard to an opponent. (Van Reijen 1992: 10)

The institutional spheres of the modern agonal order are necessarily interrelated and combine to form the ground upon which reality presents itself as the lived space of social perception and human experience: the life-world. In the following section we will examine how the life-world, as the repository of individual and collective meaning, is dialectically related to the social totality (which is the organization of power elements within society) in which it is circumscribed. This model of power will serve as a framework of analysis upon which the critique of agon culture is based.

Chapter 5

The Agon of War

I'm just a normal man
I wouldn't hurt nothing at all
but here we are

our leaders have a plan
I'd only kill if it's for them
now here we are

I drove in a car and flew in a plane
to come to your house and kick your door in
now it's down to this, it's just you and me
I'll blow your fucking head off for my country

~Lyric from the song
This Is War by Smile Empty Soul

Agon culture is the culture of war, and war is the expression of agonal rationality in its most explicit and horrific manifestation. If the gruesome reality of war is something we have come to accept as a fact of life, that acceptance has to do with the strident *normalization* of war – where war is not seen as the penultimate irrationality and absolute horror that it is, but rather is seen as something normal, justifiable, functional, natural, glorious and honourable. War, like violence, is something that often gets explained away as an inevitable and age-old problem of human society, but it remains a socially constructed reality that emerges from the rational will of those empowered to give the orders.[1]

War is mystified in many ways: as a form of solidarity, as an expression of politics, as a fact of human nature, as an expression of the innate human propensity for aggression, as a re-stabilizer of society necessary for continued growth, as good for the economy. The most enduring (non-psychological) explanation and mystification of war is perhaps the view that sees it as the material expression of the unfolding dialectic of history – that it is through the triumph of strategic "accomplishment" achieved within the contest of strength between combatant state armies that gives rise to a new state of affairs in an imperial battlefield where states vie for a larger piece of the global resources. As such, "world history traditionally is constructed out of the winners and losers of battles" (Davis and Stasz 1990: 282). It is on this basis that human societies are believed to advance themselves forward into a new phase of "progressive" history. This remains an ideological view insofar as it supports the idea that war is historically necessary in order for human progress to occur. We shall deal with this myth later on in the following chapter on the agonal dialectic of history.

While war certainly forms a substantial part of human history, war has evolved to become ever more *normalized* a part of life in modern society. Normalization is a basic strategy of discursive power. The normalization process has a fundamental cultural component to it, one contained in the disseminations of popular media texts and their ideological fetishization of competition, victory, conquest, war and warrior worship. The normalization of war also has to do with the expansion and insidious insertion of war into the fabric of everyday language and cultural meanings, and thus into the practices of everyday life. Meaning formulated on the basis of war logic makes the logic of war into a regular "problem solving" technique. So we are accustomed to hearing about having to "do battle" with this and that, and other metaphors of war action as part of our daily lexicon. We shall explore this aspect of agon culture later on in the chapter on popular agonism and the mediagon.

In agon culture positive action, power and strength is conceived on the basis of war action: war is seen as a means of resolution to the many problems of society. Public fervour is motivated on the basis of the call to war. Consequently we have many wars going on: the war on drugs, the war on crime, the zero tolerance war on youth, the notorious "global" war on terrorism, among the many other "cruel little wars" (Joxe 2002) that are mounting on top of many larger diffuse wars engaged in by the hegemonic nation states of the world. The practical strength that is believed to be war is seen as a desirable course of action in the resolution of difficulties. War is the ultimate expression of that agonal myth which believes in the *truth of force* and that force in the end proves truthful. In the agonal imaginary the progressive advancement out of problems is to wage war against them. War is always the final solution – the regress of logic into action. This has become the conventional wisdom of "problem solvers" and motivational managers within agon culture. It is also a form of regressive hysteria – another reflex action of the *hysterical agon and its spasm of power.*

The ubiquity of "war logic" as an aspect of conscious problem solving is an indication of the extent to which we are increasingly living within "a military definition of reality" (Mills 1956: 185). In such a context, and despite the lack of good results from the tactic of warfare, people have been socialized into accepting war as a reasonable course of action. The death and destruction of innocents is seen as a justifiable cost of war.[2] Such horrors are conveniently dealt with through Orwellian forms of linguistic violence in tropes such as "collateral damage," "friendly fire," and so on.

It is becoming more and more difficult, within the context of the cultural exaltation of war and warriorism, to see war for the absolute horror and senseless violation that it actually is. The sanitization of war is an essential component of contemporary agon culture – one based on the normalization of violence as a basic form of power and the instrumentality of conflict as funda-mental mode of perception within the prevailing system of social values. As such, violence and war form a significant part of the order and the reason of the modern political state which is in essence an agonal state.

The Warfare State

As Nanette Davis and Clarice Stasz write, "Critical theory holds that *it is the modern state that is most instrumental in creating and sustaining a violent social environment*" (1990: 277, emphasis in original). The problem of violence is generally recognized as among the most serious of all social problems and thus it generates a great deal of public concern. The "conventional wisdom" is that violence is something undesirable, something to be avoided. The critical public consciousness is openly against those individuals who resort to violence as a means to an end. The resort to physiological or mental abuse is rightly seen as an unacceptable type of behaviour. Many voices speak out against violence, especially against the violence directed at women and children[3] – these concerns constitute the radical ethics of public consciousness, one that disapproves of the illogicality and destructiveness of violence. Despite this concern around violence it remains a primary activity of the agonal state, which uses violence not only when "absolutely necessary" or "when it is justified," but increasingly to maintain social controls that are a regular part of state action in the post-9/11 era – including the criminalization of dissent of various forms (Colaguori and Torres 2010).

Officially, the state claims to be against violence. Heads of state publicly denounce violence and yet actively engage in the worst form of violence ever conceived – and that is war: the organized destruction of human beings and their cities, their resources, and so on. What the heads of state really mean when they say "no to violence" is that one should not take it upon themselves to personally engage in violence, and that violence shall remain the exclusive preserve of the state. The main antinomy of the civil state is that it professes an ethical and moral distaste for violence yet is actively involved in the production of violence through its support of armaments industries, increasing nuclear proliferation, and the refusal of the United States, for example, to ban land mines.

Violence, rather than something mythical, "complex" or natural is in the context of the agonal state exercised primarily as a form of social control. Such a use of violence is no different from the violence used by rapists – violence is not a metaphysical mystery, as one would be led to believe by the many ideologies of violence (Colaguori 2010). From a sociological point of view it is the means through which the subjugation of others is achieved.

It is a sociological axiom that the state claims the legitimate monopoly over the use of violent force (Weber 1946; Benjamin 1978), although this legitimacy is a matter of dispute (Wolff 1969). Violence is part of the primordial genesis of the state – its originary lifeblood as it were. Without violence, no modern state could have come into existence in the form of state we have today. The emergence of states depends on the utilization of violence in the service of power; for Hobbes, "it is the universal threat of premature death that makes the authorization of the sovereign possible" (Brown 2000: 91). The legitimacy of the state is founded in law – in legal words, but for "words to be bindingly meaningful, they must be backed by force" (Brown 2000: 92). Colonial, military and imperial forces are all based on violence as their basic type of power. Violence is thus a fundamental part of the state institutional structure, especially its military and paramilitary agencies of control (Althusser 1971). It is difficult to find a state in the world today that does not have a military apparatus upholding its power. Although Deleuze and Guattari (1986) argue that the military is an "eternal institution" and is separate from the state, this insight does little to help understand the integral relation which exists between the military and the state's wholly undemocratic monopolization of military power. Thus, the political organization of the state and the deployment of military violence are dialectical unities.

The state, born in violence, perpetually bears the mark of its catastrophic origins. Marvin Harris, writing on the anthropological origin of states, explains how this fact fundamentally dictates the character of life under the state society:

> For the first time there appeared on earth kings, dictators, high priests, emperors, prime ministers, presidents, governors, mayors, generals, admirals, police chiefs, judges, lawyers, and jailers, along with dungeons, jails, penitentiaries, and concentration camps. Under the tutelage of the state, human beings learned for the first time how to bow, grovel, kneel and kowtow. In many ways the rise of the state was the descent of the world from freedom to slavery. (Harris 1977: 102)

The totalitarian rationality of the agonal warfare state is revealed in the "total logic" (Dyer 1985) of war as represented by the functioning of the war machine. This rationality is also related to the agonal state's notion of justice: Take for example the state's self-proclaimed right to execute its own citizens in the name of "capital punishment" – it is interesting to note the heinous example of the brutality of the state which executes conscripted soldiers who conscientiously objected to the death-making of war and yet death was the final judgment inflicted upon them. This is the totalitarian judgment of the state, that it metes out death when its very orders to kill are violated.

What is the nature of the state that cancels out the right of free choice with the very denial of the right to life? Is it not disturbingly ironic that the very thing that was sacrosanct to the "offenders" – their own lives and the lives of those whom they were ordered to kill, life itself – was exactly what was denied them? Their offence was both legal and cultural. Treason is accompanied by the perhaps even greater national offence to the war values of valiant behaviour, loyalty, honour and courage – where courage is based on giving oneself over to the possibility of death. The ultimate sacrifice one is asked to make in the name of loyalty to the nation-state is "the gift of death" (Derrida 1994b).

The agonal state so demands conformity from its citizens that lives are destroyed should some choose not to comply with the dictates of the state. This death penalty does not only speak about the gruesome nature of political control and state justice as one based on revenge (another example of the truth of force), but the will behind this tactic in terms of the right over life and death is the ultimate form of power. State-sanctioned murder, as in the case of "capital punishment" in the warped justice of many legal systems, upholds the value and sovereignty of violence in so far as retribution in the form of punishment by death is an act which "repeats the exterminating gesture" (Derrida 1994a) of the mad criminal and thereby makes the state itself into a regular killer. As Adorno writes, "Murder is thus the repeated attempt, by yet greater madness, to distort the madness of such false perception into reason" (1974: 105). Capital murder is a perverse mimesis of criminality which does not challenge the value of the criminal act but seeks to overpower it through greater violence. This is precisely what is meant by the "monopolization of violence by the state" identified by Weber as the legal prerogative of the state – all agonal states reserve this right, and not just autocratic ones. Violence within this strategy of power, as a value in and of itself, is never questioned. It is a given that sacrificial violence itself is the ultimate and brutal truth – the truth of death.

The state's legal option of executing its own citizens under the euphemism of "capital punishment" – which is the newspeak term for state murder – is a fundamental part of the agonism of the state. State murder gets justified as the penultimate expression of justice as revenge: tit for tat, an eye for an eye, a life for a life. When justice coincides with killing this represents the breakdown of reasoning, the reification of logic. This both seriously compromises the ethics of the jurisprudential apparatus and completely contradicts the civilizational edict against violence.

When the state kills in order to police crime, it reveals itself as the bigger, more powerful criminal. Its actions do not challenge the value of killing but legitimates the penal system and the larger legal order to which it is attached as an expression of the state's absolute power over life and death. The war on crime is another aspect of how agonistic power is used to create an ideology that legitimates violent force as the highest form of instrumental justice.

The state's resort to violence in the attempt to resolve difficulties, either through engaging in war or through the state-sponsored killing of capital murder, sets an odious standard for power and justice – one that reveals violence as the true basis of political power. In resorting to violence the agonal state creates a cardinal precedent; it reveals an action model that symbolically filters down into the culture at large, through to its value system and its behavioural practices. In such a manner the act of violence serves as the standard of power which gets mimicked by persons in the pursuit of justice and "empowerment:" From children shooting each other in schoolyards to soldiers going of to "defend our freedom" by killing strangers in far off lands, violence is seen to form a legitimate and "effective" type of instrumental power.

The instrumentality of violence as a legitimate form of power is so engrained in the consciousness of the agonal subject that the violence of the state is publicly denied. Its wars, police repression and executions are not seen as a form of violence. "Oh, that's not the same thing!" people will exclaim. Such "things" are seen as something else other than violence – motive comes into the play of perception here and violence is mythologized as protection, as peace keeping and law and order maintenance. And as such state violence is seen as "necessary" and just. So elaborate has been the discourse which publicly legitimates the state's right to kill that it extends into the popular aesthetics of entertainment culture where death and violence is heroized, eroticized, and woven into the text of the "agonal sublime." The aesthetics of violence is part of the system of the political economy of values. This is part of the cultural adoption of the "military definition of reality" – to see things always in militaristic-agonistic terms. Consequently we have journalists reporting form the "front lines," where the "action" is, dressed in military "fatigues." The problems of the military become the problems of the Nation, the soldiers need our respect or they will lose "morale." To be critical of the military invites the risk of being stigmatized as unpatriotic – now, in the spasmodic modality of power that characterizes the post-9/11 agonal politics of suspicion, to do so is to openly invite danger. An increasingly elaborate network of espionage, surveillance, and arbitrary detention of those deemed a threat has formed in the part of the normal of warfare as an "asymmetrical" operation (Colaguori and Torres 2011).

Engaging in war is the most brutal form of power by which the agonal state seeks to maintain itself and its dominion. The existence of agonal states is coterminous with the project of domination. This imperative forms part of the agonal state as:

- a military state;
- a penal juridico-repressive state;
- a corporate state;[4] and
- an imperial state.

The fact that it is the precisely the actions of nation-states that control the balance of life and death, and not the once-feared forces of nature, speaks of the extent to which the Enlightenment fantasy of control has been realized in the destructive instrumentality of the agonal nation-state in its claims to maximize "survival" – and its mimesis of the perceived violent state of nature and thus its power over life and death. Foucault writes

> Wars are no longer waged in the name of a sovereign
> who must be defended; they are waged on behalf of

the existence of everyone; entire populations are
mobilized for the purpose of wholesale slaughter in
the name of life necessity: massacres have become
vital. It is as managers of life and survival, of bodies
and the race, that so many regimes have been able
to wage so many wars, causing so many men to be
killed. And through a turn that closes the circle, as
the technology of wars has caused them to tend
increasingly towards all-out destruction, the decision
that initiates them and the one that terminates them
are in fact increasingly informed by the naked question of survival. The atomic situation is now at the
end point of this process: the power to expose a
whole population to death is the underside of the
power to guarantee an individual's continued existence. The principle underlying the tactics of battle
– that one has to go on killing in order to go on living
– has become the principle that defines the strategy
of states. (Foucault 1978: 137)

Through this agonal strategy the survival of the state (especially
government) takes priority over any other imperative, including
that of the lives of citizens. According to the agonal military logic
of survival, the lives of others are always expendable. This credo
is at the basis of the defensive posture of the state and the persistence of its military and policing apparatus.

Justifying War

In the present geopolitical context of competing nation-states, it
is useful to understand war as a form of instrumental activity, one
that is tied to a larger economic and political purpose. While war
is recognized as an activity that fundamentally shapes the course
of human history, this does not mean that history needs wars.
Wars continue to exist not because they are eternal, inevitable
and natural dimensions of the human condition but because they
serve strategic political aims in a world of constructed scarcity
and global resource pillage.

People generally do not want wars. Even for those who
have never personally experienced war, they have to be per-

suaded. It is the state corporate rulership that needs war in order
to continue capital resource control, and in doing so needs the
consent of the population. This is a consent solicited through ideological coercion and various forms of sophisticated and persistent propaganda that foments public enthusiasm for war – the
ideological function of language is never so pronounced as in the
time of war, when all public discourse gets subordinated to bla-
tantly propagandistic aims. In a society where the political state
maintains a military and actively engages in war or is preparing
for war, it is very important from the point of view of the strategy
of such states to maintain an active interest in war among the population. The ideological conditioning for war is a necessary cultural dimension of the perpetual war society and part of what C.
Wright Mills refers to as the establishment of a "high state of war
preparedness" within the society at large.

The present global situation of war, including the smaller
wars that are raging in various places on earth, is a reflection of
a larger problematic geopolitical order – a manifestation of a historical pattern, an empire order. Empires are forms of insecure
order – they do not emerge from democratic consensus. They rely
on the use of force, both the repression of their own citizens and
the waging of war against other nation-states, to maintain control.
This is not to suggest that war represents a "clash of civilizations," as Samuel Huntington (1993) theorizes, where competing
value systems and worldviews embodied in different cultures
"clash" through the mutual contest of war to determine which is
superior and who deserves to stand victorious as the new civilizational benchmark of history. Cultural pluralism does not necessarily create conflict. Rather, the empire order of war is about
conquest and not mutual contest. Wars are merely one, albeit
odious, dimension of what nation-states, in their acting out as
institutions of insecure order, resort to in the attempt to continue
as imperial forces, to "stake their claims" on the earth and its capital, as it were. Wars are the hysterical responses of agonal states
who provoke reaction from others or who act under the suspicion
of threat, and who seek to expand their dominions on the basis
of cultivating the "spoils of war," which are then claimed as the
bounty of victory. The legal system consecrates such activities in
the arbitrary categories it invents, such as "legitimate property"
and "new territory."

The spoils of war are also part of the "fortunes of war:" the acquisitions garnered from the coffers of the vanquished and also secondary gains benefiting the force, like the raping of females by soldiers and the removal of personal possessions and dental gold from the bodies of the enemy soldiers (Bourke 1999). In World War II, first the Nazi regime and then the Americans "plundered" the art riches, oil paintings, sculptures and other items of value from the European cities. Such practices are part of the "sacking" of armies. This extra violation is a normal part of what marauding armies do. In modern techno-war "sacking" has mostly given way to "levelling." Which of these occurs depends on who the "combatants" are, and also on the level of technological power and distancing of the attacking force from the besieged. Rome was "plundered," Dresden and Tokyo were "firebombed," Hiroshima and Nagasaki were "incinerated." Chomsky writes that,

> After WW2 the US Strategic Bombing Survey concluded that "probably more people lost their lives by fire in Tokyo in a six hour period than at any time in the history of man." (Chomsky 2000: 163)

However, the true spoils of war, it must not be forgotten is human life.[5] The logic of war as a form of agonism is revealed in the brutal mathematical logic of one life for another, one for one, tit for tat, which used to be the battle tactics of soldiers confined to the front line. In comparison, contemporary warfare uses long-range weaponry, unmanned drones and other technologies that have destructive effects at a distance. The older strategy of attrition would ideally serve as a mutual deterrent to the spread of war and be based on a contest of will among armies; but in the age of postmodern war (DeLanda 1991) the old rule of one for one, a body for a body, which partially kept warfare under check, was extended to include civilian casualties as well ("total war"), and is part of the generalization of the enemy/other as a numbered body. The abstract and anonymous violence of death is the real currency of value that circulates in the totalizing agonal logic of war – "one of yours for one of ours:" Despite the changes in practice of warfare throughout the modern era up to the present, the agonal logic of tit for tat continues to inform the logic of warfare.

Abstract violence is thus about the antagonistic structure of imaginary relations that serve to perpetuate war through the violation of memory. This is why discursive efforts to label the killings of war in types such as, "unlawful," legitimate, military, "terroristic," "friendly," are all rhetorical efforts in vain.

Abstract violence is also related to the indiscriminate nature of bombing. Even the advanced (so-called "smart") techno-weapons of postmodern warfare (DeLanda 1991; Gray 1997; Kellner and Best 2001) still fail to hit their targets or involve bombs that do not even detonate at the right time, despite the reassurance offered by military tropes of "surgical strike precision." The abstract nature of killing in war also extends to the perpetuation of deathly violence out of time and context – as in the case of land mines and chemical and radioactive weapons for example, that continue to kill innocent humans many years into the future, beyond the temporal boundaries of the original conflict.

The contemporary political and economic landscape of the earth in the context of war has become a giant geopolitical agon in which empire states compete for their share of the global spoils. Modern wars are the symptoms of the dominant nation-states "flexing their muscle," asserting their claims. Such actions, from actual war to weapons testing, economic warfare, counter-attacks and all the forms of state-induced rivalry and conflict, have transformed the geopolitical landscape of the globe into a *hysterical agon*. The political hysteria of war (which is part of the insanity of war), is the ultimate symptom of the insecurity of the imposed order of inter-state competition, domination and its spasms of power. Today the spasm of power, in the North American context, is revealed in the antagonistic actions being enacted to fight the wholly anonymous "war on terrorism," in the state's elimination of the basic civil rights and freedoms that form the most coveted aspects of the political Constitutions and Charters, in the "unilateral" right to detain "suspects" without due process protections, and in numerous other occurrences which mark the regression of the social welfare state into the agonal warfare state (Marcuse 1964; Nelson 1987).

Perhaps the most glaring instance of the spasm of empire power unleashing its brutal violation most consistently and importantly is in the fight for the "Promised Land." This is exceedingly significant for Jacques Derrida (1994a) who in

Specters of Marx centres the theme of his analysis of the global problematic around a line from Shakespeare's *Hamlet*: "the time is out of joint." Derrida writes "the world is going badly," and proceeds to list what he terms are the ten plagues of new-world disorder, all of which are relational to military conflict (1994: 77). He indicates that the centre of power in this regard finds "its place in the Middle East," where "messianic eschatologies mobilize there all the forces of the world and the whole 'world order' in the ruthless war they are waging against each other" (1994a: 58). Derrida's 1994 prediction that war in the Middle East would be the epicentre of the geopolitical hot zone was accurate in its relation to the events of 9/11. At present this is a hot zone of a different variety now that democratic revolutionary movements have sprung up in many nations in the Middle East and North Africa as of late 2010. And of course military action is a part of these events too.

As is the typical case with most conflicts involving powerful nations, the resonations move far beyond the geographical immediacy of the militarized battle zone. The actions of states in their capacity as military empires are indeed threatening to turn the geopolitical space of the life-world into a perpetual agon. This is precisely what is suggested by the idea of a "permanent war economy," or a "perpetual war order." These concepts have lost their capacity even to startle any longer. So has the entire discourse of militarism, military strategic talk and the now generalized combative language of everyday war. Military discourse and military metaphors have entered firmly into the popular language of agon culture to make the military view of reality the normal one. As Orwell (1954) made clear, state power and the power of its corporate mouthpiece mass media deception are fundamentally linked to the manipulation and reformulation of language to accord with obedience and conformity. The euphemisms of war are becoming all too familiar; like advertising slogans, are "drilled into us" (Adorno) as forms of linguistic violence: "friendly fire," "collateral damage," "rogue states," "warlords," "peacekeeping," "illegal combatants," "weapons of mass destruction," "ethnic cleansing," "Operation Infinite Justice," "Operation Anaconda," "Operation Mountain Lion," "surgical strike," "hearts and minds" – the utilization of predatorial nomenclature to normalize state predation is a fundamental strategy in the normalization of war. Linguistic violence involves the reformulation of military terms into euphemisms of efficiency and justice: "getting the job done quick and easy."

The newspeak of war, which is officially issued by the military and faithfully reproduced by the corporate media, works to deflect attention away from questioning the issues and contradictions, and serves to uphold the military's view of the situation. This is the agonistic ideology in language that is essential to the maintenance of agon culture and which we will look at more closely later in this book.

Agonistic reason cannot conceive of power and history outside of an overarching ontology of war. The message of agon culture is that war is here to stay and therefore we should work to "keep it clean," quick, efficient and improve its methods. This is the extent of the normalization of war. War, at its present level of escalation, is such an essential feature of international affairs and political consciousness that the question of its total elimination seems almost unimaginable. The proliferation of war in numerous forms – trade wars,[6] peacekeeping, ethnic, regional, territorial, criminal, drugs, religious, holy, civil, technological, genocidal, among its many forms – is now so normalized a scene in global politics that the question seems no longer how to eliminate war, but how to perfect it. The "perfect" war is seen in terms of both the "just war" and the "winnable" war. This perception is certainly related to the effectiveness of the ideology of war as natural, inevitable, heroic and historically progressive. The latest twist on winnable and just wars is the postmodern techno-war which uses unmanned drones and other forms of technologically advanced armaments to perfect killing. None of it seems to make any difference anyway. The war in Afghanistan has been raging for over a decade and in the battle between advanced techno-weaponry and a rag-tag Taliban army with old guns and rocket launchers the long stalemate indicates that technological solutions do not always work as planned.

Despite this the dream of technological solutions continues to prevail. The popular discourse, as evidenced in such hegemonic media as *Time* magazine (for example, in May of 2000), which rarely questions the absolute irrationality of war but instead dreams the future of war in terms of "How Will We Fight?" The answer comes in the form of a technological solution in the listing of new and innovative weapons that will make war more efficient a procedure, more exacting, more deadly – "decisive" is perhaps the correct military term. This dream is becoming nightmare scenario in the current proliferation of drone weapons technology. Unmanned drone weapon systems are quickly becoming the preferred choice among military combatant forces worldwide. The challenges such weapons pose has raised the stakes in terms of the logic of destruction.

Meanwhile the philosophers and strategists of war continue to debate what constitutes "the just war" (Walzer 1977), falling desperately into the logic of the agon, which sees war as ultimately justifiable on some ideal grounds. The historians of war seek to assert the empirical inevitability of war as the pivotal event in the twists and turns of a progressive human history.

The ideological presentation of war in the media utilizes the horror of war as a problem created by the enemy in an effort to drive a campaign of glory such that war is presented as something necessary to wage. Consensus about how to end war quickly becomes the occasion for the financing and production of more and better weapons for a presumably quicker victory. Key players in the war are hailed as national celebrities in the mediatized ecstasy that accompanies the presentation of war in contemporary agon culture.[7] War becomes a story about honour, heroism and the protection of peace instead of a lament over the senseless mass murder of soldiers and civilians alike. Part of the sanitization of the brutality of war involves the dissemination of the idea that soldiers are not killers but that they are heroic fighters – "warriors" is the currently favoured mediagon term. This ideology works to conceal the brutal reality of war as a form of mass slaughter. Joanna Bourke, in *An Intimate History of Killing* (1999), writes against the view which seeks to "deny the centrality of killing and human slaughter" (1999: 2) as an essential part of modern war. She sets out to debunk the myth of the soldier as the sorrowful hero and demonstrates quite clearly, through interviews and letters written by soldiers themselves, that a great many soldiers actually love killing. Many soldiers claim to have been pre-conditioned by growing up with televisual combat as a sort of "basic training" – through "the romanticized canon of war" as depicted in the litany of Hollywood war scenarios. The "thrill of destruction" and the "turn on of butchery" are what makes deadly combat "orgasmic" (Bourke 1991). This gives new macabre meaning to the term "theatre of war."

The sanitization of killing is therefore not something confined to the citizens who remain at home in times of war but extends into the very act of subjective experience of the killer who actually does the killing. A number of Bourke's subjects responded that they saw the battlefield as a television screen and their adversaries as TV villains. Bourke does not suggest that TV simply creates killers; what it does is provide a conditioning and normalizing context for the act of killing. The cultural normalization and celebration of killing aids in the subjective psychic disembodiment required for the taking of another human life, and in that sense televisual fantasies of warriorism and death ecstasies substantially enables killing. Other contexts of value and meaning oriented against war and towards the sanctity of life and the humanity of the other, would not so easily lend themselves to killing and to the value-less view of human life. Televisual war therefore does indeed have a dialectical relationship with real war.

Killing in war is not easy for every soldier. Humans are not ready-made for killing. Many soldiers come back with permanent psychological damage in the form of post-traumatic stress disorder (PTSD). It seems the newspeak discourse of agonal toughness, as in the phrase "what does not kill you makes you stronger," is nonsense. Ask someone with PTSD, or even someone who has suffered a physical injury, if they are stronger as a result. How can one ever be the same? Soldiers who kill people in order to "save their own asses" or to protect the life of a friend often do end up with PTSD. That is the epitome of reification – self preservation that leads to self destruction. Because the act of killing the other is not, cannot be a true form of self preservation.

For too many years the fact of psychological damage suffered by soldiers in post-combat situations was kept hush by the military: A sign of weakness, a sign of shame and dishonour – a truth that needed to be concealed because it revealed another fact about the larger insanity of war. Sanitizing the reality of war's horror is necessary to keep the agonal system going. Thus, it is not by accident that the war society develops its play and leisure activities along the same lines: competition, combat and predation, and the methods of making things more fun and exciting.

Biblical War

The sanitization of war, however, has a substantial history to it, one which originates far back in the teachings of the Bible and which is carried forth in the destructive ideologies of the Abrahamic religions. Noam Chomsky (2000) identifies this religious dimension of killing as the "sacralization of war," which is the sanctification of savagery to serve the higher interests of God, Church and Nation. Chomsky writes:

> Probably the extremes of savagery – recorded savagery, at least – are in the earliest histories, in the Bible. I suppose that in the entire literary canon there is nothing that exalts genocide with such fervor and dedication and enthusiasm as the commandments of the warrior God to his chosen people – for example, his commandments delivered to King Saul by the prophet Samuel, who was the most just of the judges, and who conveyed the commandment to Saul to attack Amalek and spare nothing, killing all men, women, infants, and sucklings, oxen and sheep, camels and asses – the reason being that centuries earlier the Amalekites had stood in the way of the Hebrews conquering their Holy Land. (Chomsky 2000: 158)

The Bible itself is one of the most notoriously antinomical documents of all times.[8] When the slaughter of war is seen as something divinely ordained, as it still is today, the holiness of divination and the savagery of killing both lose their meaning; as such, "the old march of world history once more asserts itself" (Mills 1956: 171). This "legacy of war," as Chomsky calls it, gets inherited in modern times as the ultimate higher benevolent function and goodness of war and human slaughter.

Modern war has by no means departed from justifying itself as a sacred thing, but the idea of benevolent war has taken on a secular meaning also; a meaning which we can locate in the vulgarization of a foundational principle of Western Enlightenment philosophy, that of Immanuel Kant's maxim of the "categorical imperative"[9] and the moral/ethical edict contained in it that just as one would not want to be denied the good fortune and good reason of others, it would be unjust to not spread goodness and reason should one be in possession of it. The European conquests were ideologically and morally motivated on precisely such a basis. (It is not for nothing that colonialism was always combined with religious proselytization and missionary efforts). Slaughter was seen as a means towards an ends, a constructive activity, part of a "civilizing mission" (Nandy 1983), as an act of liberation for the culture of those being slaughtered. Chomsky writes:

> Early in this century, US troops were liberating the Philippines – liberating several hundred thousand souls from life's sorrows and travails. The press was very much impressed by this heroic and generous endeavor, and described it with some accuracy… The press reported very positively that the American forces were "slaughtering the natives in English fashion," so that "the misguided creatures who resist us will at least respect our arms" and later come to recognize our good intentions. (Chomsky 2000: 161)

What the imperial state learned from its merciless and crude colonial endeavours was how to perfect war and human slaughter into a modern form of control based on "industrial genocide." The Nazis are rightly reviled for executing their holocaustic slaughter with unbridled industrial efficiency while the Americans are heroized for the atomic incineration of hundreds of thousands of civilian Japanese. On not one but two separate occasions US forces dropped atomic bombs, one more powerful than the other, on the cities of Hiroshima and Nagasaki at precisely the time when children were being bussed off to school. The necessity of this drastic "action" remains a matter of debate on the part of war analysts, as does the firebombing of Dresden and other cities.

For the agonal state, war is never over. It is a work-in-progress, an unending exercise over time – part of the ongoing perfection of the "perfect machine" (Nelson 1987). The atomic cataclysm inflicted on Japan was the realization of a long-awaited atomic power plan: The Manhattan Project, contrary to popular belief in the American reluctance to join World War II, was begun before the outbreak of war (Nelson 1987); nuclear escalation continued long afterward. The proliferation of nuclear weapons continues to remain a serious threat to the entire globe.

The cool and calculated rationality that plans and propels war has come to see war as a grand experiment in human life, death and the perfection of military control. Scientists, who are always around the engineering of modern war, were rushed into Japan immediately after the atomic detonations and surrender of Japan to "measure" and "collect data" on the effects on human flesh and on the immediate vicinity. In an absolute military-like campaign to control public opinion on atomic matters, these scientists were accompanied by military personnel who seized control of Japanese film of the destruction, which clearly revealed the extent of the atrocity (Nelson 1987).

By the late 1960s the heavy use of chemical weapons by US forces in Vietnam was seen as a prized opportunity for American military intelligence and scientific research. Because so much chemical poison was expelled into the environment and onto the people of Vietnam, in the discourse of scientific objectivity it "furnished an extensive control group" (Chomsky 2000: 170). Today in Iraq, more than twenty years after the devastating military assault known as The Gulf War, and well into the second Iraq war, the killing persists long after the last shots of war were fired. The shells fired from American tanks were not conventional metal bullets; as if part of some gruesome tactic to get rid of hazardous radioactive waste, the American military decided to use shells made from radioactive depleted uranium cores as bullets. Consequently the sand in the region has become so irradiated from these shells that breast and lung cancer is approaching epidemic proportions among the population who live in regions where this ordinance was used, and now radioactive sand is blown into the air and is breathed into the lungs. In 2005 in Fallujah reports of increased birth defects and excess rates of cancer began to emerge. These were attributed to the use in Iraq of mutagenic and carcinogenic weapons (Busby, Hamdan and Ariabi 2010).

The weapons that remain in many previous war zones continue to kill long after actual war has ended. There are too many examples of this temporal extension of war, from land mines to chemical weapons disasters to list here. The point is that war is not just about the strategic use of force to defeat another force. It is not only discipline and mastery – modern war is also a giant Nazi-like experiment on the perfection of the techniques of killing. A number of recent wars (Viet Nam, Balkan) also replicated on the Nazi theme of cultural justification and became the occasion for racial extermination. Insofar as the decision to use chemical and radioactive weapons is often justified on the basis of the racial or cultural inferiority the enemy in question, war concentrates all of the barbarism of scientific progress in a single activity.

The rationality of war is reified rationality. The logic of war is based on a belief in instrumental goal achievement through the use of "superior" force of destruction, and that the preservation of life is based on the power of death. Agonal logic, from the punitive justice of the carceral state to the exercise of war, collapses onto itself – that is, the means overcome and absorb the ends. Agonal logic represents what Derrida terms the "fatality of vengeance" (1994a: 21). Agonistic/military logic is a false logic which reveals its antinomical character in the fact that successful military campaigns are very few and far between. Where military activity has been initiated as a means to an ends, it is the means – destruction – which endure for long afterwards. Military campaigns very rarely work to restore stability, order or "peace" (as in "peacekeeping").

The myth of modern techno-war as logically planned, precise and efficient, which is part of the ideology of "successful war," is also a false one. In actuality the military are consistently revealed as bumbling fools who communicate poorly among each other and often miss their targets or shoot and kill their own or the people they have claimed to go and defend. The military/media euphemism "friendly fire" is beginning to lose its power of persuasion. At public events like "air shows," where the military display their latest wares plane crashes are becoming more and more common. These seem to be on the rise despite superior pilot training, computer guidance systems and the whole gamut of new military "smart" technology. The military and military science has a long history of incompetence and disaster. It is a little known-fact that "rocket scientists," ironically a group whose very name became synonymous with genius in the context of early World War II rocketry, have been the most spectacularly unsuccessful group of scientific and technical researchers. If we

consider the number of accidents and deaths they have created
in the hundreds of failed rocket experiments and the massive
explosions which have resulted, the term "rocket scientist" might
be rethought as a colloquial synonym for genius.

Even though the United States is not the only country in
the world to have had numerous military and rocket catastrophes,
it is a society whose very development has occurred alongside
military development; hence, it is the model of agon culture. The
United States has the largest military and is the largest producer
and supplier of military arms on earth, as the United States continues to profit from destruction as the "world's leading dealer in
weapons of mass destruction" (Visano 1998: 17). It uses its military arsenal regularly on other people in other lands – we can
hardly get into the details of such notorious activities here, other
than to note that Noam Chomsky has made a career out of writing
at length about American military involvements. He writes that
"the US has the unilateral right to use force at will. Period" (2000:
14). The state's love of the use of force has its analogue in the
agonistic American "gun slinging" self, in the individual legal
"right to bear arms" which is a sacrosanct element of freedom
contained in the second amendment of the US Constitution.
Laurie Anderson points out:

> This amendment was written two hundred years
> ago back when people were bagging possum. So
> it's pretty outdated now as a concept. The found-
> ing fathers probably hadn't imagined that eighth
> graders would be showing up at school armed
> with semi-automatic assault weapons. And they
> probably didn't predict that at the end of the twen-
> tieth century the privately owned arsenals in the
> USA would dwarf almost every other county's
> national stockpiles – the current figures are these:
> two hundred and sixty million Americans – two
> hundred million guns. (Anderson in Bender and
> Druckrey 1994: 224)

And John O'Neill (1991), on the extent to which popular agonism
is firmly entrenched in American popular identity, an identity
based on a paranoiac, narcissistic self-fetishization states:

> The equality of Americans consists in their toler-
> ance of the ways they have of deceiving one

another, impoverishing one another, and of mur-
dering one another. The birthright of Americans
is given with their congenital blindness to America. Thus, strictly speaking, Americans have no
foreign policy other than a psychotic fear of not
being loved as Americans. This fear populates
their world with aliens, communists, terrorists,
and savages. America's weak military record
requires that its wars – which cannot be lost
because they are rarely official – be rewon by
Hollywood's collection of soldiers, spies and
cops. (O'Neill 1991: 15)

This, O'Neill reminds the reader, is the America of "MEDI-
AMERICA," "which is not entirely ruled by America." MEDI-
AMERICA is the cultural brand of American identity that lives
up to its own mass-mediated depiction of itself – a depiction
which has been formed in the context of violence and counter-
violence, and in the consequent popular cultivation of hatred and
fear masking itself as strength. In the ecstasy of the *mediagon*,
hatred has become popular, and violence has become palatable,
agreeable, joyful, and even erotic. This gives rise to numerous
perversions of subjective desire, however the mass-popular example remains the love of war.

The patriotic love of militarism that is part of MEDI-
AMERICA and agon culture is the love of violence. Violence has
become entwined with various forms of pleasure – the pleasure
of conquest, of victory, of revenge. These are themes celebrated
and exploited by the mass media and its aesthetics of violence –
which is part of the system of popular meaning in agon culture
and part of the *media-agon* which works to justify *the violent
nature of political control that gets culturally articulated as
normal.* Violence is specularized in the texts of agon culture
where it is not seen as a horror but as a thrill. This functions,
despite the "rational" call to dethrone violence, to legitimate and
sanitize all forms of violence.

The popular appeal of violence must be understood in
relation to the psychic structure of the agonal subject in which
violence is both *repressed* and *expressed.* The cultural celebration
of violence (which is accompanied by the political instrumentality of violence), is a response to the *mastery by fear.* The attempt

to achieve mastery over fear is an activity driven by the deep recognition that one is ruled by fear. This subjective relationship with fear is part of the complex psychic entanglement with fear which leads to the celebration of death and results in the disfiguration of the agonal subject.

What is the basis for such an intimacy with violence if not the fact that it is somehow lodged deep in the structure of meaning and desire? Harold Bloom's (1982) work on agonistic meaning in *Agon: Towards a Theory of Revisionism* indicates how violence insinuates itself so consistently in the structure of dramatic literature, because meaning itself has "catastrophic origins." Bloom writes: "meaning gets started by an act of violence" (1982: 43). Bloom indicates how the Western literary canon generates meaning and truth on the basis of violence. Meaning in the realm of literature corresponds to cultural meaning in general, which is reflected in literature. Thus the agonistic dialectic of catastrophe/creation is the very idea that underpins the genesis of "meaning" within the Western cultural psyche.

The catastrophic origin of cultural meaning bears a significant relation to the "ontological insecurity" of agonal fear and to the problem of violence. Throughout this study it has been proposed that the problem of agonism, which is dialectical with the problem of violence and domination, stems from a cultural problem – from the violation of the affirmative character of culture, which results in affirmation becoming entangled with the power of death and thus realizing itself as a form of cultural negation; cultural affirmation retains its aim of self-preservation but this aim is a preservation as defensivity based on the mimicry of mastery. It is an aim which mimics the power of violence in the exterminating power of death. Violence as a means entails the violation of the original self-affirmative intention as practical action. Agonistic self-preservation is therefore the subjective entanglement with death and violence, and which represents a lapsing into reification: The individual response is the agonistic reification of consciousness; the response of the insecure state is war.

Belief in the instrumentality of violence is not only a failing of agonistic reason, it is an edict that is supported by a longstanding philosophy of violence, one that accepts violence as a generative principle, that violence is "endemic to being," that violence is the "means through which self is maintained," that "determination of self now reveals itself to be what it probably always has been; determination of the Other" (deVries and Weber 1997: 1).

These philosophical understandings of violence are ideologies for agonism. They report on what agonistic action aims to achieve as a form of practical determination. Violence endures because of the persistence of these philosophies of positive violence as a part of practical agonal reason. Violence endures and intensifies also because of the particular historical juncture of "radical evils" that are merging together in the contemporary era. Derrida argues that contemporary violence has two ages that combine to produce the "new cruelty" in the present; there is

> the hypersophistication of military tele-technology – of digital and cyberspaced culture. The other is a "new archaic violence[:]" revenge… *reverts* as closely as possible to the body proper and to the premachinal living being. In any case to its desire and its phantasm. (1997: 331)

Violence, in its ubiquity, materialty and surreality nevertheless seems to escape the grasp of concrete conceptualization – could this be due to its intimate relation with the unnameable anonymity of death?

The Question of Violence

In his essay *Other Means: On the Political Economies of Violence*, James Brown writes:

> Quite apart from the damaged and destroyed lives it leaves in its wake, violence represents a couple of problems: it can be such terrible fun, and it looks useful. Of course, in conventional economics, utility and enjoyment go together. But violence is unusual and complex for all that it promises to simplify. (Brown 2000)

That violence remains a question today, despite the many ideologies about its naturalness that abound, is an indication of the vast mythology and lack of understanding that continues to surround and mystify it. Violence remains a question precisely because it has been mythologized as complex, mysterious, dangerous, powerful, even awe-inspiring and glorious. Its true contradictory nature and complexity of forms evades simple definition. John Keane writes: "Violence is clothed in an aura of strangeness: its causes and consequences are said either to be understood insufficiently to be amenable to a course of treatment or beyond realistic hope of remedy" (Keane 1996: 8). Keane indicates the resignation to violence that forms part of the reification of violence as a magical, horrible, powerful and awe-inspiring phenomenon. It is interesting to note how many of the Gods of the ancient world, both East and West, had these same characteristics imbued upon them. However, there really is no "violence" as a particular entity in and of itself. Violence is always part of some other process or action orientation. Violence is thus best understood in relation to the context of its occurrence. This does not mean that violence has no character of its own, however, as it does. Violence, "almost by definition, violates" (Brown 2000: 91) – physically, emotionally, culturally, historically and in other ways perhaps beyond measure – violence operates through destruction or debilitation. There is also the form of conceptual violence – the violence of the concept, where the idea becomes the axiom, dogma, discursive discourse; all of these insert themselves into the ideological system that supports material violence. Nevertheless, we should not contribute to the mystification of violence by reifying it as an entity unto itself, as something abstracted from social and political reality.

There is, however, an agonistic rationality of violence. Agonistic reason presumes that violence is justifiable and warranted as a means to achieve desired ends. As Walter Benjamin (1978) indicates, the ends get superseded by the means and are thereby nullified. Agonistic reason does not accept that the violence inflicted overwhelms the goals of the aims. The agonistic reason that underlies violence is a regressive form of reason; it represents a very basc form of logic – the logic of "tit for tat." Agonism leads to *antagonism,* and therefore the initial act of violence unleashes a cycle of potentially unending reciprocal violence. This cyclical response emerges from the vengeful logic of retaliation. As we have indicated earlier, revenge is so engrained in the ideology of agon culture that it has become almost synonymous with justice.

Violence does not unite or congeal. Violence lives on but does not give life – it is not virile, it is morbid and impotent. Both Arendt and Fanon point out that violence is a degenerate and regressive form of power with few beneficial effects for progressive social change. If we can speak of a true character of violence, it is certainly a negative one. Violence generally equates with horror. It is the shadow of death. Implicit recognition of this fact partly motivates the fear and apprehension of inquiring into it. Seeing violence as a form of instrumental conflict, as a means to an end, however, makes it more palatable and allows it to be dealt with as functional and productive, if not fateful. Nevertheless, there is no comprehensive theory of violence, no school of "violentology" as such, and it certainly should not remain a question.

That violence remains indeterminate and elusive is also largely because of the numerous forms of violence and the numerous occasions which can and have given rise to violence. One immediately thinks of fighting and war as archetypical forms of violence. But there are also other forms such as screaming rage and the manipulation of others to ill ends, and philosophers talk about "conceptual violence" – which is the duress of the idea, or how the concept violates reality by masking or transforming it in discursive ways. It does not serve us well to conflate these various manifestations of violence. Fundamentally violence remains questionable because, despite how it is often celebrated in agon culture, it is also commonly seen as anathema to life: "it violates the principle of the sanctity of human life" (Keane 1996: 9). This is a principle upheld by the reason of state and of religion, two primary domains of social life and social order that have nevertheless consistently violated the edict against violence; a contradiction which has not helped clarify the problem of violence very much.

Although the final result may be the same, there are numerous causes that lead to violence in the end. This is likely one reason why there has never really been a sustained school of thought approximating a theory of violence within the Western tradition of social and political thought, rather the topic has only been treated thematically, topically. This has perhaps been its largest fault. As Arendt has indicated, within social and political thought at least, violence remains an under-explored theory of study, and that there has been a "general reluctance to deal with violence as a phenomenon in its own right" (1969: 35). Why this should be so must somehow bear a relation to the truth about the causes of social and political violence; a truth which Weber mentioned only perfunctorily by way of linking violence to the operation of political states. Weber's sociology came closest to offering a theory of rationalized violence, and this was concerning the political state which claims the "*monopoly of the legitimate use of physical force*" (Weber 1946: 78, emphasis in the original). This line of theorizing in Weber however was not offered as a critique of the state. It is more of a minute sociological observation that pertains to a topic that Weber discusses at a greater length elsewhere, as the necessity of the state to engage in various forms of "legitimate domination" (Weber 1978). The current critical tradition within social and political thought has not adequately questioned the issue of violence precisely because, given the contradictions concerning violence and the modern state, it has become impossible to discuss violence without exposing these contradictions as condemnations of the abuse of state power.

Contemporary political theory does not build on Weber's insights and turns away from the question of violence and opts instead to celebrate the virtues of civil society and the cosmopolitanism of the new globalization (Ehrenberg 1999). Much of contemporary political theory is caught up in the triumphalism of capitalist empire expansion and expends its discursive energy reinventing "capitalism" into "democracy" (Held 1987; Unger 1998). If contemporary political theory were to take Weber's insights seriously, it would extend upon the relation between the state and its violence; it would contribute to the critique of the political economy of domination, which sees the growing concentration of economic power as part of the discursive project whose aim is the economic formulation of reality, rather than presenting the re-invention of the marketplace as the new global commons.[10]

While the study of violence does not form a substantial part of any of the major theoretical debates within political theory of late, there is a growing concern with social domination. For considerations of the "new suffering" (Bourdieu 1999) and the "new cruelty" (Derrida 1997) associated with the economic imperial disorder of globalization, we must turn to the growing body of texts which take the issue of domination and globalization as their primary object of study (Barnet and Cavanagh 1994; Scott 1997; Jameson and Miyoshi 1998). Nevertheless the critique of globalization, while a critique of domination, it is not a critique of violence. Critiquing violence means getting radical about the sources of violence.

Although the Frankfurt School and their radical critique of domination comes closest to a sustained analysis of human domination as the product of a violent calculative rationality, their work is not really a theory of violence as such, even though it is informed by the historical violence of the extermination camps of World War II. Similarly the para-Marxism of what came to be known as "conflict theory" within sociology is also inadequate as a theory of violence, since it is more concerned with the social contradiction and the conflict of classes and interests under capitalism and not with violence as a means of social control as such.

This inability of sociology in particular to formulate an adequate theory of violence is related to a problem identified by O'Neill, who reminds that, "sociology has always flirted with the discovery of a social physics" (1995: 27). This tendency is part of the positivism of the social sciences, which mimics the allegedly more "successful" natural sciences in their search for natural laws and for qualitative validation in the realm of the empirical. The desire of positivist sociology is a scientific legitimacy based on a utility to power.[11] It is worth mentioning Foucault's metaphor of the "micro-physics of power" in this respect as a theory that also misleads in sounding something like a "science" of power.

It is precisely this entanglement of dominant social science with power that causes it to neglect issues of violence. O'Neill writes of this neglect as a form of the "overwhelming" of the imagination of social scientific thinking:

> The experience of our century is with a scale of violence that overwhelms social science knowledge and reduces it to fictional extrapolations of the origins and consequences of violence in utopian orders beyond genuine political experience. (O'Neill 1972: 59)

The question of violence in this regard is out of the hands of the human sciences and relegated to the "natural" sciences, which is regarded as the domain of expertise in matters of "natural reality," for the surest answers to questions of violence comes from the positivists.

Violence is perhaps the most notorious example of a problem that has motivated research for natural laws in the attempt to explain human societies and social behaviour. As Brown writes, "Violence has often been thought of as natural. For Hobbes it dominates 'the State of Nature' (2000: 91). Yet for Hobbes, who is more sophisticated than the caricatured philosopher of natural brutality he is made out to be, the answer to the question of violence remained fundamentally a social and political one. It is precisely because large scale organized violence in human societies is social and political that we need to develop a more sociological study of violence in society – a *violentology* as it were – one that examines the dialectical connections between the macrosocial event of war and the microsocial elements of society that support and normalize the reality of agonism and war. This is the aim of a critical theory of society: to reveal the agonistic configuration of social life across the social spectrum and link this reality with the problem of social domination.

Chapter 6

The Agonal Dialectic of History

> Dialectics is the ontology of the wrong state of
> things. The right state of things would be free of
> it: neither a system nor a contradiction.
>
> ~Theodor Adorno, *Negative Dialectics*

> Universal history must be construed and denied.
>
> ~Theodor Adorno, *Negative Dialectics*

If one considers the legacy of oppression and atrocity which
has marked the course of human history up to the present age,
the extent to which the larger social order continues to be
based upon relations of domination and control seems undeniable. The patterns of destruction and misery which have existed
in between the conquests and wars have not subsided with the
globalization of enlightenment (which has taken the form of a
techno-militarized global consumerism), but have in fact prolif-
erated and solidified in newer hierarchical and structural relations
of domination. Conflict, it would seem, remains the "motor of
history," and continues to impact significantly on what is deemed
"development" and "social change." The conflict that forms part
of human history, however, has developed an ontological status
to it – this is its mythical nature. The view that human history is
based on cycles of cataclysm and war, which are seen to give rise
to new stable conditions and thus constitute a form of positive
growth, is a deeply engrained ideology concerning the nature of
historical order and social reality (Popper 1986). Such a view,
while corresponding correctly to the empirical reality of human

misery in that it is tied to the catastrophic character of world history and in particular the history of state formations, is false to
the extent to which its serves only as a measure of what has transpired as the history of domination. Nor is such a pattern of domination necessarily an inevitable one for the future. Adorno
concedes that although much of human history has been tied to
domination, "it is redundant to claim that such a concession
makes this domination legitimate. The fact that domination 'is'
reports on experience and cannot be converted into a law" (Jarvis
1998: 39). The claim that the whole of history is based on a
dialectical pattern of cataclysmic growth is therefore an ideology
of history. If the "reality" of human history has indeed been based
on successive cycles of destruction and production, this empirical
evidence cannot justify the reality of history as rational simply
on the basis of being deemed "real." In contrast to Hegel, who
wrote that "the real is rational" – the reality of history based on
cataclysmic cycles as the basis of growth, is a reality which is
not rational – it is the hypostatization of cataclysm in the normalization of irrationality, insofar as we understand rationality to be
a form of reason that is harmonious with the sanctity of life. The
belief that just because a certain reality has come into being
serves as proof of its rationality and correctness is the ideology
of *amor fati* – the love of fate, and forms part of the mythology
of history as positive dialectical process of production and
destruction.

That so much of human history has indeed been marked
by violence, crisis and imperial state atrocity tends to affirm the
historical objectivity of this totalizing process as one rooted
firmly in the inevitability of historical conflict. Cycles of war and
peace, economic booms and collapses, kingdoms and empires
rising and falling – all of these sorts of things are understood as
essential aspects of human progress across history. Thus the edict
that "the history of humankind is unfolding as it should" is an
ideological truism supportive of the catastrophe/creation theory
of growth, that is, of the agonal dialectic of development and
destruction. It is both a theory and an *ideology* of history developed primarily out of the philosophy of G.W.F. Hegel (1967),
whose main idea concerns "the dialectic of negativity as the
moving and creating principle," what Marx calls Hegel's "false
positivism" (Marx in O'Neill 1996: 38). The same idea, which

circulates as a popular agonistic cliché and goes, "for every negative there is a positive – so it's not all that bad," is similarly a
form of reconciliatory ideology.

Hegel's (1967) philosophy of history is based on a notion
of dialectical progression in which positive growth emergent out
of oppositional forces and their reconciliation is the cardinal principle of life and societal progress. "Self-corroding contradiction"
gives rise to positive historical growth (Durant 1953: 296):

> For Hegel every tension between oppositional ele-
> ments carries the seeds of its own destruction and
> transcendence (*Aufhebung*) into another form. That
> is how life is. Without this process of contradiction
> and dissolution, there would be no movement,
> change, or history. (Benjamin 1988: 32n)

Out of this dialectical process human freedom becomes a greater
realization because the contradictory social conditions which
exist are brought to light and cancelled out by higher social
forms, thus "Hegel interprets history as 'progress in the consciousness of freedom'" (Fetscher in Bottomore 1991: 227).

Hegel presumed that his contemporary Fichte "was right
– that thesis, antithesis and synthesis constitute the formula and
secret of all development and all reality" (Durant 1953: 295).
Hegel spoke of a history that advances through an evolutionary
progress of innovations in human development that move the
dialectic along and are seen as the expression and unfolding of a
sublime human Spirit: the Absolute, which is contained in the
heroism of individuals who make history happen – this is Hegel's
concept of the "world-historic individual." Certainly an idealistic
view of history, one which serves to sanitize the history of atrocity by emphasizing the "monumentalism" of historic achievements, which as Nietzsche (1957) criticized, emphasized the
supposed "greatness" of great events, great leaders and great
innovations, all of which mark the tyrannical progress of history
as a teleological process of "becoming." In this view of history,
triumphalism and victory is emphasized over the continuing
destruction which is the price paid for it. In the reasoning of agon
culture, it is difficult even to conceive of "triumph" outside of
the context of victory.

Dominant strands of Western philosophical thought are
rooted precisely in this Hegelian way of thinking, and agonistic/

empire thought in particular affirms it as a matter of course. Hegel's philosophy of history serves, in philosophical thought, as the primary ideological justification for conflict being "positive" if it results in the achievement of a particular goal – just as is expressed in the popular adage that claims that "for every negative there is a positive." Hegel's dialectic of history furthers the ideology of the *productivity of contradiction* in giving rise to ever-newer innovations in the "unfolding of the human spirit," which is part of the "self-realizing Absolute." Conflict and opposition are the motor of history while unity and reconciliation are understood to be the outcome of dialectical synthesis and serve, quite problematically, to normalize the conflict played out at the level of human interaction, which is understood ontologically as the "particular" reflecting the character of the "universal." Adorno states that Hegel's entire system "calls for the naturalization of the cycle of destruction." Derrida states too that "naturalism and teleologism are founded one upon the other" (Derrida 1994a: 67). The ideological element in the Hegelian theory of dialectical progress is precisely the normalization of destruction, which gives the real-world material occurrence of human conflict, violence and destruction a sense of pre-ordained logic and reasonableness, as if to suggest that things are unfolding as they must. In response to this form of reasoning Marx wrote, "reason finds itself at home in unreason as such" (Marx in O'Neill 1996: 45). Adorno, who similarly devoted substantial attention to the problem of "historicism" inherent in Hegel's philosophy of history stated "Historicism slanders its own principle, the force of history" as the force of growth and progress (quoted in Rose 1978: 146).

The form of dialectical reasoning that supports growth through destruction is fundamentally agonistic. It normalizes the principle of destruction inherent in the catastrophe/creation theory of growth. To use Adorno's words, this way of thinking, "comes all too quickly to terms with suffering and death for the sake of a reconciliation occurring merely in reflection" (1974: 74). The tragedies and horrors that mark the path of history up to the present are rationalized as the costs of some ultimate reconciliation that never seems to really occur – we are in the twenty-first century and still live the basic problems of early industrial capitalism: mass poverty and disease, war, sexism, racism, ecological destruction and pollution, exploitation of the masses as workers and consumers, etc. For some these empirical facts are reasoned away with the credo that "progress takes time!" "This perversion serves all bad purposes, from the private pig-headedness of 'life's like that' to the justification of social injustice as a law of nature" (1974: 73). Marcuse captures this ideology well when he writes about the social acceptance of misery in everyday life:

> We live and die rationally and productively. We know that destruction is the price of progress as death is the price of life, that renunciation and toil are the prerequisites for gratification and joy, that business must go on, and that the alternatives are Utopian. This ideology belongs to the established societal apparatus; it is a requisite for its continuous functioning and part of its rationality. (1964: 145)

If the eternal dialectical pattern of development and destruction constitutes the universal "whole" of world history then, as Adorno states, inverting Hegel: "The whole is false" (1974: 50). What is, is not what ought to be. Or as Marx put it (although problematically so), as the agents of history "men make history but not always as they please." Marx means that although human society is the product of human invention, free will and the outcome of "practical" action, that historically constituted entity which is (capitalist) society is not an arrangement that maximizes human freedom for the maximum number of people, but rather the opposite.

One would think that after the escalation of atrocity associated with the history of Western civilization up to the present time no one would accept Hegel's view of history as no more than an outdated expression of classical idealism, and yet Hegel's view still informs the dominant understanding of human history in both popular opinion and in positivist academic discourse alike. It is a fundamental part of the agonal imagination. Progressive reconciliation through agonistic synthesis continues to remain the big myth of social conflict.

The catastrophe/creation theory of history is a belief which inclines one to think that the destructive pattern of history is immutable and inevitable since so much of the documented history of humankind has been marked by it. It serves as a sort of natural teleology of that which has been socially and historically constructed as a pattern of domination exercising its effects on the substance of reality. Consequently the idea of "peace" can only be conceptualized as the in-between of history. Peace is the exception to the rule. The failed promise of dialectical history is contained in the perpetual postponement of a great and prosperous tomorrow that never seems to arrive.

The agonal dialectical view of historical progression is an idea promoted on the ideological belief that progress and the advancement of societies depends on social and political change that comes in the form of disturbances of large magnitude. True change must be spectacular if it is to have a lasting consequence on the course of history. A society that changes very little over the course of time is looked upon as being guilty of stagnation, thus further reinforcing the view that turbulent change is a necessary and desirable structure of advancing societies. However it is important to note that not all of that which can be deemed progress in history is based on the cataclysmic action of victory and conquest, only the history of repressive power – the power of domination – which is taken for the whole of history and is mistaken by many strands of popular and philosophical thought to be a manifestation of the Absolute and the Universal of history.

For Hegel, the realization of the "Absolute," as the phenomenal object of history, concerned the progress of the human "Spirit." The concept of Spirit has numerous meanings, including religious/messianic meanings (which is certainly retained in Hegel's conception), but was philosophically deployed by Hegel to refer to the ultimate quality of essential consciousness in mankind. He writes, "the grandest conception of all... Spirit is alone reality" (1931: 85), and, "It is the inner being of the world, that which essentially is, and is *per se*; it assumes objective, determinate form, and enters into relations with itself ...it must be presented to itself as an object" (1931: 86).

Identifying the material form of this "objective" character of Spirit was precisely what Marx set out to do when he "turned Hegel on his head." Marx understood Hegel's unfolding of Spirit through history as giving rise to a succession of clearly identifiable social *material* systems. These were identified in the "mode of production" on which a society subsisted and how the resultant

concentration of political and economic power this "mode of production" maintained gave rise to a particular type of society. As
O'Neill writes,

> Hegel regarded history as a process which unfolds
> through living ideologies, such as the Enlightenment,
> utilitarianism, and the Absolute Liberty of the French
> Revolution. Each of these ideologies is related to a
> definite cultural and social reality, through which the
> nature of human rationality and freedom is progres-
> sively revealed. (O'Neill 1995: 75)

What complicates the uncritical acceptance of the Hegelian philosophy of history is the ideological manner by which it maintains
an insistence on "progress," one which is defined without reference to the costs paid for it in human life and which proceeds in
blatant disregard for the continued unfolding of atrocity that prevails in the antagonistic constitution of society. Marx apparently
had no problem with the progressive mythological dream in
Hegel's teleology of history; the very concept of revolution
retains connotations of violent social upheaval – he believed that
the formula of historical transformation needed to be implemented in real life ("the point is not to interpret society but to
change it") – if the dialectic of change was to be realized. Marx
therefore fails to problematize the inherent positivism of Hegel's
view of history and its ideology of progress. Consequently some
of the most problematic areas in Marx's sociology of history concern his unquestioned assumptions about the nature of both the
earlier forms of social order that led up to capitalism and also
various non-Western modes of production, which Marx saw as
inherently more primitive and inferior (such as the Asiatic mode
of production). Thus revolutionary Marxism is inherently bound
up with a notion of agonistic progress carried over from Hegel.

The problem remains the question of progress in the
unfolding of history. History does not "unfold" of its own accord,
nor is a newer society automatically "better" than the one that
preceded it. It is dangerous to conflate the dialectical theory of
evolution with the theory of history. Nevertheless this conflation
is the reigning ideology of socio-historical evolution in the West
and works to justify all conflicts and developments in the name
of progress. It culminates in the present social and political order

and its new "mode of production," neo-liberal capitalist globalization, being seen in terms of a techno-cultural advance. This is
not to say that there have been no progressive advances in various
dimensions of human endeavour, because clearly there have been
profound changes in the ability to sustain and enrich human life
in various ways, even though these have not been implemented
equitably, or sometimes at all, but how little the contradiction
which belies the thinking on the ideal of progress has changed.
How is it that the myth of a perpetual historical progress is one
that is so enduring? Progress is a liberal value that is received as
a sort of historical guarantee of superiority – so that we in the
present esteem ourselves to be much better off than those of the
past, even though this is not necessarily the case for every individual alive today. The concerted belief in progress serves to help
convince modern consciousness that despite everything that is
unpleasant in our time, it is still better than before. Progress has
become a stubborn demand. The desire for progress has become
so totalitarian that it has come to mean transcendence even if that
is by way of destructive force. Destruction and production have
thus become dialectical unities of a "logical" process of historical
development. Hannah Arendt reminds us of the historical construction of the conception of progress:

> The notion that there is such a thing as progress
> of mankind as a whole was unknown prior to the
> seventeenth century, developed into a rather
> common opinion among the eighteenth century
> *hommes de letters*, and became an almost univer-
> sally accepted dogma in the nineteenth. (Arendt
> 1970: 25)

Although it remains unclear whether or not Arendt, with all evidence to the contrary at her disposal (in terms of her insights into
totalitarianism), embodies the hopeful ideology of history, which
"instead of looking toward the past now looks confidently forward into the future" (1970). She writes:

> [The] idea, borrowed from Hegel, that every old
> society harbors the seeds of its successors in the
> same way every living organism harbors the seeds
> of its offspring is indeed not only the most ingen-
> ious but also the most sempiternal continuity of

> progress in history; and since the motion of this
> progress is supposed to come about through the
> clashes of antagonistic forces, it is possible to
> interpret every "regress" as a necessary but tem-
> porary setback. (Arendt 1970: 26)

It is not the point here to dispute the fact that conflict constitutes
a major component of human history and of the character of
social experience more generally, but rather to explain the actuality of conflict as a manifestation of a particular form of rationality realizing itself through its powerful and determining
influence on social and political organization, rather than on
some hidden hand of "unfolding spirit," as in the Hegelian mystification of historical antagonism.

The History of Domination

Hegel's philosophy of history is best ingested with an antidote
supplied by Walter Benjamin, who pointed out that "history had
hitherto been written from the standpoint of the victor and needed
to be written from that of the vanquished" (Adorno 1974: 151),
and that recorded history is merely the history of empire-victory
and not the whole of human history. History as the history of victory is both "official history" in terms of what is taught as well
as that which captures the imagination of those who profess an
interest in glorious history. History we are told is the story of
kings and rulers, idiosyncrasies of past and present monarchic,
state and military figures, intimate details about their lives, loves
and sorrows – trivial information out of all proportion with the
many other facts and peoples of history that bear much more significantly upon how human realities were constituted in the
majority (Parenti 1995). It is pure mystification to understand
history as only that which has occurred under the rubric of the
power of domination at the exclusion of all else that transpired
in the unrecorded and half-forgotten lives of millions. Adorno
writes,

> We might add that knowledge must indeed pres-
> ent the fatally rectilinear succession of victory and
> defeat, but should also address itself to those

> things which were not embraced by this dynamic, which fell by the wayside – what might be called the waste products and blind spots that have escaped the dialectic. It is in the nature of the defeated to appear, in their impotence, irrelevant, eccentric, derisory. What transcends the ruling society is not only the potentiality it develops but also all that which did not fit properly into the laws of historical movement. Theory must needs deal with cross-grained, opaque, unassimilated material, which as such admittedly has from the start an anachronistic quality, but is not wholly obsolete since it has outwitted the historical dynamic. (Adorno 1974: 151)

Many lives do exist and have existed outside of the rubric of oppressive power and even today not all lives are subject to the forces of imperial state, neo-liberal capitalist domination and control. It is generally the nature of humans to resist domination when it lays bare its mechanisms. Power seeks totalization but the project of power is never thorough or complete. Freedom exists in the interstices of life that, as Adorno says, "have escaped the dialectic of control." Freedom above all else emerges from the subjective awareness of the conditions of domination, from the de-reification of perception. Insight into the condition of ideological domination is the beginning of all hope and transcendence.

If Hegel's philosophy of history has a certain ring of truth to it because it captures, in supra-aesthetic form, that pattern of human cataclysm and suffering that has accompanied development. The progress of a seemingly eternal dialectic of production and destruction that is seen to have marked world-historical process must be rejected not because of any empirical inaccuracy in reference to the actual occurrence of world events dictated by power, but because of the extent to which it has served to metastasize the destruction inherent in human history as natural and inevitable, and thus "universal." As Adorno puts it, "universal history must be construed and denied" (1973: 320). It is more politically fruitful, however, to inquire into the political economy of atrocity and to not abandon "the facts of history" to an effect of some absolute law that pre-determines the outcome of history based on an imagined mechanism of supra-human historical agency.

The Hegelian dialectic of productive negation, in both the construction of consciousness and the genesis of history, is predicated on an objectivity of hostility and antagonism that does not represent the real conditions of existence, but only its degraded form; one where conflict and antagonism have become the real and have thus instituted a false ontology of objective negation. Adorno states, "dialectics is the ontology of the wrong state of things. The right state of things would be free of it: neither a system nor a contradiction" (Adorno 1973: 11).

Beyond the false ontology that Hegelian historicism offers, the theory of agonal dialectical history is unsound if only because the history of the last five hundred years has witnessed no antithetical dialectical transformation of historical reality; there has been no steady dialectical progress of history. Instead there has been, following Nietzsche, an "eternal recurrence of the same:" the same regressive values (continuing patriarchy and religion), the same destructive social phenomena, war, structural hierarchy, exploitation. True dialectics requires complete or near complete collapse of one flawed system to be followed by a successive rebuilding and development into another qualitatively different and improved system which too eventually reaches its critical apogee and final subsequent synthesis into another more sustainable form of society that is relatively free of internal dissonance. It is not true, in terms of positive progress for example, that human history has evolved on the actual basis of dialectical synthesis since it can not be adequately demonstrated that progress, defined properly in terms of the elimination of human suffering, domination and the maximization of freedom, has succeeded in any appreciable measure. Nietzsche's idea that Western history has followed a pattern of predictable and regressive continuity is based on the societal repetition of historical themes and forces, which gives rise to a repeating morality of values. In the context of historical barbarism this historical repetition tends to recycle the values of conflict. Revenge and sacrifice get elevated and deified as the ideals of culture and consequently a self-mythology of culture develops based on the ideal of agonism.

Dialectics may be a good method for the mode of inquiry in analytical thought that pursues knowledge through a process of sustained questioning, but it is woefully inadequate for an understanding of human history as progress. The dialectical pattern of successive transformation and growth seems to be indicated in terms of the development of various systems of knowledge which have come into dominance in the West, as Thomas Kuhn's (1962) paradigmatic theory of the growth of scientific knowledge suggests, but even in the history of thought, the process of selection has been a random one based on the servitude of knowledge to dominant power interests. Truth succeeds only by virtue of its relation to power: "The relationship of knowledge to power is one not only of servility but of truth" (Adorno 1974: 56). (Foucault [1970] similarly makes a mockery of the theory of the linear/logical development of knowledge in *The Order of Things*.) Various bodies of knowledge were not known in all parts of the world and could not compete in some dialectical fashion within the totality of knowledges. In other cases knowledge was destroyed through massive book burning and other forms of the imperial elimination of indigenous knowledge and wisdom. To invoke Foucault again, he asked if it is better not to pose the question "what is truth?" but rather "how has truth been constructed?" (1980). The same goes for the truth of history – what is disparagingly called "revisionist history" is actually a challenge to orthodox history, which is the history of imperial victory. Many studies exist and are continuing to be written that present an alternative to received orthodox history (Parenti 1999; Wolf 1982; Zinn 1997). They rely on telling the untold stories that can be garnered from reading between the lines in the official documents which have remained behind, and through the anthropological evidence of what early forms of social life were like (Parenti 1999). But these have the heavy weight of tradition pressed against them. Studies of the untold histories of peoples are a necessary component of the "critique of domination."

The Dialectic of History is Stuck in the Eversame of Permanent Tension

Hegel's positivism, as has been indicated above, nevertheless opens an area of theoretical inquiry to which the dialectical method has made substantial contributions. The dialectical relation between the Universal and the Particular, and the centrality of human consciousness in the historicity of the subject are particularly appealing methods of socio-philosophical analysis. Hegel's philosophy continues to be of interest not only because his system of thought, wide ranging as it is, serves as a fruitful basis for reflection on a number of contemporary social issues but because it captures in ideological form that pattern and logic of history which normalizes the cycle of progressive destruction into which the Western teleology of progress seems so deeply immersed. If human development today has arrived at "the end of history" it is not because in any positive sense the "will to power" in history has achieved a great measure of success in finally arriving at the threshold of a social and political horizon where political consensus has liquidated all forms of opposition and thus resolved historical contradiction, as Fukuyama (1992) and neoliberals believe, but rather because the trajectory of history has been artificially held back by the forces comprising the totality of power and can not be allowed, at least at this present time, to unfold into dialectical collapse and renewal into a radical alterity. There has been a human political intervention into the very process of the dynamic of world-historical-process itself. This intervention is the high level of social, political and economic totalization and control that has been inflicted upon the unfolding of world events and which has thus arrested them in their course. Certainly, in many other respects social and historical change continues to take place. Social change is constant and inevitable (although not necessarily progressive). What remains static is the negative character of world-historical momentum. History has become characterized by a *metastasis of the same*,[1] where metastasis is a form of progressive internal systemic decay. In terms of a dialectics of history, we are stuck in permanent antagonism – stuck in the metastasis of conflict. In the metastatic situation true historical dialectics is frozen.

This notion of history as the metastasis of the same is analogous to the repetitive pattern of the eternal recurrence of history that Nietzsche spoke of. Nietzsche's (1957) critique of history, which is partially contained in Santayana's injunction that "those who cannot remember the past are condemned to repeat it," stands in contradiction to the Hegelian view where history proceeds according to its own internal logic. Nietzsche's warning is heard but not heeded – he means that the atrocities and mistakes of the past should not be repeated. As an affirmation of

Nietzsche's warning, agon culture responds by over-remember-
ing: consequently memorials of war are erected, and remem-
brance days are celebrated not to warn of the horror of war but
in order to pay homage to the "glory of our soldiers" who went
off to kill and to die. These soldiers who in the finality of their
death are denied a voice have their horror extended in the gruesome fixity into which the meaning of their death is made, a
meaning that keeps them alive as "fighters from the grave." The
death of those who go and die in war, and all the death and suffering that makes war, does not prevent future wars, but rather is
mobilized in the rally for the war to come. The price of war that
is paid for by the death of countless soldiers and civilians is inter-
preted agonistically as a cause for motivation in the future of war-
ring; as a reason why the next war should be a victory, so that the
countless past deaths may not be in vain. When Nietzsche (1957)
wrote that we should remember history in order to learn from it,
he intended precisely that the past should not determine the future
in a recurrent mimetic pattern, but should serve precisely as a
marker to be distanced from, so that society could be constantly
remade anew and not be regressively fixated on mistakes, like
the repetition of killing.

History repeats itself in cycles because humans have not
fostered the capacity for a truly critical historical consciousness
that allows them to learn from the past mistakes of history. This
is in itself a problem of the reification of culture and memory.
Dialectical history requires a self-realization of the "Absolute,"
but history repeats itself precisely because there is no self-realization, no collective consciousness of the man-made atrocities
of world history, or of the present organized misery. World-historical ignorance in this regard condemns humans to repeat their
mistakes and to perpetuate the cycle of destruction. Adorno
states, "if world history had not been shattered to pieces, then the
problem of collective amnesia probably would not have arisen"
(Adorno 1998: 295).

Baudrillard in his *Paroxysm* (1998), lends insight to the
problem of the metastasis of historical memory when he remarks
that there is an excess of historical eventfulness: "It isn't that
there are more events, but the event itself is multiplied by its dissemination, by news and information… everything has become
history that it is no longer possible to believe in history" (Bau-

drillard 1998: 7). The incapacity to believe in historical facts is based on the gross distortion of both historical perception and on what constitutes the "historical event." In agon culture celebrated history is always the history of victory. When one sports team "beats" another it is hailed as a historical event. Politicians similarly ingratiate themselves as world-historical-individuals when they cut the latest trade deal. The total violation of the very concept of history and thus the incapacity to historicize, also form part of the stultification and metastasis of the dialectic.

The idea that the dialectic has been stultified is related to the concerted organizational and administrative attempt to impose order on society, to stabilize things, to bring an "end to history" by exterminating opposition. This is, at one level, recognized as being a panic response, a frenetic effort to impose order on that which seems on the brink of autonomous self-generation. The crisis of empire/agonal history also forms part of its insecurity of power. This is why the agents of tyrannical history have always called for a "new world order." Again, the pattern of social history that has led up to the present totality has not been based on a true dialectics, since the telos of the modern period has not been interrupted by a destructive/reproductive transformation so total in form that it has given rise to a new historical trajectory and type of society – there has been no back and forth, no crisis, collapse and reconfiguration: only permanent cumulative error. If the ultimate object of dialectical history is the progressive development of "society" in formation, as a system of cumulative order and empire, as in Marx's interpretation of Hegel, it is not that the centre [of empire] will not hold. In fact it is holding up quite well. The centre (and centres of power) are holding – and being held in place by an international capitalist elite administrative order at one level and at another level, by an increasingly docile mass of repressively controlled, either reified or indentured, populations who can no longer even think about the idea of a completely different sort of society based on a non-agonal view of social life. This core-periphery setup (Wallerstein 1974), the north–south divide between economically advantaged nations in relation to other systematically disadvantaged nations, reproduces the dialectic of mastery and servitude on a geo-political scale, and constitutes what Derrida indicates is "the [dominant] order of the world today, namely the world-wide market, [which] holds a mass of humanity under its yoke and in a new form of slavery" (Derrida 1994a: 94).

The rise of the European world view has kept the history of power stuck in a trajectory of instrumental domination over nature, and now over all of humanity (Adorno and Horkheimer, 1969), begun in the sixteenth century and whose end seems nowhere in sight. This is a continuing crisis which has been contained through an extensive political intervention and bureaucratic deliberation into the political and economic core of historical-dialectical process. At least from the standpoint of a universal capitalism, total or even near-total collapse has been successfully prevented from occurring by crisis intervention strategies.

Crisis in the modern period has been artificially upheld by the various corrective mechanisms: altering the conditions of the economy through interest rate fluctuations, price-fixing, monopoly capital, massive layoffs, government bailouts, corporate welfare funding, public relations persuasion payoffs and political lobbying manipulation – all of which are efforts euphemistically known as "capitalist ingenuity" that sustain the system's antinomical imperfections and inherent discord: the vast social-executive efforts which work to keep the order fundamentally unchanged – encountering huge problems such as deficits, recessions, low consumer spending, among others. All of these are met with by pumping more and more capital into the void, the realigning and regrouping of administrative, organizational and military strategies, the creation of new political alliances; all are efforts which work towards the intensification of systems and orders to curtail the implosion that is required for a genuine dialectical transformation and the self-realization of society and its individuals.

"Crisis management," or damage control, is the real life-force/death-force of international capitalism. In the name of social stability "crisis management" has become the trope of intensified measures of social control. Crisis management aims precisely at that very problem within capitalism that Marx identified as the tendency to generate its own form of destabilizing internal contradictions. But these "contradictions" do not destabilize things very much. They are not allowed to affect the solid foundation of the economic order. They actually function to perpetuate the order of permanent crisis. Through the "success" of vast efforts and various corrective mechanisms that aim at perfecting the system's sustained imperfection, the management and containment of crisis has been made a normal part of economic order and its generalized instability. But the discord cannot be totally contained. Attempts to manage the flow and generation of capital's inherent tendency to self-regulate[2] gets socially realized as more and more restraint and discipline; not abstract discipline but discipline as increased forms of social control and domination. This is a control that gets realized in the real lives of people who suffer by it, as a form of social pressure in the name of economic necessity. It is revealed in the stress cracks of increasing dehumanization, poverty and homelessness as outward signs of inner disturbances: in the realms of labour, in the rising costs of living, corporate and civic restructurings, cutbacks, layoffs, debt burdens, and in the rising out-of-control destruction of the air, land and water upon which humans and all life forms necessarily subsist. Permanent crisis management is part of the generalized agonism of repressive forces that occur within the political economy of a frozen dialectic.

Crisis management, it must be added, also involves the Orwellian erasure and censorship of history. It is not just the market that must be contained within the agonistic dialectic of history, it is also the construction and preservation of certain historical "truths" that are necessary to legitimate the powers that contain and construct the meaning of history. Michael Parenti (1999) has indicated the great lengths that magistrates and officials throughout the past have gone to in order to preserve certain readings of history and to destroy others. He cites massive book burning by the Catholic Church throughout its history, and the persecution and elimination from history, of academics in the USA and elsewhere, for example, who have published outside of the prescribed fields of academic respectability and have "paid the price" for it through destroyed careers. His examples of how "history is made into mystery" also include blatant political and legal cover-ups that violate every freedom of speech and freedom of information, especially in the case of the FBI and other "secret" state files that do not get released, and if and when they do, they are mostly all blacked out so that the information they once contained is illegible and of little use. This state practice parallels the mobster style "disposing of the evidence" that is only a necessary measure when evidence of criminal wrongdoing needs to be eliminated to cover up an injustice that has undoubtedly actually taken place. In agonal history even information gets frozen and secured.

****

The "dissonance" of history therefore is not merely a concept. It is realized in the misery that people must endure in their lives lived in the conditions of objective decay, and in the context of an eroding life-world that is produced from the persistence of domination. The destruction of history gets sublimated into a condition of permanent social stress and strife. The history of humanity under the force of dominant power has not been the dialectic of progress, it has been metastasis of domination. Foucault writes:

> Humanity does not gradually proceed from combat to combat until it arrives at universal reciprocity, where the rule of law finally replaces warfare; humanity installs each of its violences in a system of rules and thus proceeds from domination to domination. (Foucault quoted in Ghandi 1998)

This stress that cannot hold is evidenced at a number of levels. At the superstructural level it occurs in the eruptions of numerous symptoms: the ceaseless wars, continuing violence and human suffering are outward expressions of the system's inner antinomies. The dialectic of history has been halted and stultified into the metastasis of crisis – or perhaps catastasis is the better term, which is the normality of critical breakdown and the human suffering it produces. Adorno's famous passage on this point:

> After the catastrophes that have happened, and in view of the catastrophes to come, it would be cynical to say that a plan for a better world is manifested in history and unites it. Not to be denied for that reason, however, is the unity that cements the discontinuous, chaotically splintered moments and phases of history – the unity of the control of

nature, and finally to that over men's inner nature. No universal history leads from savagery to humanitarianism, but there is one leading from the slingshot to the megaton bomb. It ends in the total menace which organized mankind poses to organized men, in the epitome of discontinuity. It is the horror that verifies Hegel and stands him on his head. If he transfigured the totality of historic suffering into the positivity of the self-realizing absolute, the One and All that keeps rolling on to this day – with occasional breathing spells – would teleologically be the absolute of suffering. (1973: 320)

In this remarkable passage Adorno, always mindful of how the Universal enacts its power on the Particular, develops the idea that historical catastrophe is not a series of singular cataclysmic events, but that catastrophe is a condition of reality that is ongoing and which exercises its domination at the phenomenal level of human experience. To speak of the "absolute of suffering" is to speak to (and also to give voice) to the painful and mostly forgotten existences that have marked the lives of more people than not in the course of human history.

The question remains: How are we to imagine a future within this catastrophic intensification of historical forces that we, for the moment, seem to be stuck in? If Marx was correct in his analysis that capitalism contains "the seeds of its own destruction" and that "the center cannot hold," and we are presently living partway between the global expansion of agonal capitalism approaching the finality of its totality, the complete globalization of capitalism, then the situation of domination will surely get worse before it gets better. This is the hot zone of history in more ways than one. In that sense it is easy to agree with Adorno's reading of the dialectic of history as the "absolute of suffering."

Adorno saw the past and the future in terms of human suffering. Postmodern theory (Lyotard 1984; Deleuze and Guattari 1977) emphasize the principle of catastrophic intensification – that things have come to pass where immense forces of power seem to be "set objectively upon collision" towards impending disaster. The theses of catastrophe and "implosion" and the "death of the social" (Baudrillard) are among the more interesting insights of postmodern thought in that they capture that character of ontological insecurity that matches the virtual uncertainty of the continuation of life on the planet. The same sentiments are echoed by nearly all the environmental scientists around the globe who are screaming and pleading with politicians that the ecology and the biosphere can take no more industrial abuse without us all suffering the consequences (Suzuki and Dressel 1999). Baudrillard, in *The Illusion of the End* (1994), posits the thesis that the apocalyptic theoretical vision which speaks of the catastrophe *to come* is a naïve one which does not understand the reality of catastrophe; the radical view he says is that the catastrophe "has already happened" and we are living in it. This is indeed a different "end of history" than the one imagined by neoliberal "bringers of good news" (see Derrida 1994a: 59-62). Baudrillard theorizes from a position which already assumes the end of the real, one which is based on a wholesale transformation in the order of phenomenal being itself.

The progressive view of happy liberalism is based on the triumphant view of the elimination of the other – the death of socialism validated and "recognized" transcendent capitalism. After the fall of the Berlin wall, for a time there in the 1990s people actually believed in the triumph of something, a hopeful global stability through a focus on civil rights, demilitarization and nuclear reduction. Today, however, with the ever-more frenzied and agitated war machine flexing its muscle in search for the new enemy, the agonistic ambition for killing and destruction has found a new cause, and an impotent dialectical history is off and running once again.

Chapter 7

A Note on Violence, Instinct and the Question of Human Nature

In order to know that people will fight for their homeland we hardly had to discover instincts of "group territorialism" in ants, fish, and apes... I fail to understand why we are asked, "to recognize that man behaves very much like a group territorial species," rather than the other way round – that certain animal species behave very much like men.

~Hannah Arendt, *On Violence*

Obviously it is part of human nature to be able to become aggressive and wage war. But how and when we become aggressive is controlled by our cultures not by our genes.

~Marvin Harris, *Cannibals and Kings*

That most of us consistently fail to consider the alternatives to competition is a testament to the effectiveness of our socialization. We have been trained not only to compete but to believe in competition... Those who argue most vigorously that competition is desirable are often the same people who assert that it is part of human nature.

~Alfie Kohn, *No Contest*

It has become a cliché of our culture to hear that violence in society results from the individual expression of a destructive, innate "killer instinct" lying deep within the animal nature of human beings. This taken-for-granted response typifies a commonly held way of thinking about violence and human nature, even though the vast majority of studies on human behaviour negate it. There is, however, a reason for the widespread belief in instincts as the ultimate cause of human behaviour, and it has to do with the dominance of pseudo-scientific thinking that shapes popular perceptions about human social life. The evolutionary paradigm established by Charles Darwin, for example, has had an enormous influence on the mind-set of the modern thought. It is not Darwin who is to blame for "the instinctual thesis," but rather misinterpretations of some basic Darwinian tenets, such as "only the physically strong are fit and thus deserve to survive;" Darwin's thought is more complex and specific in its examination of the process of "natural selection" and the "descent of man." Nevertheless, Darwinian ideas have been appropriated into a populist way of thinking that gives primacy to biological causes of human destructiveness. An entire discipline of study known as sociobiology has arisen to support the idea of biological determinations about human behaviour. The theses proposed by biological determinists are in contrast to the theses about human behaviour proposed by social scientists who argue that human behaviour is dominantly determined by culture and socialization, and not biological forces.

It is certainly true that we humans are biological beings, but that does not mean that all behaviour can be reduced to biological causes or that biology underwrites all of social behaviour through and through. The fact that we are embodied beings with drives for sexuality, that we are amenable to biological disease and have a degree of genetic predisposition, are all parts of what it means to be human, but we have to distinguish between biological needs (such as the need for love, nurturing, food and shelter) and biological *instinct*. A biological need is not an instinct. Any good introduction to sociology will state that:

> An instinct is an inborn complex pattern of behaviour that must normally exist in every member of the given species and, because it is embedded in the genetic code, cannot be overcome by force of will. It should be distinguished from a *reflex*, which is a simple response of an organism to a specific stimulus... Instincts, in contrast, are

> complex sequential stimulus response patterns
> [which] can easily be identified in non-human
> animals and have been extensively studied by
> zoologists and biologists. (Naiman 2008: 27)

Thus, a drive force is perhaps a better concept to explain the gamut of desires we humans feel. Since human drives are flexible and less distinct than an instinct is, it seems a more accurate concept to explain things like human sexuality, for example, which is quite flexible in the forms it takes. Drives are flexible and can be shaped in various directions by the dual forces of culture and socialization. All humans have a sex drive force but not all humans have identical sexualities, for example. This insight does not mean to discount all the biological bases of human behaviour. What we are trying to establish is the extent to which the nastiest of human behaviours like rape and warfare are perceived as inevitable because they are written into our instinctual hardwiring and therefore not really products of human culture and socialization, or even rational free will. Biological determinism far too often becomes a justifying ideology that serves to *normalize* human violence and also discounts the large extent to which human behaviour is *socially, politically and culturally determined.* This is a dangerous trend that has continued to grow in dominance recently. The popularity of research into evolutionary biology and evolutionary psychology has given new impetus to vulgar biological conceptions of human behaviour. Titles such as *War and Human Nature* (2005) by Stephen Peter Rosen, *The Art Instinct: Beauty, Pleasure and Human Evolution* (2009) by Dennis Dutton, *The Evolutionary Basis of Consumption* (2007) and *The Consuming Instinct* (2011), both by Gad Saad, are evidence of this trend.

The critique of violence presented here takes exception to any notions pertaining to "universal evils" inherent in the human species and other such vulgar conceptions of human nature that seek to avoid rigorous *cultural* analysis of human violence in favour of biological, evolutionary or trans-historical theories. Humans are cultural beings first and foremost. Humans cannot function normally without the benefit of culture, nurture and socialization. They do not have any useful behavioural instincts to fall back on in the attempt to survive. In animals instincts are present at birth – an ant does not need to be taught how to behave within the hierarchy of the hive, just as a baby horse instinctively stands on all fours and begins to trot alongside its mother shortly after entering the world. Human babies, on the other hand, are totally helpless. Without the presence of care-givers they most certainly die. Examples of humans who have survived in the wild, alone and outside of the presence of other adult humans, so-called "feral children," were only able to survive because they were raised by canines that provided a degree of nurturing. And the behaviour of such feral humans was very much canine behaviour – they did not speak, they barked; in some recent cases, they did not walk on two legs, they were on fours. In some cases they had been socialized into wolf society and thus could be described as wolf-people.[1] Culture is what shapes patterns of human behaviour, and yet the dominant ideology in our society asks us to look at the individual's biological makeup and the alleged bundle of unruly instincts that are seen as the reason why violent behaviour happens.

When someone with a bomb strapped to their back decides to blow themselves up along with numbers of other nearby people, is this an expression of instinct or socialization? When a man physically beats his spouse repeatedly over time in what is called "domestic violence," can this behaviour by explained by reason of instinct or by cultural and gender norms concerning domestic violence? And the behaviour of the spouse who receives the beatings – can their behaviour also be explained as instinctual? When a military commander gives the order to attack, and his army of soldiers go and attack, is this instinctual behaviour? These examples illustrate the disjuncture between various violent actions that occur in human societies and the commonly held non-sociological explanations that people hold about their causes.

Theories of human behaviour which proceed from the premise that aggression and violence in humans results from an innate drive originating in primal instincts are problematic on a number of levels. Erich Fromm undertook a study which refutes this widespread belief system in his study *The Anatomy of Human Destructiveness* (1973). Nevertheless, this sort of biological reductionism seems to be a persistent theme in the positive sciences and has unfortunately migrated into popular social and political thought as well. It is a form of thinking with serious implications for social life because the belief in the instinctual basis for violence and aggression interferes with our ability to understand the social, political and economic bases that give rise to the realities of human violence and aggression.

It is only in modern times that the question of violence began to be examined from the point of view that considers it to be an expression of an innate human nature. This mode of thought brought the question of violence under the disciplinary regime of early Freudian psychology and evolutionary sociobiology, both of which see human violence as an offshoot of innate aggression as the most powerful element in the constitution of human nature. Hence it has become common for many people, when faced with the question of human violence, to defer to its "naturalness." In the popular discourse of our agonistic-competitive culture, the pairing of "violence" and "human nature" is an almost instantaneous response – it has become a truism to claim that war, violence and the high level of human destructiveness is to be explained by the presence in humans of the innate drive for aggression and violence. Howard Zinn writes of this ideological phenomenon as follows:

> This logic is widespread in modern thought, in all classes of people, whether highly educated or uneducated. And yet, it is almost certainly wrong. And furthermore, it's dangerous... Wrong, because there is no real evidence for it. Not in genetics, not in zoology, not in psychology, not in anthropology, not in history, not even in the ordinary experiences of soldiers in war. Dangerous because it deflects attention from the non-biological causes of violence and war. (Zinn 1997: 599)

An international conference of scientists representing scholarly consensus issued a statement on the question of human nature and violent aggression, concluding that

> it is scientifically incorrect to say that war is caused by "instinct" or any single motivation... Modern war involves the institutional use of personal characteristics such as obedience, suggestibility, and idealism... We conclude that biology does not condemn humanity to war. (cited in Zinn 1997: 600)

The "naturalization" of violence, which is the type of theorizing that explains violent human behaviour as a function of instincts, absolves the theorist of the labour of social analysis, and ends up serving as an ideology for the repressive order of violence that presently exists in the world made by humans. Marvin Harris clarifies the point well:

> A perennially favorite way for anthropologists to avoid the problem of specifying the conditions

under which war will be regarded as a valuable or
an abhorrent activity is to endow human nature
with an urge to kill. War occurs because human
beings, especially males, have a "killer instinct."
We kill because such behavior has been proved
successful from the standpoint of natural selection
in the struggle for existence. But *war as human
nature* runs into difficulties as soon as one
observes that killing is not universally admired
and that intensity and frequency of warfare are
highly variable. I fail to see how anyone can doubt
that these variations are caused by cultural rather
than genetic differences, since sharp reversals
from extremely warlike to peaceful behavior may
occur in one or two generations without any
genetic changes whatsoever. (Harris 1977: 53)

Seeing violence as merely the expression of instincts actually
mystifies the complex nature of violent situations in human societies. Violence has numerous causes that depend on social and
historical context as well as the cultural value set of the human
group. Violence is not automatic among humans, nor is peace-
fulness. Human behaviour depends on situational characteristics
and the cultural values of the human actors involved, and even
on their individual personality characteristics. Behaviour that is
determined by "instincts" depends far less on situational factors
since cognition is not involved. Instincts are behavioural
responses that do not require conscious thought. Instincts determine complex behaviour patterns across all members of a particular species. If humans had pronounced instincts we would all
behave the same way in response to a variety of situations. And
we would have a society that is very ordered, with little need for
social controls. Clearly that is not the case. Humans do have basic
drives, however. These are things like sexuality, the need to eat,
to sleep and the array of emotional responses that shape human
mental life and the select facial expressions that are part of non-
verbal communication among humans. But in each of these cases
the variety of different response are enormous and can take very
different forms depending on the individual person and on cultural values.

    If humans did have instincts the social world would look
a lot different. It would be less conflictual, there would be more
order and rational organization, because that is what instincts do
– *they organize consistent patterns of behaviour across members*

of an entire species. That is why bees and ants know their behavioural roles within the hive structure. That is why baby sea turtles make a run for the water as soon as they break from their shells. Human babies on the other hand are devoid of instincts; they are helpless and entirely depend on nurturing and social learning in order to survive. Generally speaking *animals are ruled by instincts and humans are guided by culture* (Surber 1998). However, it is not the case that all animals are purely instinctual creatures. Among higher mammals such as primates, elephants, and canines, among others, a large degree of social learning takes place among members. These are species with large brains, like humans. The larger the cortex of the brain, the less there is reliance on instinct as the basis of behaviour. Social animals learn their adaptive behaviours via social learning which includes imitation or mimicry, whereas humans pass on their cultural behaviours through language and communication.

Another source of confusion about "instinct" involves its vernacular usage in everyday speech. In the English language when the word "instinct" is used to describe some aspect of human behaviour, it is often used metaphorically and means *intuition.* The problem is that the metaphor has been taken for reality. Often people use the word "instinct" in place of the more proper word "intuition," as when someone says, "I have a gut instinct about this situation," or, "I will trust my instincts on this one." But the term "instinct" has multiple connotations, and it is also used to explain human behaviour, especially the worst kinds of behaviour such as violence, rape and murder.

The widespread currency of the term "instinct" is due to the widespread ideology in our media culture which claims that we live in a predatory world where aggression and warrior values are cherished as positive and functional features of social life. We are constantly bombarded with shows about animal behaviour that depict the cruel order of "eat or be eaten," and this reality gets transposed onto human society as if the barbarism that humans inflict on one another is somehow normal and inevitable, as if human society was absolutely analogous to the "jungle," as in the popular metaphorical use of that term. The nasty behaviour of humans is not due to an essentially evil human nature. It is due to their inability to have fashioned a world of material and gender equality, where conflict and competition over basic life resources can be drastically reduced.

If there is an essence to human nature to speak of, it is to be identified in the need for human co-operation, and group organization, not the value of conflict, as in the "man the hunter" mythology that is often evoked to justify human brutality as being something inherited from our primordial history (see Axelrod 1984). There is also an innate capacity for creative *cultural* engagement with ones external environment, with the human capacity to adapt to external life conditions in the course of facilitating the basics of existence. Thus, *human nature is contained in the capacity to develop the realm of culture.* That is why the philosopher Hegel, among others referred to human culture as *second nature.* This is not to say that the human being is a *tabula rasa*, as early behaviourist psychology would lead us to believe, but that whatever inherent capacities and predispositions humans may have are generally not fixed and immutable. Rather, the elements of individual character that are quite flexible, and come into fruition primarily in the context of socialization and enculturation. (Once personality is formed, however, the self can be quite resistant to change). This idea of behavioural flexibility (also related to "neural plasticity"), is in contrast to the belief that enculturation is a process of learning in which social behaviours are mapped onto pre-existing cognitive structures which remain active and continue to exercise a determining influence on social behaviour that override cultural learning. In this sociobiological view (Morris 1967; Wilson 1975; Lorenz 1966), the process of enculturation is seen as something that develops coterminous with and in conflict with deep instincts – and that successful enculturation involves the "taming" of instincts, which nevertheless remain active even if subdued.

Culture and Behavioural Programming

It is generally accepted in the social sciences that human social life and individual behaviour are largely a product of culture. There exists an immense variety of human groups because of the varieties of human cultures. Culture furnishes people with identity and meaning and it directs the complex behavioural characteristics of each group. As Clifford Geertz writes,

> there is no such thing as a human nature independent of culture. Men without culture would not be the clever savages of Golding's *Lord of the Flies* thrown back upon the cruel wisdom of their animal instincts; nor would they be the nature's noblemen of Enlightenment primitivism or even,

> as classical anthropological theory would imply, intrinsically talented apes who had somehow failed to find themselves. They would be unworkable monstrosities with very few useful instincts, fewer recognizable sentiments, and no intellect: mental basket cases. (Geertz quoted in Jenks 1993: 6)

The theories of human nature which posit that the kernel of the human psyche contains a bundle of aggressive primal instincts adds support to the political theory that humans need to be controlled and that the "primal drives" need to be repressed (as in the religious control over sexuality) if social order is to be maintained. "Anarchy" and "chaos" are offered as the dismal prospects likely to emerge in the absence of such strict social regulation. This popular ideology proposes that if there is a lack of social regulation or cultural development, then humans may fall back onto a state of atavistic primitivism, as in a form of instinctual "species" regression as it were. Violence also should not be seen as an expression of "atavism," where aggressive behaviour is attributed to a lack of evolutionary development. This belief leads to the naturalistic myth of "animalistic ideology," where the human is seen basically as an unruly animal, albeit one with advanced social characteristics and a large brain. The idea of the human as an "instinctual being" results in the *animalization* of the human and in doing so causes us to misunderstand both humans and animals alike.

Arendt points out how the positive sciences in particular, "biologists, physiologists, ethologists, and zoologists – have joined in an all-out effort to solve the riddle of "aggressiveness" in human behaviour" (1970: 59). Aggression, it is assumed, is not the domain of political and social realities but is to be located in "animal irrationality." Desmond Morris' popular theory of the human as a "naked ape" is a typical example of the enduring authority of this sort of thinking in which observations of animal behaviour are extrapolated onto humans as a way of composing a natural theory of human behaviour (Morris 1967). The positivist view on aggression serves to *animalize* the human, and is used to explain away the crudities of human behaviour without due consideration of the cultural determinations inherent in a malevolent socialization process. Taking animals as the referent for natural brutality is fundamentally incorrect since animals very rarely kill needlessly, nor do they wage mass war or engage in mindless slaughter. These are behaviours specific to humans. It is the

height of human vanity to define violence as a quality of animals
and then to malign animals for a quality possessed in large measure by humans. Hannah Arendt deals with the issue of animality
and "aboriginally instinctual being" at some length in her book
On Violence. She writes:

> In order to know that people will fight for their
> homeland we hardly had to discover instincts of
> "group territorialism" in ants, fish, and apes... I
> fail to understand why we are asked, "to recognize
> that man behaves very much like a group territo-
> rial species," rather than the other way round –
> that certain animal species behave very much like
> men. (Arendt 1970: 59)

Thus, the theory that the ubiquity of violence and war in human
societies can be explained simply as the outward expression of
an inherently defensive, predatory, and animalistic human nature
seems to reverse the situation by citing the violence of humans
and then claiming they behave in an animal-like fashion.

Some psychological theories expound a related view that
complicates our understanding of violence. This is the theory of
"catharsis," where it is believed that humans have a storehouse
of violence within them and actually benefit from expressing
"pent up" violence and aggression, which is naturally seen to be
collected in individuals, and seeks a creative and liberating
expression. Catharsis, it is argued, reduces anxiety in people and
calms their behaviour and teaches them how to cope. As such,
engaging in aggressive, competitive activities – either actually
doing it physically through sports for example, or watching violence on a video screen, if we are to follow the theory through, is
seen as a safe, healthy and pleasurable form of "venting" violence. On the basis of the widespread belief in catharsis, aggressive, competitive behaviour is even encouraged in our culture. It
is assumed by some educators and parents that when children
engage in violent forms of play that this is a type of "healthy venting." This line of reasoning is in direct contrast to other less problematic theories in psychology which claim that to engage in
violent activities is a form of conditioning which actually reinforces violent, aggressive behaviour. The reinforcement of
aggression is further exacerbated at the cultural level where we
see the celebration of violence as a form of strength and power.
From violent sports celebrities to heads of state who engage in
war to prime time television drama – at numerous levels in our

culture violent aggression is reinforced. The psychologistic view of catharsis therefore is clearly inadequate to understanding violence and human nature.

It has generally been the position of dialectical social theory that human nature is a dynamic concept, and that "human nature," or how humans fundamentally behave towards each other, in terms of aggression or co-operation, is dependent primarily on the material conditions that mediate their existence: "Adorno ventures the hypothesis that various historical situations and social settings "bring out" and accentuate distinct types of possibilities ever present in human beings" (Held 1980: 118). Material conditions, especially those concerning the availability of life-sustaining resources and territory, can affect the extent to which some human groups come to see others as a threat to their survival (Harris 1977). But even this theory of the competition for survival is historically inadequate to explain all instances of rationalized violence, since it cannot account for why competition for resources can sometimes lead to co-operation and innovation instead of conflict. Human co-operation lies at the basis of theories explaining the survival or evolutionary success of early hominids. Without co-operation, that eminently social human trait, humans would never have made it as a species. The recognition of the problem of material conditions gets reflected in the meaning system of culture, which develops as ritualized support for, or discouragement of certain forms of, violent behaviour. As Marvin Harris states, "Obviously it is part of human nature to be able to become aggressive and wage war. But how and when we become aggressive is controlled by our cultures not by our genes" (1977: 54). One might be inclined to argue that if animals are ruled largely by their instincts acting in relation to their environment, then human beings are ruled by their cultural adaptation to their environment. It stands to reason then that it is just as likely that people will be disposed to acting altruistically and co-operatively towards each other as they are towards acting destructively. But the idea of an innate "peace instinct" is rarely imagined in relation to the determining function of instincts. Altruism, benevolence and peace are just as natural as violence and conflict. Neither demeanour is more authentically human: peace and conflict are equally plausible human realities. It is a mistake to assume that because violence is based on physical force that it is the stronger of the two tendencies, and therefore tends to prevail in the formation of human character, as if violence was an attribute that was "selected" for in terms of a preferential Darwinian selection process. Just as competition and co-operation are social values that can be reinforced, rewarded, encouraged or discouraged, as with aggressive and altruistic behaviour, either one can become dominant depending on the cultural value system in which such behaviour is circumscribed. However, it is peaceful co-operation and social group formation that has allowed humans to survive evolution and rise to dominance as a "superspecies."

Let us examine some of the intellectual basis for the widespread belief in the theory of instinctual violence in a brief correspondence between two great minds of the modern age: Freud and Einstein.

> Albert Einstein was deeply troubled by the memory of World War 1. He was horrified that human life could be destroyed on such a massive scale and worried that there may be another war. He asked Freud in a letter "if there was any way of delivering mankind from the menace of war?" "How is it possible for a small clique to bend the will of the majority, who stand to lose and suffer by a state of war, to service the ambitions of those who advance their personal interests and authority through the manufacture and sale of arms?"... [Is it] "because man has within him a lust for hatred and destruction?" Freud responded, "You surmise that man has in him an active instinct for hatred and destruction, amenable to such stimulations. I entirely agree with you...The most casual glance at world history will show an unending series of conflicts between one group and another." (Zinn 1997: 597)

The basis for instinctual aggression is most famously located in Sigmund Freud's theory of the "death instinct," which he named *thanatos,* and was an unnecessary later addition to his far less problematic theory of the "life-instinct," *eros.* For Freud the individual repression and cultural expression of eros was the life-force that gave rise to the achievements of culture and civilization. Freud's "death drive" theory was conceived later on in the formulation of his thought, and most particularly in the context of his growing pessimism with the modern age. The brutal inhumanity of World War I had a profound influence on Freud's ideas about violence and death. He makes these ideas clear in his essay, "Thoughts for the Times on War and Death" (1957). Freud was clearly shocked and overwhelmed by the total violation of law and of "moral standards" that were being committed in the atrocities of modern warfare. Freud was moved to such an extent that there could be no accounting for this unprecedented display of atrocity without recourse to some deep and uncontrollable "death instinct" that must be latent in the "unconscious of man." In this regard Freud was naïve about the barbarous capacity of states and the rational capacity of people in power to willingly engage in atrocity against others. Had he known more about the imperial politics of his day, he would not have been so surprised about the heights of atrocity that could be reached by so-called enlightened states in the acts of establishing their dominions through territorial warfare. Freud thus concluded that war was an effect of instinctual expression. But this is pure speculation. As Zinn explains, most everyone who makes the claim about the instinctual basis for war and violence relies, not on biology or psychology as explanations, *but on history.* Because history is replete with wars and conflict between states, this alone, it is suggested, must serve as proof of mankind's inability to resist expression of the death-instinct. (What it really speaks of is the violent nature of political states.) This explanation is clearly inadequate from a logical, even from a historical point of view because there are many points in history when warfare was not being waged. It also depends on how far back you go in history and which cultures are being identified as evidence, because in the historical record you can also find examples of prolonged periods of peace, especially in the long period prior to the advent of patriarchy, approximately 5,000 years ago (Lerner 1986).

It is a widely held belief that violence is the dominant force in the world. It is more accurate to argue that peace and order exist in greater amounts than does chaos. However, the effects of violence are extreme. Because violence violates, and the lived effects of violation are personally, socially and historically expansive in scope, its actions are more keenly felt and greater attention is given to its catastrophic power. Violence subordinates "the universal (society) to its exceptional particularity" – this is certainly part of the power of violence – where "violence is the state of exception which begins to become the rule."

If violence were truly the norm of society and not the exception then the social order that presently exists would be largely untenable – even in this agonistic life-world, its present degraded form: Life prevails over death; it is the ingenuity, resiliency and re-generation of life that persists. Even the economic and political development of global capitalism depends on a certain degree of functional equilibrium and stability for the social system to be maintained. Despite the popular idea that war is good for the general economy, and that much wealth is generated on the basis of arms sales, peace is altogether much better for economic prosperity in the long term.

Although peace and order tend to prevail over violence and social chaos, violence, even in small amounts out of proportion to the whole, is so disturbing a phenomenon that when it occurs in confined or localized occurrences it tends to upset the balance of the greater society. The effects of violence are also very long term and damaging, to individuals, cultures, emotional and historical memories, so even in singular amounts violence destroys lives beyond the immediacy of its occurrence.

The idea that human beings are genetically prone to conflict or have an inherent propensity towards resorting to violence is a typical example of what Theodor Adorno called "a belief guarded against reflection." People hold many such beliefs and repeat them is if they are conventional wisdom without ever pausing to reflect on their truth value. Such beliefs serve as serious impediments to the prospects for peace in their mystification of the basis by which we are able to fashion new realities based on a politics of non-violence and the development of social conditions free from socially imposed forms of domination. Yet such ill-fated ideas pertaining to violence and the human condition inform some of the most elaborate theoretical formulations of human oppression within the context of organized society. Such ideas are deeply rooted in the Western tradition of social and political thought. Such theories do not distance themselves far enough from Hobbesian assumptions about violence and human nature, where social life is based on a war of "all against all," and therefore requires the heavy hand of state regulation as a justification for greater conflict and social control. We see the same instinctual reductionism in the misleading interpretation of Nietzsche's philosophy of the "will to power" as the innate driving force in the transcendental progress of history, and in Freud's reduction of the problem of repression in Western civilization to the unruly primitivism of instincts and their precarious repression, especially in his later ill-conceived formulation of the "death instinct," is perhaps the most formidable and enduring example of a theory founded in the concreteness of innate human

violence. Freud's ideas die hard in an age where belief in instinctual aggression and "death-drives" fit so well, so "naturally," into
the prevailing order of continuing violence and destruction that
is still part of the global human condition of unending poverty
and social inequality. The vast proliferation of death and destruction that the Western ideology of violence takes as its empirical
referent – the cycle of predation and conquest, the ecstasy of continual war, and the unrelenting dehumanization and misery that
accompanies global development – all these do indeed appear to
serve as proof that we are living in a kingdom of death. The question of violence should not be a debate on its alleged origins; it
should be about how we can work towards the rational disman-
tling of organized violence to affirm life on earth. Approaching
this question is necessarily related to how we understand the
problem of violence within social life.

Competition and Human Nature

As it is with ideologies of violence so it is with ideologies about
competition. The argument that competition is a part of human
nature and is therefore inevitable and good is used as a way of
legitimating a society where predatorial competition is rampant,
and where the negative outcomes of competition – namely losership and defeat, and low self esteem – are things we are forced
to come to terms with. In a society where competition is presented as human nature we are less able to understand the sociological bases of the outcome of universal competition: which is
mass poverty and a world where too many struggle daily to
"make ends meet." So when an economic recession happens, as
it does every seven to ten years or so within capitalist systems,
the process of economic loss and all of the problems that arise
are seen as inevitable outcomes of the competitive system, in
which it is up to the individual to succeed against a challenging
set of social rules. People respond to their misery by claiming
that the game of life is unfair, and that society is an uneven playing field. All of these are true, but not for natural reasons, for
socio-economic ones. Competition is not a fixed aspect of human
nature, nor it is an inevitable aspect of human social organization
– it is a socially constructed reality that underlies the basis of
agonal capitalism. But this fact is ignored and reasons pertaining
to individual human nature are offered to explain the evident
social inequality.

The issue of "the human nature myth" with regards to competition has been eloquently elaborated by Alfie Kohn (1986), who cites a number of authors who contribute to the ideology of competition as human nature as if it was a matter of fact:

> Among those thinkers who believe competition is unavoidable are the authors of two classic works on play: Roger Callois and Johan Huizinga. Both take it for granted that we are unavoidably competitive creatures. "Games discipline instincts and institutionalize them," Callois wrote; that these competitive tendencies merit the status of instincts he did not bother to defend. (Kohn 1986: 16)

And further,

> In their 1917 essay on the subject, John Harvey and his co-authors observed that, for many people, "in games the pleasure comes from the competition itself... and not from success." From this they quickly concluded that "there is therefore in human nature an instinct of pure competition which finds satisfaction in the very act of striving to do something better than other people, even though the attempt is not successful." This is rather like claiming that because many people prefer the car ride to the arrival at their destination, humans must have an instinctive attraction to automobile travel. (Harvey quoted in Kohn 1986: 16)

And another example of this ideological discourse:

> Harvey Ruben's (1981) self-help manual, *Competing*, the first sentence of which is, "Competition is an inescapable fact of life." This, we later learn, is because "we indeed have a competitive 'code' in our chromosomes" – an astonishing claim that is not substantiated or even explained. (Kohn 1986: 16)

In case the reader clings to Darwinian evolutionary theory as evidence of the naturalness of competition in living species, Kohn goes on to point out that, "In fact, there is no necessary relationship between natural selection and competitive struggle." He cites

Stephen J. Gould as follows: "The equation of competition with success in natural selection is merely a cultural prejudice... Success can be attained by a large variety of strategies – including mutualism and symbiosis – that we could call cooperative" (cited in Kohn 1986: 18). Although competition is celebrated and promoted as the essential element that society could not do without, it is to the principle of co-operation that we owe our human evolutionary success. Ashley Montagu argues that without the cooperation of its members society cannot survive, and society has survived because the co-operativeness of its members made survival possible (Montagu cited in Kohn 1986). Kohn continues to state that human interdependence, "the fact of living and working together"... is "inherent in the very *idea* of society" (1986: 19).

Agon culture celebrates competition as the wellspring of society when the historical, anthropological and sociological evidence indicates that it is co-operation that sustains human life, and that competition remains tied to the order of social control and hierarchical organization of society.

The instinctual theory of violence and ideologies about the naturalization of competition assert that predation in the animal world is the primary principle of all living things, and when humans engage in violence they are simply living up to the "facts of nature" by mimicking the behaviours of predatory animals. This line of reasoning mystifies and "animalizes" human violence and makes it seem as if war is something inevitable and thus unavoidable rather than the result of free-will and the rationally planned, intentional conflicts emerging from powerful decision makers who control the social and political order. The danger in mistaking violence and war as something simply natural and inevitable is that we are far less likely to do anything about alleviating these problems if we are persuaded that they are eternal, rather than the planned outcomes of human intention and actions.

Chapter 8

Agonized Consciousness and the Paradox of Self Preservation in a Competitive Culture

Just as the capitalist system continuously produces and reproduces itself economically on
higher levels, the structure of reification progres-
sively sinks more deeply, more fatefully and more
definitively into the consciousness of man.

~Georg Lukács,
History and Class Consciousness

The more total society becomes, the greater the
reification of the mind and the more paradoxical
its effort to escape reification on its own.

~Theodor Adorno, *Prisms*

By offering what is repression as satisfaction,
makes the moment of self-negation permanent
and thus an unintended celebration of death.

~J.M. Bernstein, "Introduction" to *The Culture
Industry: Selected Essays on Mass Culture*

The reification of consciousness, the deployment
of its ingrained conceptual apparatuses often pre-
empts its objects and obstructs culture, which
would be one with the resistance to reification.

~Theodor Adorno,
Note on Human Science and Culture

In earlier chapters it was indicated that competition, despite being presented in agon culture as a productive, generative and positive form of social interaction, is more often tied to forms of dominating power. The popular misconception of Darwinian evolutionary theory presumes that competitive struggle is the primary modality of progressive growth and self preservation. This is more of an ideology than a matter supported by anthropological evidence. The promotion of competitive struggle as a cultural normative system has specific consequences for the organization of power and social equality in a society, just as it does for individuality and self growth. The matter of individual self growth or self preservation has been dealt with at some length by Adorno and others through the concept of "reification." This section will introduce the reader to some of the aspects of reification theory in order to develop an understanding of how agonistic thinking – that is, the competitive mode of consciousness – operates as a dominant form of reification within agon culture. As a brief definition it is useful to remind the reader that reification is an attempt to preserve the self, in thought and action, which paradoxically results in the opposite – reification is a form of self domination. Reification is a possible outcome of human consciousness when the individual is insecure, and seeks to establish security by identifying with power or by conforming to what popular culture defines as strength and success.

The Reification of Consciousness and the Paradox of Self Preservation

Reification is the consciousness of conformity. The dominant social consciousness within agon culture has become formulated to be in accordance with the values of the political and economic order. The subjective adherence to the mainstream view of social reality that dispenses with critical questioning is a form of the "happy consciousness"[1] that has been identified repeatedly in the tradition of thought known as the sociology of consciousness. One of the main features of "happy conformity" is the identification with power. The insecure subject believes that by identifying, agreeing with and reproducing the rationality of the powerful state she or he will benefit personally by sharing in that organ of strength. As Adorno and Horkheimer write,

> In the culture industry jovial denial takes the place
> of the pain that is present in ecstasy and in ascet-
> icism... In every exhibit of the culture industry,
> the permanent denial imposed by civilization is
> once again unmistakably demonstrated to, and
> inflicted upon, those affected by it. (1969: 141)

This insight represents a problematic dimension of the sort of reification that prevails in the formation of the agonal subject. It is a "happy" (falsely affirming) type of domination because, although it is objectively repressive, it takes the form of subjective satisfaction by offering a form of reassurance to the insecure subject. It is also positively stubborn because it produces a form of social consciousness that wilfully avoids inquiring into the evident contradictions of power structures such as the military machinery of the state and the promises of consumerism as forms of personal empowerment.

The structural inequalities of the political and economic system which generate personal life difficulties, daily difficulties, the blatant political contradictions and corruption, and the generalized social decay which have come to characterize the dire state in which so many people live, are not seen by the reified consciousness as being intricately connected to the society which claims to represent itself as having the monopoly on freedom. Individual complacency, political apathy, naïveté and a widespread social ignorance (induced anti-awareness) operate in the defence of a self-conditioned bondage that marks the power of conformist ideology in operation. Adorno writes: "Failing to discern the relevance of politics to their own interests, [people] retreat from all political activity" (Adorno 1991: 166). By "political activity" Adorno does not mean voting – he is likely referring to the critical quality of a politicized consciousness that engages in questioning. Even when the conditions of social injustice are exposed to conscious awareness these negative conditions of life are explained away as things to be expected. Social strife is rationalized as the eternal problem of individuals and not the outcome of human planning and an unequal social organization. To think that it could be otherwise is to be looked upon with incredulity, and even with conspiratorial suspicion. Daily life has become so entwined with domination that, as Adorno writes, "the sickness proper to the time consists precisely in normality" (1974: 58).

Part of the success of reifying cultural domination is that it remains a process of which the subject is unaware – this is a major mechanism of reification. While it is unrecognized by the conscious subject, it remains fundamentally tied to the unconscious level of subjective desire, and in particular the desire for recognition, which, we will observe below, is tied to the psychic structure of the insecure ego. The power of reification, which is the quintessential form of "cultural domination," is that in the name of subjective satisfaction the subject is offered repression, with the subject's active complicity in this deception. "Or," as Marcuse asks, has the facile resignation to debilitating social conditions come about as a result of a "transformation of the antagonistic structure itself, which resolves the contradictions by making them tolerable?" (1964: 21). Adorno writes: "It is part of the mechanism of domination to forbid recognition of the suffering it produces" (1974: 63). Foucault, years later, emphasizing the paradoxical nature of power, repeats a similar idea: "Power is tolerable only on condition that it masks a substantial part of itself... Its success is proportional to its ability to hide its own mechanisms" (Foucault 1978: 86). "If power were never anything but repressive, if it never did anything but say no, do you really think one would be brought to obey it?" Power "produces things, it induces pleasure, forms knowledge, produces discourse... much more than as a negative instance whose function is repression" (Foucault 1980: 119). The repressive function of power in consumer culture today comes in the form of pleasure, hence the paradoxical notion of "repressive satisfaction."

The Reification of Consciousness Defined

Hegemonic culture is also a paradoxical conception of culture, one that entails domination through the contradictory fabric of its system of meaning. Thus the "reification of consciousness" is dialectically related to the "affirmative character of culture," which is co-opted in the service of a form of self-incurred domination. This double effect of cultural power has been written

about in terms of the *reification* (Lukács 1971; Adorno) of culture, where dominant ways of seeing – the subjective construction
of perception – are directly linked to the project of power that
underlies the economic and political order. Cultural integration
into the dominant values expressive of this order works against
the self-realization of the individual. Reification so distorts the
dialectical interplay between self-affirmation and self-negation
that the living individual subject is transformed into a thing-like
"object" being that has lost the capacity for authentic self-determination. In this regard reified cultural domination is the aim of
the *ideological project of the domination of consciousness and
the realization of agon culture.*

Marx's thesis of "mental production," specifically the
insight that cultural domination occurs primarily through the
realm of the ideological, is the primary point of departure leading
to the thesis of reification which was first formulated by Lukács
(1971) and then reconstructed as a primary theme by Adorno.
Reification theory takes the critique of ideology and commodification a step further. The success of ideological power in
"mental production" is realized when an objective condition of
reification comes into being and the reified subject is produced.
Reification is the quintessential type of cultural domination and
refers to a social condition whose realization actually represents
the success of hegemonic power strategies realized in the constitution of personhood. Reification involves the internalization of
a particular mode of rationalization that mediates the relation
between self and the objective external world. The error of this
rationalization becomes the basis for active self-negation. Thus,
the matter of reification is a concrete problem of existence within
a society that requires the domination of its subjects in order to
maintain its power.

"Reification" speaks to a condition of domination related
to that of alienation. Lukács initially developed the critique of
reification as an appendage to Marx's critique of "commodity
fetishism," which he identified as "a specific problem of our age,
the age of modern capitalism" (1971: 84), and that reification is
the "central structural problem of capitalist society" (1971: 83).
Lukács writes:

> Just as the capitalist system continuously pro-
> duces and reproduces itself economically on

> higher levels, the structure of reification progres-
> sively sinks more deeply, more fatefully and more
> definitively into the consciousness of man.
> (Lukács 1971: 93)

Reification, however, is "a special case of alienation, its most radical and widespread form characteristic of modern capitalist society" (Bottomore 1991: 463). Further, "reification is a higher, that is the highest form of alienation" (1991: 465). Reification however is distinguishable from alienation because it does not necessarily depend upon the specific context of the capitalist mode of production within which alienation occurs.

Reification is a form of domination that occurs through the *cultural production of consciousness*; it is a product of the dialectic between the totalizing social order and the conscious character of the self. Its power of domination is based on the control of thinking, and by implication, the loss of the capacity for self-control. As Adorno writes, "The more total society becomes, the greater the reification of the mind and the more paradoxical its effort to escape reification on its own" (1967: 34). Socialization in this sense becomes a function of the order of domination. Unlike alienation, which dissolves when the conditions and relations of labour are changed, reification constitutes the normal mode of existence under cultural domination and is not necessarily confined to the capitalist mode of exploitation, although the reified production of culture under capitalist consumerism served as the primary example and concern[2] of Adorno and Horkheimer. Adorno and Horkheimer tied their critique of reification to the conflation of fascism and mass culture – a conflation which necessarily entails the deformation or mal-development of consciousness into the support for death of the other as the means for group survival.

It is important to emphasize that the condition of reification is not solely the fault of the individual or a specific problem of individual psychology as such. While the psychology of the individual is the level at which reification is manifested in subjective consciousness, it is more properly understood as an effect of the forces of cultural formation.

Before discussing how reification passes into the formation of agonal subjectivity, which is a quintessential type of reification, it is important to give a basic overview of Adorno and

Horkheimer's general theory of cultural domination. This cultural "domination of consciousness" that is essential for the realization of the society in question, the society of imposed order, is manifested in two significant ways that play upon the "affirmative character of culture." These have been identified by Adorno and Horkheimer as the tendency towards "total reification" and "absolute integration:" Both pertain to the organization of perception and the manipulation of the ways in which people think. Cultural "integration" has always formed part of the social bonding that forms part of the process of enculturation. It is normal and reasonable for people to desire socialization, belonging and recognition by others, and this constitutes the lived experience of enculturation. Enculturation is based on the subjective bonding to a system of values, traditions, conventions and social practices. While these form the ritual basis of cultural meaning and can affirmatively inform the course of life, being meaningfully bound to an objectively self-negating and inimical cultural form represents a significant type of domination: This depends on the "value" of what one is being culturally bound to. As we shall see with the problem of reification in agon culture, the dominated subject is bound into a culture that so fears the loss of life, that it affirms and celebrates death as an ill-fated logic of survival.

The problem of "absolute integration" to which Adorno and Horkheimer (1969) referred was not a form of social cohesion in the sense of being bound into an affirmative social whole, but a subjective absorption into the fold of dominant conventions of society whereby the individual reproduces these conventions in an unthinking and self-negating manner.

Mass Consciousness as Reified Consciousness

Repressive societies throughout history have utilized various means to get people to fit into the order prescribed for them by organs of power and rule. Sociological terminology sanitizes this integrative process as "social regulation," while Adorno and Horkheimer emphasized its increasingly coercive character and termed it "absolute integration," in which non-conformity is met with social sanctions. This type of integration is necessarily part of what constitutes the formation of the "mass" in "mass society"

(Mills 1956). The concept of a reified mass consciousness is akin to Gustave LeBon's characterization of the "group mind," where he identified the features of the "mental unity of crowds" (1925: 24). For LeBon the group mind is based on the regressive trans-formation of the intellectual capacity of the individual, one based not on the average of the members of the crowd, but on its descent to the lowest common denominator within it. Consequently, "crowds are not to be influenced by reasoning – the reasoning of crowds is always of a very inferior order" (1925: 60). LeBon continues:

> This explains how it is that the most contradictory ideas may be seen to be simultaneously current in crowds… Its complete lack of the critical spirit does not allow of its perceiving these contradictions. [However], this phenomenon is not particular to crowds. It is to be observed in many isolated individuals. (1925: 62)

Reification depends on the ideological harmonization of oppositions into consciousness, with the consequent subjective incapacity to reason and see through social contradictions and make sense of one's lived reality. George Orwell described this phenomenon like no one before or since. In his *Nineteen Eighty-Four* (1954) the state is actively involved in the mass dissemination of contradictory ideas such as War is Peace, Love is Hate, Freedom is Slavery. This newspeak doublethink as he terms it becomes the basis for a campaign of autocratic behavioural control. The effect of such conflations of contradictory ideas is to destroy the capacity for individuals to develop any significant critical, independent conscious awareness that will assist one in understanding the world around them and one's place in it. Doublethink controls by controlling the subject's capacity to think through contradictions and thus opens the subject up to greater manipulation and control. Reification in agon culture functions precisely on this basis: through the destruction of perception and thus through the formation of the subject as a controllable conforming object.

Absolute integration colonizes the desire for social belonging by rewarding people to behave in certain culturally prescribed ways in order to "fit in:" "Fitting in" socially means faithfully reproducing the dominant cultural conventions, speaking in clichés and generally sacrificing the tendency to depart from convention and develop the self in an autonomous way.

Absolute integration into mass society is therefore directly related to the reification of consciousness – to the undermining of the subject's capacity to think. The population is constituted into the mass when it has been successfully socialized into accepting, even celebrating the order which represents its own negation. Mass mentality prevents the critical awareness and questioning that is necessary for freedom to exist. The motto of reified conformity is "don't think about it," "Just Do It;" being tough means going blindly into the challenge. The injunction to living without thinking, the "unexamined life" or "ignorance is bliss," has been so engrained as a reified cultural value that such slogans, which are cherished as comforting remedies in times of stress, have the ring of charity to them. In Kant's time the King at least said, "think as you please but obey" (Kant 1970). Mass enlightenment today dispenses with independent thinking altogether and in agon culture is based on the assembly of "facts." Cerebral stimulation offered by the next entertainment spectacle or news broadcast. Unthinking pleasure has now become a market demand, one which the culture industry gladly delivers.

The loss of critical consciousness is thus a necessary precondition for social conformity, manipulation and reified cultural domination. The culture industry today functions primarily in this manner, wherein certain forms of uncritical or conformist modes of perception are inculcated into public-mass consciousness. This promotes self-negation as self-affirmation.

It is important to note that not everyone is subject to the project of reification. Nor is everyone persuaded to think identically on all issues in society. But there are definitely dominant ideological modes/trends of thinking which get established in terms of the ways public perception gets constructed. Nor do minor differences in matters of personal opinion necessarily constitute any significant departure from the dominant view of things. So effective, in fact, has the construction of popular consciousness been that general opinions on social issues have become fairly accurate in the ability to predict public opinion (which is at the same time a measure of social consciousness). Opinion polls are accurate in this regard insofar as they correspond truthfully to how effectively social perception has been formulated. Opinion polls are among the main insidious ploys of media-democracies: The media disseminates "information" which gets publicly internalized and is reported back to pollsters as personal opinion. Democratic consent has come to mean that the dominant ideology gets faithfully reproduced. This process of the subjective internalization of dominant ideology was elaborated by Althusser (1971) in his concept of interpellation. Interpellation is a process that refers to individuals repeating ideological discourse as if it were their own formulation and which has thereby taken on the status of personal opinion. The interpellation of subjects is a documented phenomenon in the formation of a conformist consciousness (Williamson 1978). The work of George Gerbner (2002) examines the same phenomenon with a different set of concepts. He talks about how mass media "cultivates" a "mainstream" perception of reality among those who engage heavily with the offerings of the culture industry.

Jere Surber (1998) writes of the problem of public "common sense" through the invocation of Socrates' distinction between opinion (*doxa*) and knowledge (*episteme*). Socrates held that some of the views of people in the public held up under questioning more than others, and that it is popular opinion – doxa, the view shared by the majority, which is found to be full of contradictions and is thus "self-cancelling and amounts to saying nothing at all" (1998: 2). "Opinion," which is much more common than "knowledge," thus constitutes one of the lowest forms of understanding. Absolute integration or opinionated loyalty to dominant conventions is not identical to reification, although they are dialectically related in the context of a totalizing and imposed social order.

The charge of academic elitism that is launched against social thought, which identifies how the public is transformed into the mass and rendered incompetent through a reified or otherwise socially *constructed* ignorance, is a false one. While stupidity is a fact (as is a vast difference among humans in intellectual capacity), so is ideological manipulation on a mass scale. It is a reactionary claim that seeks to silence the critique of power in the name of the integrity of the public mind. So effective has the campaign against this sort of critique of the problematic of mass consciousness been that contemporary cultural studies, which claims to be "critical theory," has reduced the parameters of its concern with social domination to the institutional axes of "race, class and gender." Consequently it risks redefining "domination" as mere social exclusion or inequity rather than engaging in a critique of consciousness. Such degraded forms of critical theory, ironically enough, have actually come to favour the forms of popular consciousness that have emerged in conjunction with the culture industry as an expression of social resistance (Fiske 1989). In this respect Cultural Studies merges with postmodernism in supplanting the radicalism of an authentic critical theory, which consistently located the problem of domination in the reification of consciousness. It is important, therefore, from the point of view of the critique of domination, to retain, reconstruct and re-apply the concept of reification to the poverty of mass-cultural consciousness in the present.

Reification as the Disfiguration of Consciousness

The concept of reification is a complex one and deals with some of the most fundamental issues pertaining to freedom, social control and the problem of domination as these were addressed by the critical theory of the Frankfurt School (Jay 1973; Rose 1978; Held 1980; Wiggershaus 1995). The general theoretical area, which Habermas (1984) refers to as the "philosophy of consciousness," has initiated some important scholarly debate within critical thought concerning the general problem of domination in contemporary capitalism. This study opts to reconstruct and apply the concept of reification in the context of agon culture, where the value texts of conflict substantially inform the production of the reified subject as a type of agonal consciousness.

Although reification as a concept/problem has been traditionally discussed in relation to the mental processes which negotiate the psychic life of the individual, most of the scholarship on it remains confined to a philosophical discussion concerning the history of the concept, and in particular pertains to the debates concerning the philosophy of subject/object relations (Rose 1978; Habermas 1984; Adorno 1998). This analysis discusses the concept of reification in relation to the material realm of the life-world, including the realm of subjective experience, personal meaning and social suffering. Adorno, for whom reification is a fundamental concept, was concerned with the "corporeal, sensuous, and suffering human being" (Krakauer 1998: 4) and it was primarily this concern that drove his interest in reification, and not its relation to foundational principles and debates within the history of the philosophy of mind.

There is a tendency within certain receptions of reification theory to think that all cultures tend towards reification. This has to do with reading the theory of reification in the context of anthropological cultural authenticity: that because certain non-industrial, secluded, tribal societies engage in sacrificial rituals and self-mutilating behaviours, that this serves as empirical validation of reification occurring in "pristine" cultures, and therefore reification is normal, inevitable and unproblematic in capitalist consumer society. Reification theory would reject all forms of culturally sanctioned self-destructive behaviour as reified behaviour as long as reified cultural practices serve the interests of maintaining a hierarchical system of power and social subordination. The frequency of its occurrence in human cultures past, present, local or distant, has nothing to do with the naturalness of reified consciousness in modern society. Nor should such examples be used to defend the authenticity of reification as a functional element in the growth of economic systems. A culture should not be immune to criticism simply because it has not fostered the capacity to develop a meaningful tradition based on affirmative practices, in which the sanctity of life and the sacredness of the body are not upheld as imperatives of the culture.

Reification is a paradoxical condition of consciousness because it is not subjectively experienced or recognized as a type of domination. It can be seen as a type of "repressive satisfaction" because it transmutes repression into contentment. Reification is thus a form of unwitting self-negation because its processes remain concealed from conscious awareness and are actually perpetuated by the active (self-preservation seeking) subject. Reification operates as a form of social domination because it coincides with the subject's removal from conditions (of conscious awareness) that enable a true process of self-realization based on a de-reified consciousness.[3]

The socialization of the individual into the subject-position "consumer" also represents a type of reified "positive domination" through the commodification of desire on the basis of the satisfaction of pleasure and want. In the traditional discourse of the "philosophy of consciousness," reification is conceived of as a form of domination which entails the transformation of the self as "subject" into a thing as "object." Objectification in this sense is thus the manifestation of domination unto a mode of non-being. In reified culture individuals are socialized to see others as calculable objects and are themselves objectified in turn. This seeing the other as object is part of the competitive mode of perception that predominates within agon culture.

Cultural domination is realized when the subjective state of reification comes into being. Reification, as a particular quality of consciousness, does not exist in and of itself as an aberration of enculturation. It is a reflection of power and order realized in the formation of subjective consciousness under a culture based on domination. Reification attaches to the larger system of domination, especially the political and economic order of domination, and its system of values. The reified subject is socialized into believing that internalization of the superiority/victory values of the dominant order will assist in the struggle for individual advancement and self-affirmation. Reification thus plays upon *the subjectivity of self-interest.*

Agonistic reification operates by a form of self-deception based on the mimesis of that force which represents the power over life and death, which is attractive because it seems to represent strength but in actuality reproduces negation. J.M. Bernstein writes about this in terms of the "postmodern sublime… [which] by offering what is repression as satisfaction, makes the moment of self-negation permanent and thus an unintended celebration of death" (Bernstein 1991: 22). By transmuting that which is objectively repressive into forms of subjective satisfaction, active participation in reified culture masks and normalizes domination as a self-incurred process of psychic defeat: The principle of self-preservation (which is inherent in the affirmative character of culture) is realized as self-destruction. Simon Jarvis writes, "Energetic self-preservation is replaced by the indissociable entanglement of self-preservation and self-destruction" (1998: 83). Adorno and Horkheimer explain the paradox of preservation/destruction in terms of the primordial history or prehistory of reified subjectivity:

> As soon as man cuts off his consciousness of him-
> self as nature, all the ends for which he keeps him-
> self alive – social progress, the heightening of all
> his natural and spiritual powers, even conscious-
> ness itself – are nullified; the enthronement of
> means as ends, which under late capitalism is tan-
> tamount to open insanity, is already perceptible in
> the primordial history of subjectivity. Man's dom-
> ination over himself, which grounds his selfhood,
> is virtually always the destruction of the subject
> in whose service it takes place; for the substance
> which is dominated, suppressed and undone by
> [efforts at] self-preservation is none other than
> that very life for which the accomplishments of
> self-preservation are supposed to be functional; it
> is in fact what is supposed to be preserved [that
> is destroyed]. (Adorno and Horkheimer 1969: 54-
> 55, translation modified)

This dense passage indicates the critical idea that preservation of
the psychic self follows the formula for general preservation, in
terms of negotiating the natural realm of necessity – by domination over it. This formula is transplanted into self-preservation as
a *domination* of (control over) the self by the self to culminate in
self-negation. Reification emerges from the panicked conflation
of domination with preservation to, and becomes a reversal of,
the intended primary aim.

Adorno thus argues that reification is a "death mask" of
identity, a form of self-expression as self-negation, the paradoxical result of subjective efforts at self-preservation through identification with cultural values, commodities and life-choices
which present themselves as enabling and "positive" yet are inimical to subjective well-being. Examples of this include the agon
culture directives that discipline over the self is the key to pre-
serving the self, that the body is more important than the mind,
and that strength defined in terms of aggression and violence represents a positive mode of transcendental action. Entire industries
have arisen in response to the personal pursuit of these pastimes,
not surprisingly we have "competition-bodies," "predator cham-
pions" and "karate kids" to name only a few, emerging as normal
reified cultural types. Because reification involves the internal-

ization of antinomical means and ends that guide individual behaviour in various maladaptive ways, it results in all sorts of debilitating life difficulties.

Agonistic reification thus gives rise to the *disfiguration of consciousness*, where the subject proceeds to take pleasure in dominating acts and in their own domination. The disfiguration of consciousness is realized when people are successfully persuaded to act in ways which are inherently self-destructive but which are not subjectively perceived as such. Reification denies the critical judgment required for true self-preservative action by mistaking physical strength over others for power. The resulting multiplication of life difficulties that one must endure is made worse by a weakening of the capacity to self-reflect on issues and thereby further multiplying a situation of difficulty based on the loss of the critical capacity to self-reflect on whether or not "personal challenges" defined in terms of competition are really going to result in transcendence. Reification involves a self-defensive reaction to life, a lack of results by which the reified subject ignores negative feedback, and deliberately persists in the same strategy but with greater force.

In a culture that celebrates negation as a form of power, the efforts of those who desire self-preservation and emulate the power of the force of negation are only thrust deeper into existential turmoil. A common response in this regard is the belief that strength and power are the modes through which one can be victorious within the general order of domination. This motivates the agonized individual to aspire to the status of becoming a "winner" in the attempt to transcend his or her negative condition. As we will examine below, the frenzied desire for winning is a fundamental dimension of agonal subjectivity. Reification installs itself precisely in these moments where activities inimical to self preservation are actively engaged in. Thus the critique of reification extends beyond a consideration of the integrity of consciousness and into a critique of the mal-development of the individual's life-path choices. This often entails the sorts of disfiguration of the individual that are realized in the despair and trouble that plague the lives of so many who fall prey to reified cultural pastimes based on conquering death (we shall explore these further in the chapter on popular agonism and the mediagon). The fear and despair that people endure in cultures of domination is part of the more generalized erosion of the life-world which agon culture tends to foster and to which the condition of reification fundamentally gives rise.

Reification is relational to the *disfiguration of perception* because "it impedes the development of autonomous individuals who judge and decide consciously for themselves" (Adorno 1991: 92), and thus complicates personal thought on what course of action in life best serves the interests of self-preservation. The reified subject is trapped deeper in the disabling web of dilemmas that impoverish their social and interpersonal existence. It thwarts the decision-making process and supplants critical thought (the negation of that which is inimical to well being – the real element underlying affirmative culture) with conformist thought – which is the positive acceptance of that which is merely presented as affirming. Reified consciousness is therefore fundamentally a form of "false consciousness" (Engels 1968).

The critique of reification as a form of "false consciousness" needs to be explained without recourse to the problematic term "false," which opens up an onslaught of reactionary defences pertaining to the inherent authenticity of *all* cultural forms, and drastically simplifies the complexity of cultural domination as simply a matter of value judgment. Reified culture can be seen as an extension of Marx's original formulation because it misleads the subject in the self-directed ways described above as the co-optation of the process of self-preservation that occurs through a mimetic identification with the very power that represents domination and subjective negation. This is the ultimate paradox, and the tragedy of the affirmative character of culture – that self-preservation becomes realized as self-defeat. "The ideology which affirms life is forced into opposition by the immanent drive of the ideal" (Adorno 1967: 29).

Resistance to Reification

Even though the order of social totalization in which reification operates seeks universalization, the project of power is never complete. Not all people succumb to domination. And even in those that do there seems to be a glimmer of insight, however degraded, alas an insight that may never be pursued unless social conditions are ripe for a transformation of consciousness. Lukács, for example, "counts on their being some reservation within the subjective nature of human beings that is resistant to reification," a "type of resistance that subjective nature opposes to rationalization" (Habermas 1984: 368). Adorno and Horkheimer similarly write that people live with a "dim recognition" that things in life are amiss, that there is a subjective awareness at some basic level that things are fundamentally unsound in social life. But the motivation that drives the gesture towards exploring the insight into one's negative condition is immediately met with resistance, and pursuit of the transcendental idea is avoided and the insight repressed. This is especially the case in agon culture where the very mechanism of resistance is cast in terms of competition and conquest. The insight that would otherwise inform a course of transcendence is avoided precisely because of the appeasement of anxiety that comes from absolving oneself of the hard responsibility that pursuit of the insight would necessarily demand. *The pain of self-reflection is related to the burden of self-transformation and to the resignation to one's life situation.* The fear of failing at freedom is as great as the fear of social deviation, so inactivity and conformity are self-rewarded: the reified subject retreats deeper into forms of conformity and integration. Adorno writes, "for the individual, life is made easier through capitulation to the collective with which he identifies. He is spared the cognition of his impotence" (1991: 174). A similar idea is expressed by Horkheimer:

> The individual as a rule must simply accept the basic conditions of his existence as given and strive to fulfill them: he finds satisfaction and praise in accomplishing as well as he can the tasks connected with his place in society and in courageously doing his duty despite all the sharp criticism he may choose to exercise in particular matters. (1972: 207)

The resignation to one's ill condition in life is thus related to the reification of the critical faculty inherent in cultural consciousness. Adorno puts it thus: "The truncation of their imagination deprives them of the faculty which made the state of freedom pleasurable in the first place" (1991: 167). The level of people's willingness to ignore the obvious foolishness and idiocy of much of what passes for popular culture, entertainment and leisure activity is proof of how integrated domination is with freedom and especially "free time."[4] For reified subjects, "the rule of such unfreedom has been abstracted from them" (Adorno 1991: 165). It is a form of self-incurred repression motivated by a fear of transformation and an objectifying desire to remain the same. The desire on the part of the individual to retain a static and unchanging self forms part of the reifying dimension of personal identity. We wear our identities as they mask us in turn; this is the impasse of identity as the ultimate mask of self, part of the reifying "death mask."

Reification involves the clinging ever more firmly to one's identity and deeply held beliefs; so much so that even when the time for the possibility of questioning arises and new knowledge may emerge, the reified subject "sticks to his guns" and obstinately refuses the chance at transformation: One lives in total disregard for the insight to transcendence, for "knowledge obtained in the denunciation of illusion" (Adorno and Horkheimer 1969: 23) and "the infinitesimal freedom that lies in knowledge as such" (Adorno 1974: 26).

The individual susceptibility of reification is inherently related to the construction of the insecure/agonized subject, where insecurity becomes the primary cultural mode through which defensive power gets manifested in social behaviour. The insecure subject is one whose response to feelings of powerlessness (as an ill-fated response to felt oppression) comes to identify with the agonistic character of power that circulates in the general order of society. This happens to such an extent that both narcissistic personality types and social insecurity become dominant modalities of self-expression (O'Neill 1991; Lasch 1979). Agon culture, with its ever-present climate of insecurity and universal competition, cultivates narcissism as a social norm. The very order of domination that promotes power as the highest virtue, even to those who are oppressed by it, becomes the occasion for the public stimulation of insecurity. The narcissistic response to the perceived threat to self and feelings of a "loss of self" is met with an overreaction to the threat and through the emulation of the power of that which threatens. What results is an unconscious capitulation to domination through a cultural process that mimics the domineering characteristics of power, one that is not made available to conscious awareness. The subject of racism becomes a racist; the subject of physical abuse becomes an abuser, and so on. Recognition into this agonistic-antagonistic dilemma is met with a subjective reaction that culminates in self defeat and is thus a fatal response to insecurity. It is notable that in the clinical psychological literature, narcissism is associated with deep aggression, rage and hostility (Kohut 1972). Aggression is a characteristic feature of agonism and part of its destructive organizing principle.

The aggression that emerges from narcissistic reification is one possible response to felt insecurity. Adorno and Horkheimer write, "self-preservation repeatedly culminates in the choice between survival and destruction" (1969: 30). Insecurity and aggression are subjective responses to fear, and fear is what motivates the threatened, dominated subject. Ontological fear is the "primordial" fear of death. As Adorno and Horkheimer write, "physical injury cripples the body, fear the mind" (1969: 256). Motivation by fear creates an unconscious susceptibility that predisposes the subject to respond by mimetic identification with the power of danger. Mastery, or the superiority of danger, originates in the fear of death. It is the mimesis of mastery contained in the Hegelian dialectic of self-consciousness – which we will look at more closely below.

Cultural Mimesis and the Dialectic of Recognition

Thus subjective mimesis of insecure/agonal order (the order that represents power) becomes the mode through which cultural reification emerges and gets expressed as a dimension of self-hood. Adorno called this type of reifying mimesis "identitarian thinking" (Adorno 1973), where the rationality structures of the dominant power/order are mapped onto the cognitive structures of individual consciousness. While Adorno recognized the anthropological truth contained in "the mimetic heritage" of culture where "the human is indissolubly linked with imitation: a human being only becomes human at all by imitating other human beings" (Adorno 1974: 154), individuation is possible only by way of inter-subjective socialization. Adorno (and

Horkheimer) take exception to mimetic social learning when cultural "imitation enters into the service of domination" (Adorno and Horkheimer 1969: 57), as it does under the reification of culture, where the striving for self-preservation is tied to the mimesis of that which represents defeat and death (Adorno and Horkheimer 1969: 57). Identity thinking, "Adorno tried to show, correctly registers but falsely affirms dominant ideologies" (Held 1980: 202). "For Adorno and Horkheimer a non-coercive integration of the self could never be realized in an objectively antagonistic society" (Jarvis 1998: 33). The dialectic between reification, mimesis, artifice and death is an important nexus in the critique of agon culture and domination. Simon Jarvis clarifies the point further:

> Mimesis, for Adorno, it needs to be borne in mind, is not the attempt to make a copy of nature but the attempt to become like nature in order to ward off what is feared... Death is an inextinguishable reminder of the nature in culture. The whole nexus of self-preservatory thought and action, Adorno and Horkheimer suggest, mimics death, strives to become inorganic, object-like in its attempt to ward off death. Self-preservation has thus become intimately entangled with self-destructiveness. Individual psychological self-destructiveness and collective (military-industrial) self-destructiveness are alike interpreted by Adorno as this kind of desperate miscarried self-preservation, a mimesis of what is dead. (Jarvis 1998: 31)

Identity thinking, or self-negating mimesis, which drives the self-incurred process of domination in reification, is not unrelated to the psychic processes of mastery and bondage that construct the psychology and the docility of the colonized subject. As has been indicated above, the reification of culture is the new mode of cultural imperialism in the agon. As such, the mental mechanism identified in Hegel's (1931) paradigmatic master/slave dialectic of self-consciousness is useful as a hermeneutic of psychic domination, yet it remains a problematic construct. Its initial attraction is based on the way it establishes and recognizes the relationship of oppositional/antagonistic power as the determining force of the subject constituted under the pressure of domination. The dialectic of self-consciousness, which for Hegel is the dialectic of becoming, sees the subject as the construct of power relations that come to inhabit the psychic structures of consciousness and identity. The dialectic of domination finds fertile ground in the individual's original insecurity, which forms part of the *psychology* of domination and which stems from the genuine social "need for recognition" (Hegel 1931) that as humans we all possess. A number of disciplines have extended Hegel's dialectical philosophy, including sociology, phenomenology, critical theory and psychoanalysis.

The argument is as follows: The need for recognition by social others as the basis for our own sense of self worth is a need which establishes both self identity and social interdependency. As Jessica Benjamin notes, "A condition of our own independent existence is recognizing the other" (1988: 53). Yet, "the need for recognition entails [a] fundamental paradox: at the very moment of realizing our own independence, we are dependent upon another to recognize it" (1988: 33). "We might call this the dialectic of control: If I completely control the other, then the other ceases to exist, and if the other completely controls me, then I cease to exist... True independence means sustaining the essential tension of these contradictory impulses; that is, both asserting the self and recognizing the other" (1988: 53). "They [master and slave] recognize themselves as mutually recognizing one another" (Hegel 1931: 230). Recognition – which becomes the gauge for self-worth, is based on the desire to identify with and be identified by a meaningful/powerful external figure/object. The self-seeking subject begins with this predicament, this ontological condition of lack and desire, which also becomes the occasion for the consent to domination. For Hegel, what ensues at the inter-psychic level is a nasty drama, an agonistic interplay of social recognition and self destruction. Hegel writes:

> This presentation is a twofold action; action on the part of the other, and action on its own part. In so far as it is the action of the *other*, each seeks the death of the other. But in doing so, the second kind of action, action on its own part, is also involved; for the former involves the staking of its

own life. Thus, the relation of the two self-conscious individuals is such that they prove themselves and each other through a life and death
struggle. They must engage in this struggle, for
they must raise their certainty of being *for-them-
selves* to truth, both in the case of the other and
in their own case. And it is only through staking
one's life that freedom is won... (in O'Neill 1996:
31)

This seminal passage, where self-authentication depends on
negation, is the architectonic of imperial-psychic domination.
Self-preservation is seen in terms of combat. Hegel's famous formulation carries forth a fetish of the other inherited from the sub-
ject/object dichotomy, which in real life gets formulated as the
master/slave relation and serves to understand how the psychological problem of inter-subjective demand for recognition as
self-authentication becomes the genesis of domination. "Domination does not repress the desire for recognition; rather it enlists
and transforms it" (Benjamin 1988: 219), both in the instance of
cultural domination as well as in the more deeply ontological
predicament of domination where the individual as subject gets
structured in relation to an objective externality – which can be
either another (objectified) subject or external "hostile" Nature,
the latter two serving as the grand totemic referent that is the
threat against which subject/self develops identity. In the classical
Hegelian subject/object distinction the Other is seen as threat to
self/subject, and part of the strategy of dealing with this threat
involves a drive to over power through destruction. When actual
domination cannot be acted out, it gets symbolically registered
(sublimated) in the possessive dynamic of mimesis – copying that
which has power over us as a strategy of overcoming it.

Mimesis is a way of coming to terms with the predicament of subjective mastery through copying the master as a form
of appeasement and docility to power. However, the mimesis of
mastery is a form of deformative self-othering. Mimesis is based
on copying: To endeavour to be like the other is already to take
leave of one's own self and thus forms the basis for a rejection of
self; in fact, it is a form of self-negation and self-hatred. (We see
this deformation of the mimetic tendency of individuals in the
rituals of popular culture in which young boys wear the hockey

jerseys of their favourite players, or young girls strive to look like their favourite female celebrities). "Mimicry" generally demonstrates docility – the term comes from "simian," which means "ape," and refers to ape-ing, a mere copying of another's behaviour and identity, as contained in the saying "monkey see monkey do." The term, in its charge of atavism, is an affront to intelligence. It indicates action before reflection and therefore is demonstrative of a lack of thinking and self negation. Mimetic behaviour in this sense is non-cognitive, it is reactive, and is driven by insecurity. In the mimicry of mastery the subject concedes defeat in seeking to be like the Other/Master, albeit in a degraded form, but is nonetheless ensured a degree of self-preservation through the false hope of recognition by others who can relate to the identification. The process appears to be like the relatively benign "mimetic faculty in cultural learning" or the "analogical consciousness of resemblance" (Bhabha 1994: 49), but because it is driven by coercion and domination, it is entirely reifying and subjectively disfiguring – it speaks of the loss of self in the pursuit of another presumably higher self. The process of identification in the mimicry of the master/slave dilemma (despite the discourse of reconciliation that is often associated with the dialectic of recognition), is spoiled due to the original imbalance of power inherent in the actors which comprise it.

It must be stated again here that the Hegelian dialectic of self-consciousness is not an unproblematic conception. At one level we affirm the master/slave dialectic of self-consciousness as useful for understanding the production of domination in the violated, threatened and insecure subject. In this context it has been a useful analytic for understanding colonial forms of domination where the oppressed strives to be like the oppressor (Fanon 1952). At another level the dialectic must be rejected because its architectonic of psychological disfiguration begins with the presupposition that the fragility of the human psyche – its Achilles' heel – is the innate master pattern of a presumed incomplete consciousness and not merely that which gets fostered in the context of cultural – even inter-familial – insecurity. It also proposes as a universal in the development of human consciousness that the other is a perpetual threat and that self-growth depends on the possession, control and eventual destruction of the Other. Thus an unreconstructed appropriation of the

master/slave dialectic involves the problem of the false universalization of ontological insecurity. The other problem, as previously alluded to, is the presumed "reconciliatory" movement
between actors that abolishes the master/slave dichotomy,
resolves the contradiction/conflict, and seemingly collapses the
imbalance of power between master and slave – dominator and
dominated. The master/slave dialectic becomes an ideology
which preserves the authenticity of the original distinctions
between master and slave and leaves mastery and slavery intact
– or at least until the synthetic implosion of oppositional characters occurs as false "reconciliation." The much-touted reconciliation speaks of a freedom which is always in the process of
becoming and is never achieved – antagonistic consciousness
gets preserved and transformed. Certainly there is another way
of theorizing the "birth of the subject" that is not "vacuously
apocalyptic" and self defeating (Eagleton quoted in Bhabha
1994: 64).

Fundamentally then, the Hegelian formulation of dialectical production of self is quintessentially agonistic. That it rings
true is only because it captures the socially fabricated condition
of what exists within agon culture – the economic, political and
cultural formation of antagonisms between human beings who
have been socialized into seeing one another as a threat and thus
must be conquered. For Adorno, the dialectical ontology furnished by Hegel develops on the basis of objective antagonism
as a condition of reality it simultaneously represents and solidi-
fies as the only true condition of being. In offering a historical
construct as the ontological condition of all reality, the Hegelian
dialectic of self-consciousness becomes an ideology for the normalization of conflicted relations amongst human beings. The
critical approach would be to see the negation and antagonism
inherent in the formation of dialectic inter-subjectivity as a historical construction of antagonistic social relations that are
merely reflected in the constitution of the social world, in the relation between dominator and dominated, and not essential to it
(Adorno 1973).

The tendency to naturalize the antagonistic sub-text in a
system of thought like Hegel's is supported by the theory of
human nature that sees humans as innately aggressive and competitive creatures. The ideology that couples violence to human

nature is an important one to consider in terms of the critique of agonism, and has been examined in some detail above in chapter 7. Nevertheless, although the motivation for self-preservation has been incorrectly explained in terms of innate "survival instincts," we enter onto problematic terrain when we biologize the will to life that forms part of the subjective need for accommodation with the objective realm of necessity. It is more theoretically worthwhile to examine the culturally constructed psychology of lack and desire rather than to consign the human to biological predispositions that result in conditions of the inevitability of relations based on mastery and domination. If humans are indeed born with a predisposition towards insecurity and are thus subsequently amenable to domination (as psychoanalysis claims), and that this condition forms the basis for life as an "unhappy consciousness" in the Hegelian sense, then it is the fault of the agon cultural order that both feeds upon and colonizes this frailty rather than "affirmatively" working to alleviate it. As Marcuse states, in a one-dimensional society there is a "conquest of the unhappy consciousness" (1964). Similarly, the economic conception of the individual, as *homo economicus* – which is the classical liberal-utilitarian conception of the individual (Abercrombie, Hill and Turner 1986), where the "acquisition of goods" is seen as the basis of freedom – is also a conception that contains a dialectic of lack and desire: the desire for goods to fulfill needs is met by the abundance represented in the consumer marketplace. This is the ideology of self-preservation based on the "maximization of utilities" as the basis of transcendence through possessive individualism (Macpherson 1973). The idea of self-preservation thus exists alongside the reality of objective need, which plays upon the realms of the biological, the economic and the psychological. These are merged together to form a complex matrix of subjectivity that configures the insecurity of the subject and its desire for freedom. This conundrum leads to the subject's vulnerability and readiness for domination, a readiness that the forces of the unfettered marketplace are only too willing to oblige.

What happens at the cultural level of reification, where there is a subjective identification with power (and this power can also be represented by the promise of the marketplace of goods), is thus a classic example of the master/slave dialectic of domination operating at the cultural level, where the dominated attempts to accommodate for subjective weakness by identification (false internalization) with the strength of mastery. The mimicry of mastery becomes the paradox of the identification with power and gets realized as a form of self-incurred defeat. This cultural "mastery," through which the reification of consciousness occurs, is bound up with forms of social regulation that operate at the level of subjective desire. This strategy of lack and fulfillment is repeated in the ideology of the market society where the promise of commodities to alleviate needs becomes the occasion for a self-negating formation of the individual.

To restate: Agonistic selfhood is supported ideologically through the celebration of competition as part of the self-preservative (virtuous) pursuit of being a "winner" and the fear of being a loser as the driving ethic in agon culture. Competition forms a substantial part of the mode of sociation in consumer culture. It permeates the interpersonal world of public association by becoming the organizational ethic mediating human relations. Agonism as a social value, then, relates directly to the formation of reified cultural subjectivity by the way it informs the relations of self to self and self to others within the sphere of culture. Agonism is the primary text of value within the narrative of culture that informs the reification of the self at the level of desire. The manner by which the agonal subject seeks to reconcile with fear determines the value structures that come to dominate subjective thought and action. The reification of the subject thus has two dominant levels of manifestation in agon culture: the *political* and the *cultural*, which as shall be indicated below, also represent the two realms that have become increasingly conflated in the rise of modern agonal society.

Popular Modes of Agonal Subjectivity

Although political subjectivity is not necessarily identical with the production of the consumer subject, in the context of agon culture, they are related on a number of levels. The formation of the political/patriotic subject overlaps with that of the consumer/utilitarian subject in so far as they both depend on the *subjectivity of self-interest* – which is the ideal contained in the constitution of the modern individual and has culminated in *possessive individualism* (Macpherson 1973) as a popular cultural norm. Possessive individualism is based on the classical liberal ideal that freedom is based on the subjective power of accumulation: It is an eighteenth century solution to an ancient concern with the problem of scarcity and basic satisfaction of the realm of necessity which consumer society tries to capitalize on with its abundance of "goods."

The problem of agonal individualism is that the pursuit of seemingly rational self-interest contributes to the creation of various forms of self-negating behaviour. Agonal individualism manifests itself in both the "possessive individualism" of the consumer subject and in the "defensive individualism" of the political subject. Both subject formations identify with the idea that strength over another is a positive form of power. This association tampers with the subjective capacity to critically self-reflect, insofar as it reduces the world to the schema of "positive" and "negative," which is the binary frame of perception in the agonal imaginary. The automatic labelling of things in life as either positive or negative constitutes a significant reduction in the capacity to understand the complexity of things. Seeing things, issues, decisions and so forth as either positive or negative works to suspend the questioning that is necessary to sustain critical cultural awareness. Questioning gets supplanted by quick decision making and practical action: "Just Do It." Is the very act of questioning is itself seen as a negative waste of time. In this manner agonistic socialization brings with it preformed judgments. As such "positive" means social conformity, consenting to the general order of things, "going with the flow," and not "being difficult." In the appeal to positivity people are rewarded for their complicity with power. Positivity and the positive acceptance of the dominant social order tends to reproduce the military model of command-obedience as the consensual model of social integration. It reduces the scope of freedom to a choice between positive-conformity or negative-nonconformity. As Adorno writes, "freedom would be not to choose between black and white but to abjure such prescribed choices" (1974: 132).

When large sections of the population, as in the context of contemporary agon culture, have been socialized in such a way that their capacity to reason has been compromised in various ways, it is not surprising that the condition of reification has become the norm. The condition of reification as a quality that mediates the contents of consciousness forms part of the ideological mode in the production of a type of mass psychosis – a sort of phenomenological coma where a useful comprehension of one's social conditions and of how oneself is circumscribed within them becomes near to impossible. Only under such conditions of the ideological manipulation of consciousness are popular formulations such as the love of agonism and the celebration of death culturally possible. The integration into society involves the shaping of identity as a citizen-consumer; consequently cultural socialization includes directives about what to buy, what to love, who to hate and how to respond to the major issues of the day. The dominant ideology that underwrites the thinking of the political subject is that most important element of political being: the question of freedom. It is on the issue of freedom that consumerism and patriotism become dialectical unities in the ideological production of the agonal subject.

The production of the modern consumer subject, as has been briefly indicated above, is based on a dialectic of desire and lack, where lack – the subjective recognition that one requires the satisfaction of certain basics in the realm of necessity – is believed to be alleviated by the abundance potential of the accessible free-market and its cornucopia of goods. This is basic liberal utilitarianism as it has been made to correspond with the capitalist free market. Similarly political subjectivity is formulated on the basis of the maximization of benefits to the self. This introduces a paradoxical situation because the individual is permitted such liberal freedoms only to the extent that he/she belongs to, and is integrated within, the larger social order. The subjectivity of self-interest is thus appeased through a type of conformity to the dominant social order, presented as the marketplace of freedom.

While the political subject is dominated through being "subjected" to power and thus is *constituted in subjection* (in terms of subordination or being *subject* to order and/or rule), the consumer is dominated through the process of *objectification*. Both are forms of individual reification, however. As will be indicated in the brief discussion below, and paradoxically so, while the respective ideologies that pertain to the idea of the autonomy and sovereignty of the individual, both conceptions of subjective freedom involve deeper forms of social regulation through integration into an order of conformity. The doctrine of individualism glorifies "sovereignty" but works to produce isolated individuals whose very condition of isolation and social atomization work to increase the desire for social integration. This results in an integration that involves the reification of belonging and actually works to intensify forms of conformity that work against social cohesion. The prime example that comes to mind in the context of agon culture is that of the mass audience, especially the spectator/consumer audience at sporting events – of which more will be said in forthcoming chapters.

Citizens who have been successfully ideologized – whose thinking does not depart from that which has been "drilled into them" (as Adorno remarks) – get defensive about the questioning of the freedom they are believed to enjoy, and immediately remark on the unfreedom of other places as proof of the authenticity of their own highly esteemed brand of freedom. Such impassioned defences often conceal the anxiety of influence. Adorno and Horkheimer remark that their "anxiety is none other than the fear of social deviation," a fear of "departing from the facts which, in the very act of perception, the dominant conventions… have already molded" into the consciousness of individuals. "Any negative treatment of this realm of facts, or of the dominant forms of thought" (1969: xiv) is wholly discouraged in a stultifying appeal to conformity. The success of reified domination is that it attaches to the subjective efforts which strive at self-preservation. By identifying with the popular ideas and political structures, the mimetic faculty in cultural identity realizes itself as an affirmation of the status quo and becomes a dominant modality of conformist belonging within agon culture.

1) Political Subjectivity: The Citizen

Through the production of a patriotic consciousness, the hegemonic political order secures popular consent through the offer of liberty, statehood, national affiliation, and the personal pursuit of freedom. This is a strategy of mass conformity to a political system which represents the individual's own negation, seizing upon the moment of subjective insecurity in the rallying of consent. Patriotism conflates love of the nation with unquestioning support of the agonal state. This serves in the approval of various state practices that would otherwise be seen as questionable. It is precisely at moments when the state is "flexing its muscle" that patriotic fervour is unleashed in the population at large.

Public allegiance to dominant power is an implicit acknowledgement of the system's enormous power, one which compels individuals to cling ever more firmly to this system, lest they be "on the other side," so to speak, as one of its enemies. Political socialization in agonal societies teaches patriotic subjects to see in terms of "friend" and "enemy," which is the fatal dichotomy of association in the agonal political imaginary (Schmitt 2007). Adorno, remarking on the totalitarian cultural pressure to conform, to publicly align oneself with power, wrote in the context of World War II that "it is a basic feature of domination that everyone who does not identify with it is consigned for mere difference to the concentration camp."[5] One can only wonder at this present point in agonal history as to what extent this suspicious and predatory perception, based on an "us or them" mentality (as was characteristic of McCarthyism, and is repeated today with increasingly threatening biblical overtones[6] by politicians who, in their war-lust cry, "either you are with us or you are against us") will take hold in the population at large; and how the cultural notions of social belonging and multiple identities, which are celebrated as the emerging cosmopolitan virtues of the new globalization, will be tested under such conditions which intensify the forms of racist mass suspicion and cultural paranoia that an "us versus them" mentality necessarily creates.[7] The feelings of subjective fear and insecurity that are produced in a disciplinary society (Foucault 1979; O'Neill 1995) only serve to align the insecure subject more with the side of repressive power, and to favour the security measures, however draconian, that are believed to create a necessary barrier of defence, protection and self-preservation within a generalize climate of agonism.

The hegemonic project under agon culture speaks of an intensification of this form of disciplinary power where the formation of the agonal subject, the subject that is enamoured of power, becomes totally loyal to the order of the state. This identification with state power occurs to such an extent that the subject reproduces the rationality of the state in individual form: as a monadic representation of the state. In this regard Adorno writes: "the individual owes his crystallization to the forms of political economy" (Adorno 1974: 148). The classical conception of the self as the sovereign individual is thus analogous to the notion of the empire of the self. The political liberation of the individual as such, through the proviso of constitutionally guaranteed rights, is a re-orientation of the arena of freedom under the dominating umbrella of the state, which remains the dialectical master of the "sovereign" citizen. The "freedoms" said to be granted upon becoming a citizen of the state result from a fiduciary belonging to the power of empire and are meant as an "enlightened" replacement of the *sensus communis* which once existed in small-scale societies outside of the rule of a centralized authority. This is particularly so when we consider that in agonal modernity we have the formation of "nation-states." "State" originally had little to do with "nation." Nation refers to a historically developed indigenous way of life and culture into which people are born. The state appropriates all of this in an attempt to further its program of totalization as an economic nation-state.

In such a context social belonging remains, however, a discursive relationship between the individual and the state and creates a fundamental reconfiguration of the "social bond" (O'Neill 1995). The "civic" invention of the individual as a unit of sovereignty corresponds to the rationality of state rule through the construction of a dependency of the individual on the state, which thus grants these much touted rights, freedoms and utilitarian potentials. The individual under the state remains a jurisprudential construction. "An individual is, when defined fully, a legal personality. It is on these grounds that children, women and lunatics at various times have not been regarded as autonomous, separate persons" (Abercrombie, Hill and Turner 1986: 34) under the law. Today recognition under the law has extended into the problem of a growing international migration and the need for displaced persons to be granted official status as citizens under the state, lest people be permanently displaced and disparaged as "aliens" who are denied the freedom of national belonging. Sovereignty of selfhood used to be touted as a Right, today it is exalted as a privilege.

The self as a "sovereign individual" is thus a unitary analogue of the state and so reproduces the rationality of the state as a form of civil consciousness. Recognition of this conflation between citizen and state is realized in the formation of the patriotic subject and the empire of the self. Domination thus extends itself into the consciousness of individuals by deceiving them to engage in a positive defence of the very system through which they are debased, the monumentality of which the patriotic subject proudly declares to be a measure of one's own liberty. Power operates by mimetic effect, by mimicking the exalted authority of the state, in the social reproduction of domination. Domination becomes linked to self-preservation: Siding with power is seen as a form of security. This affirmation of self in relation to the larger system is a manifestation of the adherence to "positive thinking" as a dimension of psychic colonization, the result of strategies of conformity to a system which represents the subject's own negation. This is a determination which victimizes people doubly. In their misrecognition of the tyrannical interplay between the universal (state order) and the particular (the individual), subjects are made servile in defending the order that debases them and contributes to the misery of countless others. Ideologized subjects both identify with and reflect the domination of the universal order of control – in that sense there is an extent to which people are keenly aware of the power of the state and its capacity for domination.

Today belonging to the nation-state is seen as an extension of individual empowerment by virtue of having a share in the power of domination. Liberty, in this patriotic conception of the individual, involves the right to participate in the political sphere, which is the order of power that the state erects, defends and shares with its citizens. Patriotism, as the mode of loyalty to the political system to which people belong, by national affiliation and "personal honour," is a measure of the docility that has been successfully produced by the political project of subject formation. It is the mark of a successful indoctrination into the order that reproduces itself precisely through the medium of human consciousness, its cultural susceptibility and inherent frailty.

If there is an inherent frailty in human consciousness, one that leads to an unwitting consent to domination, and which crystallizes in the process of reification, then this frailty is seized upon by the forces of the consumer marketplace and becomes a further occasion for the psychic domination of the individual.

2) Cultural Subjectivity: The Consumer

Both "possessive individualism" and the "subjectivity of self-interest" figure prominently in the cultural formation of the consumer subject. Consumer subjectivity develops on the basis of the commodification of the self, and on the fetishism of commodities. Commodification of the self through the attachment to objects reproduces the subject/object dilemma indicated in the master/slave dialectic of domination. This is not the sort of reconciliatory dialectic offered by Hegel, where the distinction between master and servant reconciles into a disappearance of power imbalances, but is precisely an example of the critique of Hegel's dialectic offered by Marx. Marx looked upon the master/slave dialectic as the *dialectic of domination*, where the positions of mastery and slavery remained intact: The slave wishes to be like the master and the master's position depends on the subjugation of the slave. It is not a relationship that leads in the end to reconciliation. In Marx's reading of Hegel, it is the very system of social relations under capitalism that created master and slave relations, and thus it is the system itself which must be abolished.

As Marcuse states, a sort of false reconciliation takes place between individuals and their possessions, one that extends the problem of social control into the very intimacies of their experience of the life-world:

> The people recognize themselves in their commodities; they find their soul in their automobile, hi-fi set, split-level home, kitchen equipment. The very mechanism which ties the individual to society has changed, and social control is anchored in the new needs which it has produced. (Marcuse 1964: 9)

People learn to take pleasure in what the culture industry offers them. Desire and affirmation get channelled into object consumption – the world of objects becomes the new repository of personal meaning. Baudrillard's analysis in *The System of Objects* (1996) examines how meaning gets formulated in and through commodities and the sign systems which promote them. He explores "the proposition that the new world of consumer goods represents a new form of language in which brand names, in particular, are said to stand in place of and signify quite complex social meanings" (Lee 2000: xxi). Baudrillard's early work belongs to a school of thought interested in the critique of the commodification of culture, informed by the work of Guy Debord and Roland Barthes. This school of thought identifies the production of meaning, the new "empire of signs" (Barthes) and the new mass consumption of images as part of the spectacle that consumer culture has become. It is a production of meaning that grows alongside numerous forms of social disenchantment, alienation and the loss of meaning.

Joyce Nelson refers to the "loss of meaning" that has come to characterize modernity and the problem of alienation (1987: 24). She writes:

> In past ages, given collectives of people had their own unique face-to-face rituals by which each member felt [meaningfully] contained and valued within the social matrix. Fully participatory and communal rituals – like story telling, song, dance, religious festivities, apprenticeship in a craft, rites of passage to mark the stages in life – all provided the shared "ritual container" for the immense conscious and unconscious energies of a people. The traditional rituals channeled these energies along pathways that all met at a shared center of meaning purpose, and harmony. Individuals felt themselves to be contained, body and spirit, within the larger matrix: encompassed in meaning, and contributing to that meaningful whole through the living out of their individual lives. (Nelson 1987: 24)

The "thesis of the loss of meaning" (Habermas 1984: 346) in modernity constitutes a substantial concern for critical sociology and takes as its major concern the alienation of the modern life-world. In terms of the historic human break with nature represented in the Enlightenment era, the natural cycles of life ("the body's rhythmic ties to nature and the cosmos" [O'Neill 1991: 32]), were replaced with the modern industrial momentum of atomized, rationalized, time-work-discipline life (Thompson 1967), popularly known as "the grind." Modern alienation, in terms of how Weber characterized it as the "disenchantment" of life, speaks of the paradox that lies at the basis of modern social order: At a time when humans have been able to substantially construct a new way of life based on rational efficiency and the unparalleled potential for new freedoms unlike any other time in history, the individual finds her or himself increasingly out of place and disconnected within this new world.[8] This existential feeling of being "out of place" and disoriented in a world that was supposedly re-organized to maximize the service of human interests, but fails to do so at some fundamental level, is the basis of "the thesis of the loss of meaning" in modernity.[9]

The problem of meaning in modernity is therefore significantly related to the rise of forms of consumer cultural meaning that arose in replacement of traditional ways (Ewen 1976). The transfiguration of meaning in terms of the rise of the consumerist commodification of culture has become the most pronounced part of this modern disenchantment process, and is directly related to the malformation of the psyche in the formation of the reified consumer subject.

The loss of traditional systems of meaning has become the occasion for the re-invention of a new meaning system, one furnished by the synthetic culture of the culture industry, where the subjective desire for meaning and the need for recognition become sublimated into the falsely affirmative pleasures of consumer culture and the commodity dream. Advertising, the discourse of consumerism, John Berger notes, "proposes to each of us that we transform ourselves, or our lives, by buying something more... Publicity [advertising] persuades us of such a transformation by showing us people who have been apparently transformed and are, as a result, enviable" (1972: 131). Further, "the publicity image steals the love of oneself as one is, and offers it back for the price of the product" (1972: 134). Therefore,

> the purpose of publicity is to make the spectator marginally dissatisfied with his present way of life. Not with the way of life of society, but with his own within it. It suggests that if he buys what it is offering, his life will become better. It offers him an improved alternative to what he is. (Berger 1972: 142)

Berger's formulation contains two important insights. The first is that the consumer subject is a "spectator buyer," one to whom the world is revealed primarily as an image-text. The world of consumerism is a collection of representations about the real world, another possibly attainable world. Hence the world of consumerism is a collection of representations that *simulate* a kind of reality, one presented to subjective perception on the basis of *sight* and *spectacle*. Baudrillard (1983) has argued that the modern world of consumerism is so deeply immersed in the order of fabricated images that it has entered the phase of hyperreality, one based on a logic of *simulation* where the order of photo-image representation has actually supplanted and become the real. This has the ontological effect of eliminating any authoritative reference for the authenticity of cultural perception. Consequently, the simulation of culture opens up numerous possibilities for cultural deception. When we have simulation passing for reality, then we have another problem in people's ability to perceive and understand what is actually going on in the world around them. This distortion through simulation represents a more fundamental level within the general problem of perception in the mass-mediated culture of the consumer subject. Although the "specular" (O'Neill 1991) world of media culture works to regulate perception through the presentation of images and their ideologies as the real, reality actually exists outside of the media-simulated world of the photo-reproduced flow of images (Williams 1974). The conflation of the two realities prevents critical perception of the distinction between them; this forms much of the basis of mass communicative power over the construction of culture.

Berger's second important insight concerns the consumer culture's appeal to the "real you" – advertising addresses the spectator buyer as a sovereign individual in search of fulfillment. The deep motivation in this production of consumer desire concerns the feelings of dissatisfaction and subjective lack that generate the motivation for personal improvement. This is the system of manufactured needs upon which consumerism feeds (Galbraith 1998; Marcuse 1964). A subject constructed on the basis of lack and insecurity will more readily fit into what is prescribed by the order of consumerism and its promise of fulfillment. Consumerism thrives off of the production of insecurity because this becomes the basis for self-improvement and self-affirmation. The insecurity of the subject in this sense has been economically, culturally and hence ideologically produced. This does not mean that the insecurity is not real. Insecurity is subjectively felt and it is based on subjective feelings of powerlessness and the fear that the recognition of powerlessness produces.

Berger speaks of this phenomenon in terms of the social production of envy, where the individual conceives of success as a condition realized when he or she becomes the object of admiration, recognition and envy by others. Success is therefore dependent on social recognition and becomes equated with self esteem. This is a form of possessive individualism that is a fundamental part of the reifying apparatus of consumer culture; the self-identification with objects in turn objectifies the consumer. Debord writes that "the domination of the economy over social life brought into the definition of human realization the obvious degradation of *being* into *having*" (1995: 17).

As consumer culture colonizes desire, human cultural creativity gets instrumentalized into various forms of consumer behaviour. The passion people have for life is stolen away from them through the re-construction of the means of its expression. Human creative, affirmative energy becomes entangled in the culture of trivia and nonsense, in the waste of labour, in the pursuit of empty fun, and by taking pleasure in "killing time;" as Marcuse says in an interview with Magee, people exhaust their lives "in full time alienated performances" (Magee 1978: 47). The "loss of meaning" is dialectically related to the loss of self, where the restoration of the self is sought in a dream-world of commodities, a consumer world which conflates wants with needs in the artificialization of the realm of necessity. The lost self searches for meaning and affirmation in the superficial world of consumption. As Adorno and Horkheimer write, "Artifice is the means by which the adventuring self loses itself in order to preserve itself" (1969: 48).

The artificial self is the reified self, where the colonization of ambition results in the perpetuation of self-defeating behaviour. Reification gets realized as a form of agonistic domination in the very manner by which it propels the subjective will to self-destruction. As agonism is based on competition, agonistic self defeat gets realized in the competition with oneself as a form of inimical selfhood, as self-hatred. Competition with oneself develops when one begins to see him or herself as inadequate, as in need of improvement, and begins to see oneself as an impediment to one's own happiness, as one's own enemy.

Self as Enemy

To see your own self as an enemy is actually an extreme form of self-negation. It is the working towards the destruction of self. The culturally induced desire to be a "winner" in the battle against the enemy-self is precisely the form of reified personal motivation that contributes to the self-incurred spiral of agonistic self-defeat. De-reified cultural awareness would realize that it is the very notion of aspiring towards being a winner, a victor, that should be discarded, in so far as victory is achieved at the price of vanquish and victory is therefore entangled with domination. Inserting oneself in the context of victory and defeat sets the stage for the likelihood of defeat. The agonistic ideal of the pursuit of victory is not so easily rejected, however, because it is so fundamental in the maintenance of the order of consumerism. As such, agonistic values form a substantial part of the dominant cultural meanings into which the subject of consumerism has been socialized. The socialization into agonism is a fundamental part of the project of consumerism and its transformation of the individual into a subject of compliance to the social regulation of desire.

Let us look more carefully at the psychic configuration of agonistic self-defeat in the reified consumer subject: The competition with oneself has a cultural motivation behind it. This motivation stems from the internalization of consumer cultural values. The system of values in a culture constitutes the conceptual realm through which people are able to invent meaning for themselves. Values in this regard represent a fundamental level of meaning that pertains to the realm of the *life-world* – which relates to how perception translates into reality.

Consumer values emerge from the idea that self worth is based on the capacity to consume and thus acquire commodities and the consequent formation of a lifestyle on the basis of what money can buy: the clothes one wears, their travel dreams, the car one drives, houses, possessive desires in general – even the idea of a prosperous future is dreamed of on the basis of the enjoyment of what money buys. The reified consumer subject has difficulty conceiving of selfhood outside of the commodity form.

Consumerism accurately identifies and enlists "the loss of meaning" and the "loss of self" that are characteristic of modern alienated urban subjectivity, and it offers a remedy to this in terms of what is offered in the world of consumption. Success in life thus comes to be defined as the ability to overcome subjective lack and non-fulfilment through consumption. Consumerism proposes, therefore, that if one consumes in the manner prescribed by lifestyle advertising for example, that he or she may attain happy success. Success in this context becomes agonistic when it is defined as a competitive pursuit in relation to others. There is a popular phrase for it – "keeping up with the Jones's," or as Veblen (1953) puts it, "conspicuous consumption."[10]

Without these advertised forms of socially produced insecurity (Williamson 1978; Leiss, Kline and Jhally 1990), and the corresponding commercial *structures of inadequacy* that promote subjective lack and feelings of inadequacy, commodity consumption will not be as frenetically engaged in. When the population's capacity to inquire into their own life-situation, as a measure towards its amelioration, has been tampered with through the colonization of desire, it is not surprising that large numbers of people resort to a lifestyle based on consumption, where it is believed the more one has, the happier one will be. Self-esteem and self-worth become based on the power one commands through money and what it can buy.

Insofar as consumerism defines success as something based on the capacity to consume and to partake of the cornucopia of "goods" in the capitalist marketplace, those who are unable to do so are castigated as "unsuccessful," as "losers" in the "game of life." Happiness and success in life becomes a game, a contest, in the competitive order of consumerism. Consumerism therefore reformulates self-affirmation on the basis of the capacity to successfully consume. The production of the consumer subject is therefore fundamentally about the commodification of happiness.

The agonistic formation of the consumer subject is a classic form of reification in so far as it is a form of self-incurred psychic defeat, where negative self-perception is antagonistic to self-esteem. The antagonistic relation to self, which culminates in various forms of personal debilitation, is fundamentally related to the problem of the insecurity of the subject. In such a context, where the subject is convinced of their own inadequacy, such subjects are *divided against themselves.* It is important to note that this is a form of socially and culturally produced insecurity. It does not stem from biological or psychopathological causes, however, it is certainly manifested in the psychological structure of the insecure ego.

The distorting lens of the insecure ego reduces everything in its purview to the narrow parameters of its own threatened realm. Insecurity and self-delusion compliment each other. *This malformation of the psychic structure of the insecure ego is substantially related to the formation of egoistic success and failure under agonistic consumerism.* The perceived threat to self that is inherent in the insecurity of agonistic subjectivity is believed to be alleviated if one consumes in a prescribed manner, and competitively in relation to the level by which others consume. Insecurity is therefore based on the fear of being a "loser" in the competitive game of life as a struggle of accumulation. The reified consumer subject has been successfully persuaded to buy into a particular lifestyle characterized by commodification where the act of consumption and possession is believed to alleviate feelings of insecurity and unhappiness. What ensues at the level of cultural and personal awareness is an inability to understand the implications of what one is participating in.

The life-distorting capacity of the insecure ego is a theme written about by R.D. Laing (1969), who develops a theory of "ontological insecurity" to explain the condition of psychic disfiguration and its relation to self-destruction. Laing uses the concept of "ontology" to theorize on a mal-formation of "being," which gives rise to a "divided self," a self which is inimical to its own well-being. He writes about the pathology of split-being as a "divided self" where the anxiety stricken subject lives under the conditions of "ontological insecurity" (1969: 39). Laing's analysis of the disfiguration of consciousness that gets produced out of the maintenance of a "false self" (1969: 94) is analysed in terms of the schizophrenic construction of self. A divided self is a self whose efforts at self-realization have been thwarted due to its enculturation under the conditions of what Laing has termed a type of schizophrenic culture. Laing's thesis in *The Divided Self* (1969) is that schizophrenia, as an extreme example of the division of self, is not necessarily a form of psychosis in terms of being out-of-touch with reality, but in fact is just the opposite; it is a form of hyper-awareness and hyper-sensitivity to the inherently schizophrenic, destabilizing and contradictory nature of a debilitating external social reality – one that gets subjectively internalized to the level of psychic disfiguration. Distorted recognition of the interplay between life, death and psychic survival thus plays a large part in Laing's conception of the "divided self" and provides a hermeneutic of psychic insecurity through which we can understand the fear and suffering that arises through the domination of the reified subject.

To reiterate: Consumer subjectivity is fundamentally agonistic because it is produced through the colonization of the "dialectic of desire and recognition" (O'Neill 1996) inherent in insecure subjectivity. The consumer subject who has been successfully convinced that she or he is a body in need of repair and improvement, a body of lack and not a complete person, begins to see him or herself as his or her own enemy.[11] The struggle against the self results in the development of a particular kind of a reified person and it augments particular kinds of social formations that reinforce agonistic selfhood where competing with oneself occurs. The lack and insecurity which have become the occasion for consumer spending begins a cycle of self-denigration that is informed by agonistic values – namely competition and defeat. Competition as a supreme value leads, in the culture of reification, to competition with oneself. The reified/agonized subject contains within its psychic structure the means of its own negation. Thus the insecure subject begins to, in effect, compete with itself, and this forms the basis for an unconscious self-hatred. When we compete with ourselves, "do battle" with ourselves and see our own self as enemy, as an impediment to our own happiness, then a spiral of self-destruction ensues at a very personal level of being. This is a socially produced process of psychic disfiguration directly related to the sort of divided-self type of psychosis Laing describes. A self that is divided cannot work towards its own self-authentication, but in fact is a self pre-disposed towards its own destruction. When this strategy of self-hood becomes the norm then we have the basis for a highly alienated society, a society of divided selves. Insecurity gives rise to competitive anxiety because competition naturally breeds mutual suspicion among combatants. Competitors in the "pursuit of happiness" are seen to pose a threat to one another. If one cannot keep up with the frenzy of consumption he or she is made to feel unsuccessful – in the terminology of agonistic defeat: She or he is seen as a loser, the ultimate failure and loss of status. "Losership" or reified self-hatred is the end result of the personal "battle" with insecurity; endless consumption keeps the battle going.

　　　　This scenario of the insecure consumer subject as ago-nized subject furnishes the motivational apparatus that stimulates the ambition of the consumer subject – the "shop till you drop" mentality that has resulted not only in the cultural mal-develop-ment of individuals under consumer culture, but also which results in the staggering depletion of natural resources that are necessary to support this high level of consumption.

Chapter 9

Popular Agonism, the Mediagon and Competitive Sport

In the opening scene of the film *Little Miss Sunshine* (2006) Richard Hoover, a down and out father struggling to set up his own self-motivation business, speaks to a room of youngsters. In the background his PowerPoint presentation displays slides that mimic Darwin's "evolution of man" chart, except that they show a lumpy, hunched over, sad-sack "Loser" evolve into a smiling, triumphant, arms over his head, "Winner." Richard exclaims:

> There's two kinds of people in this world – Winners and Losers. Winners and Losers. What's the difference? Winners see their dreams come true. Winners see what they want, they go out and they get it. They don't hesitate. They don't make excuses. And they don't give up. Losers don't get what they want. They hesitate. They make excuses. And they give up. On themselves and their dreams. Inside each of you – at the very core of your being – is a Winner waiting to be awakened... and unleashed upon the world. With my nine step "Unleash the Winner Inside" program, you now have the tools, the know-how, the insights you need to put your losing habits behind you and make your dreams come true. No hesitating! No excuses! I want you to go out into the world... and be Winners! (Arndt 2006)

A gon culture is the culture of competition and militarism. As such it is not surprising that the social values associated with competition and war are consistently to be found in the fabric of everyday language and other popular forms of human expression such as movies, promotional literature and leisure activities. As indicated earlier in this book, a society that maintains an interest in war will reflect this interest throughout its cultural realm creating a condition where competition and war are normalized aspects of human social life. In agon culture the value of competition and war have become the dominant texts of meaning. Although this has been part of the fabric of Western culture for a long time, it has become a more prominent phenomenon in the post-9/11 era and has been noted by many critics including Boggs (2005) and Giroux (2005), who identify an intensification in the "culture of militarism" and new forms of authoritarianism and imperial thinking as popular cultural themes. Their analyses are correct in identifying intensifications of power in the post-9/11 era, however, they fall short in ignoring the larger ideological structures which have been in place for a long time and which have created a welcome context for a hyper-military society. This cultural context goes beyond increasing patriotism in the news media and movies and attaches to the more seemingly benign forms of the cultural celebration of conquest, championship and victory as based on the defeat of the other. Thus, many critics fail to recognize the role of competitive sport in the culture of militarism. Another point worth mentioning is the tendency of many critics of power in the post-9/11 era to speak of a mounting authoritarianism as if it was something new. The Frankfurt School's critique of power, including Herbert Marcuse's, always maintained that the sort of political power established after the "events of World War II" was not a form of politics that transcended fascism and other elements of totalitarian tyranny. Instead the new reconfiguration of the global hegemon post-World War II was based precisely on authoritarian forms of social and political control. In the midst of the much celebrated "democracy" there are always spasms of totalitarian power. These are witnessed in many forms, including: the criminalization of dissent, corporate autocracy versus public well being, neoliberal imperialism, and the increasing homogenization of popular culture as a commercial entity that fosters conformity to the orders of competition and mass consumption. "Culture," that area of social life that Adorno focused on so well as the text of meaning where mentality and consciousness gets shaped, was recognized as the principle medium through which power is exercised.

In capitalist modernity part of the reformulation of culture entails, as Theodor Adorno and Max Horkheimer observed, a "melting down of all values in a giant crucible" (1969: xv), where political and economic values support the affirmative tradition of culture so that the cultural integration of the individual becomes a form of subjective conformity to a totalizing social order. The critical insight and questioning that traditionally formed part of culture proper, and the "sense of belonging" which produces cultural identity as well as inclusivity, has become transformed into what Adorno and Horkheimer called "absolute integration" into the dominant order (1969). These developments have contributed to the new poverty of culture ever since it has become subordinated to the demands of political economy and the new imperium of power that is part of the *agonal* order of the world today.

Agonal Discourse and Popular Ideology

The new "front" of agon culture and its perpetual war system is the frontier of culture. This includes the battle over public opinion and the regulation of desire, and thus agon culture aims at having victory over individual consciousness and getting individuals to conform to the ideals of competition and victory as the modes of transcendence. The discursive construction of popular agonism is the primary manner by which it sets out to exact such a form of cultural domination. Agonism is popularized in a number of ways. We shall briefly examine two of them through:

1) the regime of discourse and the colonization of language;
2) the regulation of desire by the entertainment spectacle of the mediagon.

The construction of discourse is part of the destruction of understanding and the incapacitation of critical awareness. This is a standard mechanism of discursive domination within agon cul-

ture. It is based on the de-valuation of certain words, the reformulation of their meaning and the constriction of the universe of
possibilities to the restrictive binarism of agonal discourse which
reduces the mode of perception to positive and negative, black
and white, winner and loser, good guy and bad guy, hero and
rogue, and so on.

Discourse is a highly structured narrative that articulates
its point of view mostly on the basis of assumed premises and
shared ideological assumptions. Its aim is to persuade, to convince, to have victory over the subject – such is its *discursivity*.
Discourse carries ideology but is not synonymous with it. Ideology is a form of public knowledge that seeks to make socially
constructed relations of power seem natural and inevitable. Ideologies span longer periods of history, while discourse is often
the specific utterance of a more long-standing ideology in a specific place and time, or which reflects the understanding of a
given event. Discourse fulfils its discursive aim in various ways,
from rhetoric to the institutional regulation of the realm of pleasure and desire. For Foucault discourse is essentially bound with
power, especially the institutional power that seeks the legitimacy
of its practices over subjects and across history. The success of
discourse thus depends on institutional authority. Agonal discourse aims to persuade the subject of the natural correctness and
practical utility of competition and violence as positive, natural
forms of power. It does this by labelling things in a binary way
as either positive or negative depending on how they pertain to
the dominant order of power in society; for example, the
dichotomies of good and evil, or friend and enemy, fall into an
agonal way of looking at things. Agonal discourse labels that
which is supportive of the dominant order as positive. That which
goes against the status quo of dominance is castigated as negative. Political leaders, forces of the repressive state apparatus,
successful business tycoons and champion athletes are celebrated
as warriors for good in agon culture, while those who question
the agonal corporate order and are openly against war are reviled
as "peaceniks," radicals, anarchists or trouble-makers.

It is a contradictory (falsely dialectic) agonal logic which
claims that to halt destruction you must be more destructive – to
be one-up on the other yet to do so without transcending the
established terms of might, without questioning the "rules of the

contest." This is the perverse transcendentalism inherent in the philosophy of the agon where the exaltation of violence as an instrument of transformation serves as the productive model of progressive action. Agonism informs cultural values as the one behind the notion that competition is valiant and good as well as the one behind the "tit for tat" or "an eye for an eye" logic, which reduces justice to retaliation, and victory is seen in terms of conquest and defeat of the other. The list of ideological truisms which are supportive of the agonal way of thinking, this way of valorizing violence, are infused into the popular consciousness and contemporary capitalist discourse ad nauseam: "might is right," "survival of the fittest," social strife as "the cost of progress," "for every negative there is a positive," and other forms of agonistic talk. These are the linguistic manifestations of a popular philosophy of aggression that has become all too quickly absorbed into the public discourse of self-preservation. Such sayings are the slogans of agonistic perception, pre-packaged forms of conformist thinking which are the mark of the agonal subject with its characteristic resignation to power, what Adorno called the language of reified consciousness: "Resignation and delusion are ideological compliments," "we want what we have been drilled to resign ourselves to" (1973: 52).

Agonistic value circulates as a cultural norm primarily as a justification of the socially produced reality of everyday conflict: its productivity, its fatefulness, as a painful necessity. Enduring the pain of conflict has become the ethic of agonism. How closely this ideology parallels the belief that out of personal tragedy comes wisdom: The philosophical tid bit that "no one can traverse the pathway to knowledge and return unscathed" (which is a recasting of an idea from Sallust into an agonistic credo), parallels the popular truism which reduces this simply to "what doesn't kill you makes you stronger." Such an adage, which is tied generally to athletic training and to the "pursuit of excellence" within the universal competition of the agonal order, is meant to promote a questionable value, one which claims that pain is necessary to succeed in life, as in the saying, "no pain no gain." This belief legitimates the political and economic order that produces pain as a daily norm. It proposes that one must endure pain in order to gain. While what is to be gained is largely left unclear; what one is taught to endure on the other hand is the normalized trauma of pain, violence and injustice that the agonal order of domination regularly exacts on its subjects. Adorno remarks that the prioritization of pain in sports training, the training of the body to endure pain, toil and physical exhaustion, is a sublimation of that which is required for the dutiful and productive worker under competitive capitalism: "It is in sport that people first inflict upon themselves (and celebrate as a triumph of their own freedom) precisely what society inflicts upon them and what they must learn to enjoy" (1991: 168).

Because power affects the content of language and language reproduces relations of ideological power, meaning gets distorted and remade anew in the interest of perpetuating power. It is a normal and desirable part of culture that words are generated to adapt to the changing reality and discursive shifts within agon culture. In consumer-democracy the language of the free market propels itself primarily through a discourse of agonistic reason. The agonistic reason of predatory capitalism penetrates both academic discourse and the realm of interpersonal relations. Agonistic discourse invents and propels the ideology of competition in a way that the idea of competitive struggle becomes axiomatic. The rise of agonistic discourse and the subservience of all other ideas to it mark the contemporary poverty of language as an instrument of a monopolistic order of cultural meaning. That everything today can be related to the grand referentialism of sublime conflict is a mark of the autocracy of conflict and the level of violence in language.

The success of repressive power depends on the ability to disguise the flawed reasoning which supports the false freedom of agonistic discourse. Yet this mode of unfreedom at the level of the construction of consciousness conceals and reveals its operation at the level of language. In the doxological duplication of consumer language through media discourses, popular trivia, and the litany of truisms and clichés which have re-signified language into a subservient mimicry, cultural intelligence is measured by how well one can parrot the dominant view on things. The talk of freedom within consumer-democracy,[1] its proliferation as a discourse indicates how subjectivity reveals itself in public discourse. People reveal themselves in language, in the content of their talk, which is the verbal manifestation of their subjective world-view. This matrix of language and perception is precisely the ground through which the values of agonism are reinforced as a component of selfhood.

In a culture of repressive conformity, social communication is so thoroughly debased that what passes for conversation becomes the exchange of "trade-marks that trigger off conditioned reflexes" (Adorno and Horkheimer 1969: 166) so that consensus is maintained and new thought is socially discouraged, "in the stultifying appeal to conformity." Those ideas which conform to "the way things are" get more widely circulated and thus made more publicly valid. Ideas which do not conform to the status quo are uttered at great social risk. As Adorno writes:

> Today anyone who is incapable of talking in the prescribed fashion, that is of effortlessly reproducing the formulas, conventions and judgments of mass culture as if they were his own, is threatened in his very existence, suspected of being an idiot or an intellectual. (Adorno 1991: 79)

This conformity to formulaic language Adorno speaks of is the totalizing dimension of the reification of public discourse as domination, its social perpetuation into a mode of dominant perception which mimics a second nature. Language and perception are dialectical unities in the manifestation of reification. An oft-repeated utterance serves as self-evidence of its consensual truth and ethical validity. "Whatever lacks the familiar trace of such pre-formation lacks credibility" (Adorno 1974: 108). As such, the most meagre and base articulation of opinion is greeted with a wide acceptance in so far as it accords with the dominant view of things, while critical thought is frowned upon. And thus the "dislike of thinking rapidly becomes incapacity for it" (Adorno 1974: 124).[2]

Similarly the agonal discourse of business and politics, which is the jargon of "success" within agon culture, emits the world view of the "sovereign-self" revealed in language. When people acting in accordance with the capitalistic principles of despotic self-interest behave towards others in a manner for which no apology can justify, and say "this is not personal, its just business," it is precisely the realm of the personal which is destroyed and reformulated into the arena of justifiable and thus socially normalized interpersonal domination where antagonistic self interest is explained away as part of the universal order of things. Similarly, Adorno writes, "the eye for possible advantages is the mortal enemy of all human relationships" (1974: 33). The liberal principle of competitive self interest is precisely that element within agon culture where the values of competition thrive on people seeking competitive/predatorial advantage over each other. In a thoroughly economized culture of constructed inequalities, the clichéd values of competitive business practices operate as the foundational values of the culture at large. The values reproduced in the rituals of sport, commerce and militarism translate into the anti-wisdom of "might is right" to infuse the inter-subjective spaces of social relations with an everyday conflict that is not denied, but rather is acknowledged and popularly affirmed through repetition in language and celebration in ritual.

The agonistic view, which sees the other in terms of a self-serving utility and as a potential threat, is part of the larger criminogenic order of agonistic capitalism that produces a culture where mutual mistrust prevails and a "culture of suspicion" (Visano 1998) is created. In the culture of privatism, which contributes to the culture of suspicion, control of the other is fetishized as a necessary pre-condition for the preservation of self: The instrumental objectification of the other into a calculable and controllable thing/object is also the negation of the other (which is rendered enemy). This self-other relation serves as the basis for self-affirmation in the recasting of the social bond on the basis of strategic advantage. These statements are not to be taken as ontological absolutes – they are purely the social realizations emergent from the ideology of agonistic inter-subjectivity. They describe a reality which arises out of the discursive strategies of a generalized political and social insecurity. Thus both the insecurity of the political state and of the individual ego lapse into a defensive posturing in the attempt at self-preservation.

Thus agonal rationality realizes itself not only in the actions of nation-states, but in the system of social values which are constructed to accord with the power interests of the nation-state. The "fact" of conflict and violence has been naturalized into the workings of the social to such an extent that it has been *normalized*. Always the last resort of insecure reason, the turn to aggression, to the values of the agon, serves to justify the unwillingness to think otherwise, to imagine a politics, a global politics, a local

politics, a politics of co-operation outside of the resolute measures of applied conflict: a politics of peace. Through the cultural
re-formulation of thinking that exalts agonism as virtuous, the
monstrous aggression which is fundamental to legitimating the
actions of the imperial consortium of nation-states, violence has
become an approved value of the population at large.

Military Metaphor

Violence infects language through the inclusion of military
metaphor as a normal part of the vernacular. Metaphor is a particularly powerful linguistic device which uses the ancient form
of the communication of meaning generated out of resemblance,
verisimilitude, the analogon. In agon culture the grand referent
of meaning is war – its categories, its logic, its principles, its aspirations and directives, its means, its expressions. Agon culture
thrives by using war and combat metaphors for virtually every
conceivable aspect of life. Beyond the obvious discourses of business and sports, military metaphor enters the intimate interstices
of the personal realm. One can hardly watch the latest news
broadcast or engage in casual conversation without hearing military and combat metaphors used – even when such forms are
exaggerations or misrepresentations of what is being described,
people rely on them as if they represent clarity of communication.
Even when speaking of sex and love, military metaphor redefines
the realm of romance as an agonistic pursuit.

Military metaphor descends into everyday language also
from the corporate mass media which disseminates it regularly
in the course of explaining its news stories and providing entertainment. War news itself is chock full of militaristic Newspeak:
"friendly fire," "surgical strike," "collateral damage," "rules of
engagement," and numerous other euphemisms which are all
becoming too familiar in the public mind. Military vocabulary
functions to normalize war and legitimate the fact that society as
a whole, the social totality, is erected upon a military model of
reality. In such a context words themselves and the language in
which they construct have become forms of symbolic violence.
Words are used in opposition to their original intention. As
Adorno and Horkheimer remark in regards to the reformulation

of language to accord with power interests: "All the violence done to words is so vile that one can hardly bare to hear them any longer" (1969: 166). So it is with much of what is offered in the realm of popular culture where the agonistic dimensions of social reality are affirmed at all levels of discourse within the culture industry.

The Mediagon

In chapter one, the culture industry was examined as the primary apparatus through which ideological hegemony is maintained in agon culture. This repressive function makes culture the instrument through which domination is exercised. Hegemony functions in part by creating a subjective allegiance between individuals and state power. It is able to perform this function in the way that issues and themes are mobilized as information that unites common interests. Adorno and Horkheimer write, "automobiles, bombs, and movies keep the whole thing together..." (1969: 121). The power of the culture industry has grown substantially since its inception and has now become a global phenomenon. The significant intensifications it has undergone since the 1940s, the time when Adorno and Horkheimer (1969) first wrote about it, is due to a number of changes including:

- The unheard of increase in the monopolistic power of the mass media as a corporate apparatus – what is known as the media monopoly;
- The increasing amount of time people engage with the offerings of the mass culture industry and with media technologies in general;
- The new forms of media technology and the increase in the compelling visceral power of technological interfacing with the electronic image-text. This results in a greater intensity of subjective/perceptual immersion into the media spectacle; and
- The nature of the dominant ideology embodied in popular media spectacle, which is the ideology of agonism and includes various representations of competition, war, and predation. The culture industry has become the *mediagon*.

The mediagon is the contemporary cultural manifestation of the ancient Roman coliseum where the spectacle of brutal combat unto death was the main attraction and the source of viewer pleasure. Agon culture retains the heritage of gladiatorial spectacle, its violent pleasures and casual brutality, and replaces the ruined coliseum with the virtual electronic architecture of the mediatized coliseum of consciousness. The coliseum now extends into the living rooms of the Nation, into the movie theatres of local neighbourhoods (some of which are even named "coliseum"), and into the very hands of technology users whose "personal communication devices" provide an ever-increasing interface with interactive media and the world wide web.

The mass demand for gladiatorial spectacle is today met through a number of culture industrial products from televisions shows and movies to the promotion and sell-out of hugely popular competitive/destructive public events such as the WWF, Mixed Martial Arts and Robot Wars among the many others. The standard sports fare of baseball, hockey and football now seem almost benign in comparison to the frenzied mania and death ecstasy represented and celebrated in the new *extremification* of competitive spectacle as seen in the many programs that extend the theme of competition and predation as the main ingredient of their events.

The public thirst for gladiatorial entertainment also extends to the "trash TV" talk show format where certain individuals are paid to appear, held up for public ridicule and made the object of audience hatred.[3] Agonal entertainment is based on having something to despise, either hating the one on trial and/or taking pleasure in the viewing of combative destruction. The unruly mob of LeBon's (1925) atavistic crowd has become the model audience at agonal spectacles.

The content of the new coliseum – the mediagon – consists generally of the following six genres:
- the spectacle of competitive sport;
- Good versus Evil crime texts;
- Darwinistic-type predator and survival texts;
- Imperial history conquest texts;
- military texts; and
- necrophilic texts.

These six genres of agonism are among the many forms of the valorization of competition and conflict as a popular norm. As the new popular aesthetics of violence, they function ideologically to fetishize predation and celebrate conflict and violence to promote various fantasies of aggressive control as forms of subjective empowerment. Empowerment is not transcendental or self-actualizing, it is the reified identification with the destructive-coercive power of the agonistic *protagonist.*

Agonistic empowerment and agonistic spectacle form the basis of viewer pleasure in the spectacle of the mediagon. The genres of entertainment embody agonistic reason and combine to form part of the ideological legitimation of the repressive power of the agon at the popular level. The ideology of conflict to which they contribute is part of the naturalization of domination that is fundamental to agon culture and forms a large part of its dominant text of meaning. We shall look at some of these genres more closely by examining the basis by which entertainment pleasure is generated in them.

The fascination with "good versus evil" is a primary cultural mythology developed as a recurrent formula in the mediagon. This archaic mythological binarism is played out daily in the litany of crime shows where justice is constructed in terms of revenge, where "might makes right" in the historic continuation of an agonistic jurisprudentialism that marks the regression of law to the base level of agonistic reason. Contemporary crime and criminal justice narratives in particular constitute a substantial portion of media-culture programming and exploit the agonistic formula ad nauseam. Crime dramas are particularly important because they reproduce the discourses of the juridical state and in particular draw the viewer into siding with the repressive state apparatus, its policing and legal powers as the dominant force of revenge. In such dramas too the production of meaning involves the subjective participation of the active viewer who is structured to identify with the vengeance dimension of the agonistic interplay.

Harold Bloom (1982) argues that all drama is centred on conflict, and that dramatic meaning originates out of the primacy of a violent act from which drama unfolds. He refers to this as the "catastrophic origins of meaning." The agonal economy of drama is played out in the modern televisual drama precisely on the basis of the unfolding of conflict, where the "plot thickens" with each successive dilemma introduced into the story. Each turn in the narrative flows from an instance of antagonism, which in the end culminates in the resolution of the drama through the final judgment in the contest of conflict. This dramatic structure forms the basis of audience tension, anxiety and emotional immersion into the story. The ultimate alleviation of such anxiety constitutes the "pleasure of the text," which also furnishes its "entertainment value." Thus reader/viewer pleasure is tied in to the very agonistic structure of the text and through subjective identification with the victorious protagonist. This is a familiar discursive strategy of popular narratives where subjective pleasure is based on siding with the protagonist, as police officer or as the castigating judge dispensing justice with forked tongue. The agonal resolution of conflict is the reformulation of justice as it conforms to the power-logic of the repressive state. Agonistic viewer pleasure is thus based on the satisfaction of revenge. This is a theme fully exploited by the law and order crime genre of the mediagon.

This revenge discourse of the popular media also includes the daily news broadcasts and the coverage of world affairs where the state's monopoly on the use of violence in terms of capital punishment, the waging of war and the squashing of democratic dissent through both the military and the paramilitary agencies of the repressive state all serve to *legitimate the violent nature of political control which gets culturally articulated as normal.* To a large extent agon culture is criminogenic culture. Not simply because crime is a normalized part of contemporary life in societies which claim nevertheless to operate under the Rule of Law, but because crime is not merely an aberration within the social order, it is the outward expression of its sinister inner workings (Taylor 1999). When the values of competition, aggression and destruction of the other are seen as the legitimate mode of justice and self-preservation and normalized within the culture at large, it becomes difficult to understand criminality as a form of social deviance when what it actually represents is a form of hyper-conformity to the agonistic values of repressive state order, values which are consistent with agonistic ones celebrated in the legally sanctioned modes of capitalist organization. If "objective" reason is measured by the extent to which behaviour is conducted as an expression true to the essential character of the social totality, then subjective criminality, as a reflection of the corrupt and criminogenic order of contemporary capitalism, lives up to it with great fidelity. It thus remains a form of "reasonable" conduct by virtue of the extent to which it pays homage to the agonistic reason of the universal order of corruption and domination that is tacitly recognized in the structure of society ("society as a racket" [Adorno and Horkheimer 1969]).

From the warriors depicted in movies that cover themes of military history, martial arts mastery and science fiction fantasy to the competition programs of the reality television genre – identifying with the warrior-victor is a main source of viewer pleasure. The warrior theme is blatant in so much of what is offered by the culture industry and is becoming a theme in places where it previously did not exist at all. For example, cooking shows and car enthusiast shows have now ramped up their entertainment excitement value by adding the element of competition – so we now have *Car Warriors* and *Iron Chef* and *Hell's Kitchen.*

The subject position "warrior" has been completely invested with positive meaning. Doing battle, increasing empire and gaining superiority over others are all unproblematic values in agon culture. This warrior theme is again a blatant feature in the world of video gaming, where the vast majority of games are based strictly on outright killing – either in the context of urban gangland shooting or military warfare (*Grand Theft Auto* and *Street Fighter* are examples of the former). In the 1990s computer era there was the game *Doom* which allowed the player to choose a variety of high-powered weapons to blast opponents to smithereens on their way through a maze of sorts. With the internet we now have this full kill format intensified into a multiplayer online game in real time where many players compete with each other in a pay-per-use service that earns millions in revenues. The most notorious game in this regard is *World of Warcraft*, a game that has over eleven million subscribers, a significant number of whom have developed serious and debilitating addictions to it and have exhausted great amounts of time and money playing in a virtual agon.

There have been many debates over the sociological and behavioural effects of excessive exposure to symbolic violence in media form. The conservative view claims that such exposure does not create violent behaviour among users or viewers of violence, and even goes so far as to claim that engagement with representations of virtual violence has a cathartic effect that reduces violent acts in real life. The more rigorously researched view is the one put forth by George Gerbner (2002) and his colleagues whose studies indicate that violent forms of media add to the overall culture of violence and can cultivate violent attitudes in persons who spend large amounts of time engaged with violent media representations of reality. There is no doubt that what exists in our culture at large becomes an aspect of the human socialization process. Whether such forms of exposure affect people in the same way is certainly a matter of debate. Gerbner's "cultivation model" is of great relevance in that it indicates the extent to which the social and cultural values depicted in media come to form a part of the culture at large.

Agon culture is the culture of the warrior and the culture of war. These themes are interspersed alongside the related themes of competition, predation and death. Toying with death, producing death, celebrating, lamenting and depicting death are all elements in the cultural process that entwines subjective reification with cultural agonism.

The Pleasure of Fear and the Thrill of the Death Response

As indicated earlier in this book, agon culture shapes subjectivity in various forms of reification. One form of this "agonized self" emerges when people compete with themselves. This is often a prescription for self defeat. It is seen throughout the culture where self growth is often measured in terms of the physical contest such as "personal challenges" where one engages in various rituals of "testing and honing one's survival skills." The ideological theme that is all too apparent in such programs is that "life is a struggle" and that the challenges we face in society are the same as the challenges of nature that humans faced before the civilized era. The cold calculation of natural selection remains the primary principle in the agonistic-Darwinistic drama that has come to define the injustices of social life. This is a form of mystification that conflates natural selection with the economic mechanism of selection that humans have erected in the mimicry of nature – a system that justifies human-made social hierarchy, inequality and scarcity as if these were merely natural conditions we must continue to face.

Survival aspirations have become a new dimension of the leisure and entertainment marketplace within agon culture. The rise in extreme sports and extreme danger activities is on the rise in the past decade. Bungee jumping, sky diving, shark swimming, adventure travel, paint ball warfare, extreme martial arts fighting and so on can all be seen as agonistic rituals that exemplify the agonistic ideal which claims that to survive a gruelling ordeal is somehow a measure of excellence and championship of which one can be proud. In Toronto a new activity of precisely this type is to be found in the EdgeWalk, where people can pay to be daredevils who teeter off the edge of one of the largest freestanding buildings in the Western hemisphere. Although safety is relatively assured through the use of restraint cables, there is always the risk of death in any such activity. Regardless, the nervous system produces the desired response in any case. Whether one participates in such activities directly or watches them on a television program – the point is that toying with death and inviting danger are becoming more common themes in a culture which, on a geopolitical level, is indeed more dangerous and risky.

One of the primary bases through which pleasure and desire is constructed in an agonistic manner is through the mediation of fear as an obstacle one confronts in challenge. Fear is the explicit theme in a number of recent entertainment programs such as *Fear Factor*, where "contestants" are "challenged" to "brave" dangerous activities and engage in dreadful and nauseating behaviours such as swallowing live creatures, or lying in a pit of snakes or rats. In another version of the individual versus nature genre – the "survivor" type of program – contestants have their survival skills tested by trying to find food and shelter in the wild as a team. Members who do not pull their weight are sent away in an elimination process.

The theme of agonistic Darwinistic survival is central to a litany of entertainment programs that have come onto the popular culture scene in the last decade. On such programs, contestants are rewarded on the basis of testing their "resolve" under gruelling conditions in which their survival strengths are proven against the will of other contestants. In the television show named *Survivor* a group of people is selected to remain alone in a deserted place and a contest of survival ensues whereby on a daily basis the group (the social collective) ejects a member from that group until only one member is left in the end. *Survivor* reproduces the problematic atavistic regression of the scenario in Golding's *Lord of the Flies* and adds to it a blend of soap opera, sex, and social science field study in inter-group agonism. Its popularity is matched by its ideological exactness to the mythical order of agon culture where "survival of the fittest" is the cardinal principle. The ideological danger is that *Survivor* confirms the widespread view that some people just cannot get along and that the process of elimination of the other remains the best strategy for social engineering. This mythos contradicts the anthropological truth that human survival is based on co-operation and not on elimination of the other.

Fear is also at the basis of the new "extreme" sports. Extreme sports take relatively conventional sporting activities and add a degree of intensification and danger to them. The aim in such activities is to simulate the conditions of pure physical and psychological danger. Whether the activity is actually life threatening or not is less relevant than the fact that it is supposed to be based on the pure visceral shock of evoking the *death response* as the basis of excitement and pleasure. The bodily death response is achieved upon entering conditions of extreme fright and recovery and is based on nervous system excitement – the familiar "fight or flight" phenomenon. It is an autonomic response of the central nervous system and bypasses conscious thought. It is not unrelated to the death mask of reified subjectivity.

Seeking pleasure in the death-response involves the loss of the mind and the absorption of the self into the agonal body. The agonal body is the competitive sport body, the rigorous body, the self that seeks victory over the body. It is a body tested and tortured under the rigours of military discipline and abuse. Today physical fitness means conquering the body. In the regime of sport, Jean-Marie Brohm (1978) writes: "the body is reduced to the status of a machine or a quantity of energy… It is clear that *the vocabulary of the machine dominates the language of sport.*" Dreaming the body as a machine forms part of the mental strategy of determination that underpins the disciplined confrontation with fear.

Competitive sport should not be confused with physical fitness and good health. Humans have been using their bodies in ways that keep them physically fit for eons before competitive sport was instituted en masse. It may true that playing certain sports can contribute to physical fitness but there are other, perhaps better ways. It is equally true that many competitive sports are quite hazardous to one's health, by way of crippling injury, brain damage, exhaustion of the heart, extensive focus on one single type of movement and more. Those who encourage kids to play competitive sports in order to stay physically fit and healthy are being disingenuous about what they are really promoting.

The fear factor of extreme sports is based on panic reformulated as pleasure. For the reified agonal subject, satisfaction and pleasure requires the feel and taste of death in order to feel alive. Provoking the death-response as a form of entertainment is a type of death-ecstasy. People "get off" on fear, just as Joanna Bourke's (1999) soldiers derive pleasure from killing. Here we have the classic example of reification as defined by Adorno when he remarks that reified culture pays homage to the very thing that presents the threat to life by honouring it and upholding it as a virtue to be respected.

There was once a time when the pleasure provided by challenging leisure activities had something to do with the nature of those activities being related to an engagement with the elements of nature. The practices of cliff diving or mountain climbing, or outdoor hiking for that matter, find their meaning based on the ethic of utility and integral connection to survival in nature such practices can evoke. They can be seen as extensions of the same activities our hunting and gathering ancestors needed to hone in order to live. Thus such practices are integrally connected to a type of life where rigorous activities based on negotiating terrain serve as a type of visceral knowledge of the landscape. The pleasure in such activities was thus based on their being tied to essential life activities. Even mountain climbing, cliff diving and hiking have become competitive thrill and self-testing events far removed from any organic meaning they may have once had. Now climbing a mountain is a metaphor for the challenge of life itself. Long distance mid-life crisis running has become a running away from the effects of aging and an attempt to escape the "full time alienated performance" (Marcuse) that is one's life. Because people cannot "brave" life and refuse to engage in a de-reified knowledge of it, they opt for the easier physical challenge of a weekly excursion up the side of a frozen cliff or a sky dive parachute jump from an airplane, and the reified sense of accomplishment these provide. However many sports extremists may care little for the organic pleasure of engaging with the outdoors in any truly redeeming way, they willingly opt for the straight-forward thrill of pure fear and the evocation of the death response. Extreme sport of this type dispenses with all the frivolities of other players and delivers the death-response in pure distilled form as the primary objective of self pursuit. The pursuit of the death-response is part of the "negative ecstasy" (Baudrillard) sought in extreme sports. Pleasure in this sort of activity is obtained in having experienced the taste of death, in defeating death, and conquering fear and presumably coming out on top more resilient and victorious. These are all essential themes in the psyche of narcissistic reification. In the ritual of extreme sports agonism and reification are merged.

It used to be the case that Darwinistic-themed programs on television were confined to animal shows. And although the popularity of animal programs has remained, the focus continues to sharpen to a particular kind of animal, the apex predators: lions, tigers, sharks, dinosaurs, wolves, raptors, and so on. Again, such programs disseminate an ideological subtext that makes predation and hierarchy a natural fact of all living things – a rule of life as it were. This rule gets applied to the ways in which viewers are socialized into understanding their own life-worlds. In such a context predatory capitalism, consumer scams and political corruption are explained away as simply a part of the natural order of things.

The mediagon of television nature and survival programs reproduces the death aesthetic of the agonal life on a regular basis. This agonal aesthetic is increasingly coming to define the content of films as well. The number of feature films which are being released that either celebrate or convey their stories through various forms of violence are becoming so common that one could argue that violence defines the number one genre of film making. These movies range from a focus on vampirism, militarism to criminal violence, gangs and serial killers to Armageddon and total destruction. There are too many of them to list here, but to name a mere few, there has been *Gladiator, Fight Club, Saving Private Ryan, Flatliners, Patriot Games, Pulp Fiction, Black Hawk Down, Pearl Harbor, Predator, Terminator, Mars Attacks, Independence Day*, the *Rocky* series, *The Silence of the Lambs, Star Wars*, and *Scarface*. One can hardly find a major Hollywood blockbuster release that is not based on some form of agonism as its primary theme. Although the patriotic support for the status quo of the hegemonic military state is evident in feature films as much as it is in the mainstream corporate news media (Boggs 2005), it is only one form of the agonistic celebration of death within the mediagon.

Agonistic necrophilic pleasures also form part of the growing pop-cultural fascination with vampirism in which the celebration of death is also a feature. People today aspire to become vampires as a form of subversive personality type; the fashion mode of all black clothes and make-up whitened cadaver-like skin is still a popular fashion "look." Vampirism has reached new heights of popularity in a number of recent films and television series where the eroticization of death forms a part of viewer pleasure and identification with the anti-hero vampire protagonists. Vampire worship has also become a new context for teenage identity empowerment in what is known as "Goth culture." What is subjectively believed to be resistance against a marked, perhaps unconscious, cultural awareness of the ubiquity of death and destruction is actually a reaction that unwittingly supports it – in paying homage to death Goth culture and vampire fetishism is not resistance to what agon culture represents, but actually is an explicit manifestation of what it seeks to confront. Again we see evidence of Adorno's idea of reification as a "death mask" of identity. In the fetish for vampirism we see reification played out: recognizing death as the threat to life, the subjective response is not the affirmation of life but instead what occurs is the capitulation to death – to conquer it by becoming like it.

How can we ignore the fetish for war and the cult of warriorism, predatory elimination and death cultivated within agon culture? The examples are too numerous to list. A few hours glance at prime-time television displays all.

The Agon of Sport

> It is in sport that people first inflict upon themselves (and celebrate as a triumph of their own freedom) precisely what society inflicts upon them and what they must learn to enjoy.
>
> ~Theodor Adorno, *Free Time*

> Sport itself is not play but ritual in which the subjected celebrate their subjection.
>
> ~Theodor Adorno, *The Schema of Mass Culture*

The following is a sample of "news briefs" put out by the Canadian Broadcasting Corporation (CBC), which flashed them at the bottom of the television screen while coverage of the civil protest events in Egypt were unfolding on February 10, 2011. These news briefs slide-repeated every few minutes. Most of them refer to the main story of the day which was the events leading up to the removal of President Hosni Mubarak in Egypt. They read as follows:

> "Teenage suicide bomber kills 31 in Pakistan;" "Facebook, Google face 10 billion dollar bid to buy Twitter: report;" "Senators trade Mike Fisher to Predators for first round-pick;" "Mubarak speaks to Egyptians in National Address;" "RCMP addressing taser recommendations: watchdog;" "Strong Canadian dollar shifting production offshore: report;" "Woods received 55.4 million to promote UAE golf resort: report;" "Sidney Crosby says he expects to play this season;" "L.A. judge grants Charlie Sheen divorce from his wife Brooke;" "Mubarak pledges to prepare for honest elections;" "Toronto mayor Rob Ford in hospital with kidney stones;" "Ex-WikiLeaks insider attacks Assange in new book;" "Mubarak says he will stay on till elections;"

"Mubarak will not listen to 'dictates' coming from abroad;" "Minimum wage hike to cost 7000 jobs across New Brunswick: report;" "Mubarak will relax emergency laws when security improves;" "Protesters disrupt Toronto city hall budget meeting."

This is a random sample of news bits that is typical of what the media puts out as news on any given day. It represents the general thematic focus of media discourse with all of the ideological biases intact. Out of seventeen news briefs that make up the total flashed on the screen, five refer to the situation in Egypt, three are business reports, one of them implies that paying people a fair wage "costs jobs;" three are sports related (as if the details of corporately owned competitive sports is sufficiently newsworthy as to be included amidst real news); one is news of a killing caused by a suicide bomber abroad – terrorism is a dominant discourse of news broadcasting that keeps up the public support for the "war on terror" – one would imagine that many other deaths occurred around the world that day that were not mentioned because they are unrelated to the politicized issue of "the war on terror." Another brief refers to crime control policy and appeases public concerns over taser-related deaths by police forces in Canada who have come under much scrutiny in the use of tasers against people in instances when much less force would have sufficed; one is celebrity gossip, which is an example of how celebrity trivia is given equal consideration to real social issues in the news.

The media focus on information about the world of sports (which should properly be called the sporting industry) seems somehow out of joint with the newsworthiness of the other items mentioned, except for the celebrity gossip, which is equally base in terms of its social significance to human lives. Why would the average viewer be interested in the details of sports player's career decisions? What assumptions does the news broadcaster make when it disseminates sports items as newsworthy, that is, of such social value that it warrants public attention alongside world historical events? Only in the fabricated reality of the culture industry are such perverse juxtapositions allowed. Boorstin (1961) writes of the making of the "pseudo event," where an occasion that is captured by the mass media and televised or otherwise displayed comes to take on a significance of its own – it becomes something real and historic. Sports events are very much the pseudo event constructions of the imagistic media, and we often hear of "historic victories" of this team or that player. Competitive sport is a significant aspect of reality partly because of its promotion by the mass media and partly because competitive sporting is an institution funded by and of great importance to the nation-state. In this context it is not surprising to see how sport is a major dimension of the culture industry in numerous ways: its transmission of agonal cultural meanings, its economic nature as a corporate profit-making enterprise, its use of resources and roles production in schools and universities, its symbolic significance as a marker of national identity and moral fibre – and of specific relevance to this study, its role as an ideological text of meaning that supports the agonal order of society, from war to the competitive mechanism of selection.

Progressives who, in mainstream fashion, see sport as a mode of transcendence conveniently ignore the basic sociological dictum that competition is the wellspring of capitalism at its worst – its most basic and functional ideology of inequality. Progressive aid organizations see no problem going into impoverished communities around the world with donations of sports equipment, soccer balls, and knee pads, as if encouraging poor kids to consume their days running around each other in a frenzy of competition was somehow going to help alleviate their misery by teaching them something they already know all too well – that life for them is a struggle and that winning is rare when the odds are stacked against them. What are the real effects of teaching children to spend their time and effort engaging in competitive sport? What is the purpose of creating hierarchical filtering mechanisms that promotes the more aggressive kids and demoralizes those who would rather be doing something else with their time? Teaching poor children to exhaust their energies learning to compete with one another in the midst of material scarcity is both an affront to their dignity and a woefully insufficient replacement for real action that can bring substantial change into their lives.

There have been many sociological treatments of sport. Mostly these are functional analyses that examine the role of sport as a form of social bonding and ethical training. Others are slightly critical of sport in that they examine the violence within sports and are thus forms of organizational sociology whose main interest in solving problems within the institutions of sport. Other critical analyses of sport link go much further and link the values of competitive sport to the problem of hypermasculinity and male-centred violence (Burstyn 1999; Katz 2006). Few analyses of sport take the position developed by Jean-Marie Brohm (1978), who is among those few who have written critically of the ideological function of sports. In contrast to the dominant ideology of sport as something based on communitarian values, Brohm writes:

> While educationalists all stress the potential of sport for peace-making through the bringing together of individuals, peoples and nations and development of mutual understanding, in fact the opposite is true. There is a steady increase in violence in sport, primitive aggression, deliberate brutality, collisions, clashes and conflicts, which at the inter-state level reach war-like proportions. Tough tactics are spreading in every field of sport. There are more and more refereeing incidents, vendettas between players, invasions of the field by wild crowds, gratuitous violence on the part of spectators and so on. The wave of violence in sport, totally contradicting the ideology of sportsmanship naïvely peddled by the promoters, is merely the transposition of the violence of the social relations of capitalist production, the rule of every man for himself and the "struggle for life." All the values of the capitalist jungle are played out in sport: virility, sexual athleticism, physical dominance, the superman, muscle worship, fascistic male chauvinism, racism, sexism etc. (Brohm 1978: 14-15)

The ideology of Olympic games for example is also a blatant representation of competitive Nationalism and is directly tied to the values of pride, honour and identity. Olympic athletes are hailed as National heroes and share an exaltation equal to that of their cultural analogues, war heroes. Cultural heroism is constructed precisely on the basis of victorious accomplishment, and consequently the notion of heroism is thereby degraded (Boorstin 1961). Brohm cites from the "Anti-Olympic Committee" declaration:

> We stress that the mystification operated through the Olympics is just the most flagrant expression of the regimentation of the masses and especially of young people by means of competitive sport, which has become a true opiate of the people. (quoted in Brohm 1978: 31)

The identitarian fervour that is part of the sports audience creates a level of emotive unreason that allows for the acceptance of brutality in sports, and by implication everywhere in life where victory is desired. Brohm says of rugby:

> The masses are expected to mindlessly cheer [and they do] on a series of pitched battles and wild mauls in which new-style thugs knock each other about. Rugby is a text book case of tolerated violence and the deliberate cultivation of brutality. It reflects the torture mentality and the cult of physical force and confrontation typical of the goon squads of creeping fascism. (Brohm 1978: 17)

Rugby never really caught on in North America, but the desire for Rugby-style brutality certainly has. The thrill of gladiatorial-style destruction is furnished in North America by Monster machines, Robot Warriors and the plain old boxing match reinvented into its extreme form, mixed martial arts, where pugilists engage in full contact combat. These serve up agonism in its aesthetic simplicity in terms of a one-on-one violent battle to the end. For Brohm there is "a reactionary ideological function in sport, especially at the level of mass psychology" (1978: 26). Sport contains:

    a)   all of the values of traditional repressive morality and hence all of the models of behaviour promoted by bourgeois society: the cult of duty for its own sake, the sense of sacrifice for the community, the ideology of the super-ego, obedience, discipline, etc.;

   b) a *libidinal substitute* and a sublimation of aggressiv-
       ity... a controlled process of self-inflicted punishment
       or even self-destruction... a mortified sexual pleas-
       ure... a *schizophrenic relationship to the body* where
       one "gets pleasure from pain" (Freud); and
   c) a veritable *ideological apparatus of death,* physical tor-
       ture, tolerated and put on as entertainment... It condi-
       tions people to accept as "natural" all the aggressions,
       injuries, mutilations and physical suffering liberally dis-
       pensed by most contemporary governments. The mass
       capacity for revolt and struggle is transformed into
       organic self-repression. (Brohm 1978: 26-28)

For Brohm sport is inseparable from the state and has become an "ideological state apparatus" in the Althusserian sense. All regimes and repressive orders utilize the regimentation of sport as a means of inculcating discipline into society. Sport disguises repression and discipline into subjective satisfaction. Adorno writes: "Sport itself is not play but ritual in which the subjected celebrate their subjection" (1991: 77). The pleasure of sport is not only confined to the individual who partakes in sporting behaviour but also extends to the spectator fan (fanatic). The production of the sports fan certainly has an ideological state-national function, but can also be understood as an expression of the productive apparatus of corporate capitalism. Sports have become a mega industry. The profitability of sports extends from ticket sales to product endorsements by prominent athletes. Sports have become so integrated into the economy, society and national identity that cities go into mourning (or conversely into a destructive chaotic frenzy of ransacking and looting) when their teams lose or win or when they lose a team itself. Teams themselves are forms of private property. They are capitalist ventures that co-opt and exploit the idea of community property and collective identity. Sports teams follow the logic of capital, blended with the ideology of agonism in a most perverse mixture. Of this ideology of agonism, which sports transmits through its distorted "aesthetic" of play, something must be said: It is a widespread belief that the aesthetic of sport is carried in the beauty of execution, the gracefulness and precision with which the physical task which leads to victory is performed. The physical task itself however is meaningless and deemed not beautiful outside of the context of victory. A "great play" is not good enough if it does not result in a "win."

The aesthetic of sport is tied to victory just as agonistic spectator pleasure is becoming increasingly tied to the thrill of destruction, of vanquishing an opponent, and death. The sacrificial gesture that attempts to pay honour to death is there in another sporting event, one which is not based on teams competing against one another. This is what Don Atyeo (1979) refers to as "death as a spectator sport" – events such as bullfighting, cockfighting, dog fighting and other sacrificial ecstasies that abuse animals in the spectators' sublimation of human fear and weakness. This practice is the singular invention of human beings, a morbid and disgusting inheritance based on rites of sanctimonious sacrifice and contest, and which has been carried into the present to ensure that death reification persists in contemporary form.

Agonal death ecstasy is revealed in a more diluted form, perhaps, in traditional boxing matches, and in a more intensified form in the illegal, underground and very brutal "street fighting" competitions in which young men are "pitted" against each other like dogs in a fight with "no rules" that ends when one man

It is not that one is "against sport" per se, although such a position is certainly defensible. Rather, it is that the agonal values within sport – its conflict, violence, discipline and authoritarianism –needs to be tempered by a value set which counteracts the ideological indoctrination that is inflicted on the young who are thrust into sport against their will. Often, sport is imposed upon children by their parents and teachers in a cult-like fashion. The children are inculcated into sport through the enthusiasm and determination of their superiors (parents, coaches, teachers, sports celebrities, and so on) and this is reinforced further by their peers and by the sport-centric media. They are denied any vision of alterity that encourages them to come out against competitive sport should they feel they would rather be involved in something else more meaningful to them.

finally goes down. Men who behave in such ways are not mimicking fighting dogs. Rather the horrible practice of pitting dogs
against one another is an activity prompted by humans, since the
behaviour of dogs in such a context is a coerced one, because
"wild animals never kill for sport. Man is the only one to whom
the torture and death of his fellow creatures is amusing in itself"
(Froude quoted in Atyeo 1979: 93).

Many people are alarmed at and take offense to the mere
suggestion that competitive sport is ideologically related to war
and the normalization of violence in society. This defensive posture is what makes sport almost immune to total criticism. Like
religion, it is a belief system that is guarded against evidence to
the contrary. Its success is based on feelings. These are feelings
of fun and play and pleasure and accomplishment – which are all
certainly tied to sport but do not invalidate its negativity and problematic status as a discourse of domination.

In Vancouver in the summer of 2011 a crowd of 100,000
hockey fans rioted in grand fashion after the Vancouver Canucks
lost against the Boston Bruins for the Stanley Cup final. They
caused 5 million dollars in damage, burned the flag of a small
band of Boston fans and generally engaged in various acts of
destruction. Police cars were burned, store windows were crashed,
tear gas was used unsuccessfully to stop their destruction. The
initial media reports tried to claim that it was caused by "anarchists" but this ridiculous bit of propaganda quickly wore out and
the nation came to accept the reality that many young sports fans
behave this way as a normal practice. Violent displays of nationalism and hatred are not an abnormal response at sporting events.
Fans often resort to violence – usually alcohol – inspired young
males (the same general demographic of the military) – it is the
exact same reason that prevails in the military agon – the resort
to violence – the lowest form of reason.

In other countries such violent behaviour takes on a more
organized form; it is called hooliganism and is a regular part of
the pseudo tribalism that develops around soccer teams. No less
barbarous, it represents how the mass culture of competitive sport
is not inseparable from the Machiavellian and Clausewitzian
form of international politics of empire pride and national championship. How is this any different from the geopolitics of the
Olympics when in 1936 Hitler used them as a forum to promote

Aryan notions of superiority and Nazi imperial grandeur? In 1968 there was slaughter at the Olympics in Mexico. In 1972 in Munich 11 Israelis were assassinated. In the Moscow Olympics of 1980 there was an American-led boycott that kept 62 nations from participating, ironically for reasons of the Soviet invasion of Afghanistan. The 1984 Los Angeles Olympics became a frenzied display of American patriotism, nationalism and corporate sponsorship. The 1988 Olympics in Seoul, South Korea were also marred by boycotts and acrimony among nations. The 1992 Olympics in Barcelona also reflected the geopolitical climate of the times with new entries from South Africa and from members of the former Yugoslavia and the Soviet block. The Olympics are not just about displaying the athleticism of each nation's top athletes. Nor is competitive sport synonymous with general health and fitness. On a dialectical scale the Olympics represent in macrosocial form the variety of social relations that exist within agon culture: the global politics of nationalism and competition between nations, and the generalized set of competitive relations that exist even between individuals who are on the same team.

Competitive sport affirms the order of the agon. As indicated briefly in chapter one, sport is the largest – that is the most popular and vast – ideological belief system that works to maintain the agonal society and its various institutions. Sociologists speak of the "institution of sport," but sociology as a discipline does not really consider sport to be a major social structure of society. Even Althusser minimized the role of competitive sports in his treatment of the ideological state apparatuses in his famous essay on the topic (1971). Introduction to sociology textbooks offer chapters on the state, the family, religion and other institutions but not exclusively on sport. The popularity of and the generally positive attitude that people have towards sport should not make it immune to criticism and blind social thought to the significance of such a fundamental institution.

Chapter 10

Conclusion: The Agon – Life Under Tension

This study of Agon Culture is based on the premise that agonism represents the current form of the reification of reason realized in societal form – a reason that prevails in the geopolitical order of domination operating in the world today. The positive thinking that leads to destruction is nothing but the destruction of reason. How has this come about?

- How is it that human consciousness is negatively structured so that it lends itself readily to the self-destructive complications of reification?
- How is it that the structure and organization of society tends towards lapsing into systems of domination and war?

Answers to these questions have been explored here in terms of the "reification of culture" in terms of agonistic rationality in particular. This agonal rationality is evident in the structures of society but originates in the realm of culture. Reified culture is troubled by the tension between the human desire for *affirmation* and practices that end up failing at life affirmation and paradoxically support the forces of *domination*. This essential dialectic forms the frailty and fragility inherent in the nature of human culture, and this dialectic serves as a hermeneutic device for inquiry into the reign of irrationality that occurs within the *thinking* of culture in the present era where humans have not yet been able to realize reasonable amounts of progress in an equitable, global manner. Human life, indeed the myriad forms of life on earth remain "under tension" – with the basic contradictions of modern industrial society unresolved. An element of the failure of a reasonable and shared human progress is the proliferation of agonism which justifies the *rationality of irrationality* in a type of dominating reason that conceals contradictions, props up myths about conflict and transcendence, and serves to perpetuate a historical cycle that curtails true dialectical growth.

This book has examined five manifestations of agonistic reason:

- the agon of reified consciousness and the problem of competitive self defeat;
- the Enlightenment agon of the domination of nature; the war machine of the agonal state and its order of domination;
- the agon of history and the mythology of dialectical progress; and
- the competitive-ecstasy of the mediagon, including the collaboration of death in entertainment and sport.

The *agon*, which is the society erected on the basis of agonism, actually recognizes the fact of agonism and affirms it as the *forceful way to truth*. It is self-reflexive on the matter of its complicity with domination and submits to it, attempts to come to terms with it – it does this through the creation of rules. The agon therefore justifies the system of agonism through the *ideal of fair play*. It lays down the rules of the game and posits that if these rules are followed, order will emerge and freedom will be protected. These rules are ethics, law and the entire apparatus that *normalizes* crisis, inequality and war – they are deemed the great counterbalances to corruption and disarray. This is the "Democratic Agon." If we look closer, however, we begin to realize "that rules are allowed to be broken if you are strong enough to get away with it." This "creative capacity" for rule-breaking is "the cunning of reason," which violates the principle of cultural creativity and subsequently rationalizes all violation and violence with the credo that "might makes right."

The illusion of "just war" is maintained through the myth that war can be conducted in a civilized manner, and that the agon is the ideal configuration for working through conflict. But evidence in the continuing violations of the Charter of the United Nations against wars of aggression and conquest and the ongoing barbarism and war crimes that exist in presumably lawful wars belies this myth and counterposes the unrealistic ideal of just war with the hideous actuality of open slaughter.

In agon culture the Universal is dialectical with the Particular. War in the actual fields of battle are dialectically related to the ideological forms of everyday culture in which war-like activities are promoted in the language of the workplace and the discourse of entertainment and popular culture. Somewhere in between these two realms exist the middle-range softer wars – the war on drugs, war on terror, war on poverty and so on – that are to be found in the conflicts on city streets, where crime, unemployment, beggary, and other forms of social violation emerge when conditions of scarcity and need are informed by cultural values of predation, domination and disrespect.

The problem of agon culture is the problem of domination. When we speak of agonism and the massive *human* problem of a destructive and oppressive social order that has been identified in this study as *agon culture*, we are speaking of that particular dimension of life which is constructed in dominance, of that which is specifically enthralled by the social totality and its power. As has been emphasized throughout this book, however, the totality of domination is not thorough nor is it complete. The problems of human domination illuminated here grow alongside an increasing awareness, albeit on a restricted scale, to the project of power taking place culturally and politically on a global level. Outside of the gargantuan scope of the agon and its attempt to reformulate the earth as a production/destruction machine, there is a renewed awareness to the power of globalizing forms of autocracy and their relation to the perpetuation of atrocity. Thus it is important to note that the process of power described in this study is by no means total or universal in its grasp so long as it remains within the realm of political recognition (although the process itself makes claims on the universal in its thrust for totalization).

Today the public critique of domination which protests the globalization of corporate capitalism, and the protests against anti-democratic dictatorial regimes in numerous places, are the most prominent counter-hegemonic social movements at the beginning of the twenty-first century. They are bound up with an increasing recognition of the extent to which the empire-order of power is tied to the perpetuation of suffering and injustice, one which is not going to be resolved by a mere tampering with the maladjusted and inefficient institutions that administer society.

Bourdieu writes:

> We must put an end to the reign of "experts" in the style of the World Bank or the IMF, who impose without discussion the verdicts of the new Leviathan, the "financial markets," and who do not seek to negotiate but to "explain;" we must break with the new faith in the historical inevitability professed by the theorists of liberalism. (1998 : 26)

It has been over thirty years since the human sciences has had a consistent paradigm of truly critical scholarship, ranging across the disciplines, that amounts to the concerted critique against domination, the kind of domination we are seeing today. One can scarcely walk into a bookstore without encountering the latest denunciations of globalization. This does not mean that this new critical discourse has achieved the level of radicalism of earlier efforts, nor has it supplanted the official dominant positive discourse which still governs the development, funding and application of the human sciences, and thus still directly upholds the policy and trajectory of the State-Corporate apparatus of power. Nevertheless there is a treatment of the critical issues that corresponds with popular protest which together contributes to a culture of dissent that is necessary for the maintenance of an emancipatory consciousness and a co-ordinated struggle for human rights everywhere.

The hegemonic project of domination is not absolute. There is a culture, and there are cultures, which do not fall under the domination of the agon, which are not mediatized, simulated, competitive, conflicted, promoted or profitable. There is also a growing awareness of the empire of destruction. There is however pitiful little awareness of the dangerous ideology of agonistic competition and conflict which affirms this order as natural: It is still far too popular and deeply engrained a passion for many, even among the freethinkers and others who esteem themselves radically opposed to domination. The popularity of agonistic affirmation and the pleasures of competition will certainly continue to obstruct the potential for a critical awareness of its inherent problematicity to emerge.

It is hoped that the global-intellectual imagination has been shaken by the events of conflict that have come to characterize the post-9/11 era, and that scholarship will be catapulted into looking more directly at the root of war, but it seems, even when staring at war in the face, recognition of its integral truth is obscured by the overpowering positive rhetoric of agonal discourse.

The critique of agonism is also about the philosophy of peace. If ideals pertaining to peace have been "spectacularly unsuccessful" (Ursula Franklin) in our times, it is not because of the poverty of these ideals, their invalidity or naiveté as such, but because of the poverty of the context of their reception. Peace is far more difficult to achieve in a society that believes transcendence is possible through conflict.

Notes

Chapter 1

1   The affirmative character of culture refers to the will to survival that is inherent in culture as a form of collective historical knowledge oriented towards the preservation of life. The affirmative character of culture thus signifies the self-preservative element in culture proper as something enabling and meaningful. Cultural awareness is affirmative in the sense that it offers critical insight into the predicaments of one's life situation and thereby informs ways in which people are able to shape their lives and fashion new realities for themselves outside of the constrictions of imposed domination. Culture, in the affirmative sense, is thus a form of knowledge that is oriented towards growth, sustenance and adaptation to constantly changing conditions; this constitutes the predicament of culture. Culture is therefore a form of knowledge based on creative ingenuity, one oriented towards the preservation of human life. This creative intelligence is the most profound expression of human culture.

The critical theory of culture maintains that there must be an objective basis by which we can determine if cultural practices and cultural values are either supportive of the primacy and sanctity of human life, or violate this fundamental principle and unwittingly or overtly promote and/or celebrate death. In most cases however, including in that of non-industrialized indigenous cultures, affirmative and repressive cultural values often occur alongside one another. Human culture, while aiming at preservation, has a tendency to celebrate that which it fears and thus may "lapse into infidelity." Adorno writes:

> Culture, in the true sense, did not simply accommodate itself to human beings; but it always simultaneously raised a protest against the petrified relations under which it lived, thereby honoring them. In so far as culture becomes wholly assimilated to and integrated in those petrified relations, human beings are once more debased. (1991: 86)

See also Marcuse's "The Affirmative Character of Culture" (in Marcuse 1968: 88-133).

2   A "synthetic" that has been "materially invented" does not mean that it is purely artificial in terms of its human experiential content, but in the form of its genesis. Top-down culture has become a field of power where human wants and needs have been tampered with by market forces that have shaped the content of value and influenced the realm of necessity through the regula-

tion of desire. Adorno and Horkheimer (1969) refer to culture as the product of calculation in contrast to a way of life made by and for the people in an indigenous sense.

3   See John O'Neill's *Plato's Cave: Desire Power and the Specular Functions of the Media* (1991). O'Neill's analysis begins with Plato's allegory of the cave as a primary metaphor for contemporary communicative media and its power of deception.

4   McLuhan writes:

> After three thousand years of explosion, by means of fragmentary and mechanical technologies, the Western world is imploding. During the mechanical ages we had extended our bodies in space. Today, after more than a century of electric technology, we have extended our central nervous system itself in a global embrace, abolishing both space and time as far as our planet is concerned... As electrically contracted, the globe is no more than a village. (1964: 11-12)

5   For a thorough discussion on the relation between Marshall Mcluhan and technological determinism, see John Fekete (1977).

6   Carl von Clausewitz, strategist and lover of war, reverses the claim but the idea remains the same when he calls war "the continuation of politics by other means" (1997).

7   See Benedetto Fontana, *Hegemony and Power* (1993).

8   See Ewen, *Captains of Consciousness* (1976).

9   Walter Lippman's term from his *Public Opinion* (1922) that referred to the need for the deliberate manipulation of public consciousness in democratic systems was revived in a critical sense by Herman and Chomsky in their *Manufacturing Consent* (1988).

10   By contemporary empire I am referring to the formation of economic, political, cultural and military power (Derrida 1994; Parenti 1995; Jameson and Miyoshi 1998; Hardt and Negri 2000) that prevails in the new world order of capitalist expansion and corporate control. This is an order based on the hegemony of the American business model, the English language and Western techno-military control. Cultural imperialism forms a significant part of this through the globalization of the culture industry.

11   See Benedict Anderson, *Imagined Communities* (1983).

Chapter 2

1   Michel Foucault (1980) indicates that power can be modelled on the totality or on the particularity, at the macro-logical level of a universalizing discourse or through the micro-physics of power. We can deduce three useful conceptions of power referred to in Foucault's text, which he builds upon in varying degrees in his own conception of power:

- Power is primarily a juridical conception, in which power is taken to be a right that one possesses or has conferred upon them by a sovereign authority – power is therefore a jurisprudential/legal phenomenon. "Right [is thus] in a general way, the instrument of domination" (1980: 95).

- Power within the context of capitalism is something modeled upon the commodity form, and thus upon the economic order that emerges from it – from the commodification of desire to the relation of commodity exchange. As such the commodity is the basic unit of social analysis in the critique of capitalism (1980).

- Power is that which "exists only in action" (1980: 89) and is "above all a relation of force" (1980: 89). Power in this sense is that which represses in terms of "struggle, conflict and war – in terms of the hostile engagement of forces" (1980: 90-91)… "the set of relations of force in a given society constitutes the domain of the political, and politics is more or less global strategy for coordinating and directing those relations" (1980: 189).

Foucault writes: "It is only if we grasp these techniques of power and demonstrate the economic advantages or political utility that derives from them in a given context for specific reasons, that we can understand how these mechanisms come to be effectively incorporated into the social whole" (1980: 101). It is important to note, however, that Foucault articulates these different conceptions of power as examples of forms which "can be deduced from the general phenomenon of the domination of the bourgeois class" (1980: 100). Foucault's conception of power tarries with the meanings listed above, however the conception of power that seems most apparent in his writings departs from them. Foucault's formulation of power as discourse is both something subjects possess rather than something which acts on them and thus is both something which is simultaneously repressive and potentially liberating. This contradiction exhausts the critical meaning in Foucault's concept of power and invites its liberalization and co-optation. What remains of power's centrality is the virtue of power – such as the subjective ideal in the term "empowerment." Agonal critique takes exception to the concept of power as simultaneously that which one possesses as strength and also that which the state exerts as domination. Agonal critique emphasizes the third conception of power listed above, that is, power as a "relation of force," especially the antagonistic orientation and coerciveness of the forces that exist in an unequal society where competition is rampant.

2   Best and Kellner discuss the implications of the new chaos theory in their book *The Postmodern Adventure* (2001).

3   Walter Benjamin's thesis that "there is no document of civilization which is not at the same time a document of barbarism" (1969: 256) indicates the extent to which recorded history was the history of victory and conquest. Hence historical domination gets valorized, and the triumph of victory is celebrated as historical progress. In the agonal imaginary of progress, history which occurs outside of the dialectic of domination is not considered to be authentic history.

4   In his *Totem and Taboo*, Freud (1986) develops a related argument to the development of this point, relating the origin of religious deification of the oppressive father to the collective guilt of paternal sacrifice.

5   See Marvin Harris *Cannibals and Kings* (1977), who also discusses the cultural meaning of death-sacrifice.

6   Rene Girard in his *Violence and the Sacred* (1972) is usually credited with having formulated what is called the "mimetic theory of violence," however the formulation is also contained in Adorno and Horkheimer's *Dialectic of Enlightenment* (1969), and is a part of their theory of reification as the sacrificial mimesis of death.

7   Ong writes that, "with logic, ancient Greece formalized adversativeness as no other culture had done... In fact, deliberate cultivation of the adversative lies at the deepest roots of intellectual development, particularly in the West" (1981: 20-22).

8   John O'Neill gives a fine example of what Horkheimer means by being in "harmony with the totality" (1974) when he describes "civilized humankind's [break] with nature" (O'Neill 1995: 84) in an earlier order of life, which was inscribed by a set of values through which

> the peasantry could encounter the totality of meaning ordained for them in the feudal order and die at peace with their station in life because their daily life was congruent with the whole of their life. But because the modern individual pitted against an ever-expanding universe of ideas, problems and values... always encounters death as meaningless, for death robs them of infinity. "And because death

is meaningless, civilized life as such is meaningless; by its very 'progressiveness' it gives death the imprint of meaninglessness." (Weber 1946: 140)

9   See Abercrombie, Hill and Turner's *Sovereign Individuals of Capitalism* (1986).

10   Among the many cultish texts of "objectivism" that explicate the theme of capitalist self-interest is Rand's *The Virtue of Selfishness* (1964).

11   The question raised in all of this concerns how the ethical rationality of enlightenment was superseded by economic rationality to culminate in the moral justification of capitalist individualism and its translation into social exploitation. This transformation in the very fabric of ethical meaning marks a monumental task undertaken by secular order dedicated to undoing an ancient religious edict against profit and compound interest in money lending, which had to be transformed into a system of unbridled consumption and excess based on the system of credit.

12   Held indicates that "the principle of individualism and the pursuit of rational self-interest... was nurtured in the sixteenth and seventeenth centuries" (1980: 67).

13   The agonal state in this study is seen as the political-military state that depends on the use of force to maintain its sovereignty. An "agonal" state would include most contemporary capitalist states in the world today that maintain active military forces, but the term can also refer to political-military states of antiquity and more recently to entities such as the Stalinist and the Maoist states, which nevertheless sustained themselves through forms of brutal repression. Agonal states use military force to wage war against other nation-states as well as employ repressive force to prevent progressive social change among their own people and within their own borders.

14   See Gillian Rose (1978: 4).

15   See Frederick Pollock, "State Capitalism: Its Possibilities and Limitations" (1989). Marcuse states: "Pollock wrote the first article which argued that there were no compelling internal economic reasons why Capitalism should collapse" (in Magee 1978: 50), thereby basically indicating that the life of the economy was entirely supported by a state politics of intervention. Pollock argued that in the "genesis of monopoly capitalism... the crisis growth patterns of liberal capitalism had not been destroyed under the system of monopolies" (Held 1980: 57). The fusion of capital (the economy) and state (politics) was intensifying to an extent that they were becoming mutually dependent on one another to form state capitalism. This idea was already prefigured in Marx's notion that all economies are ipso facto political, hence the

concept of "political economy." Liberal theory had insisted on the separation of state and economy because the state was supposed to protect the interests of the individual and not administer the corporate financial sector of society. Today it is clear that the state in capitalism is a political-economic-corporate agonal state. Its central agenda (outside of war) is the negotiation of strategic advantage in trade. An economy is not merely an appendage of society for the generation of wealth – it is also a way of generating a political order to facilitate the multiplication of capital.

16   It was actually Herbert Marcuse who was openly critical of Western imperialism and was engaged with Fanon's work. See Wiggershaus (1995: 611-12).

17   Max Weber writes:

> There are three pure types of legitimate domination. The validity of the claims to legitimacy may be based on:
>
> > 1. Rational grounds – resting on a belief in the legality of enacted rules and the right of those elevated to authority under such rules to issue commands (legal authority);
> >
> > 2. Traditional grounds – resting on an established belief in the sanctity of immemorial traditions and the legitimacy of those exercising authority under them (traditional authority); or finally,
> >
> > 3. Charismatic grounds – resting on devotion to the exceptional sanctity, heroism or exemplary character of an individual person, and of the normative patterns or order revealed or ordained by him (charismatic authority).
> > (Weber 1968: 215)

18   Kant's infamy for colonial theory is not only due to his ambivalent concept of the "categorical imperative" and its imperial legislating overtones, but also his racism. Goldberg writes:

> the historical record of moral appeals to race by many of the greatest intellectuals and political figures in the liberal tradition is overwhelming... Kant, citing with approval David Hume's likening of learning by "negroes" to that of parrots, insisted upon the natural stupidity of blacks. (1993: 6)

19   I am deliberately invoking the title of Kant's famous essay on the establishment of peace as the goal of governance and universal law insofar as it has gained some new prominence in the wake of deliberation over civil society, human rights and international order. See the collection edited by Bohman and Lutz-Bachman (1997).

Chapter 3

1   Marcuse says, "All domination in recorded history has been patriarchal domination..." (in Magee 1978: 53).

2   See Wolfgang Sachs' essay "One World," in which he writes: "languages are dying out every bit as quickly as species... at present roughly 5,100 languages are spoken around the globe... many indicators suggest that within a generation or two not many more than 100 of these languages will survive" (1992: 102).

3   The agonistic nation-states that call themselves liberal democracies consistently demonstrate the falseness of that claim. Derrida writes, "all the evidence bears massive witness to the fact that neither the United States nor the European Community has attained the perfection of the universal state or of liberal democracy, nor have they even come close" (1995: 63). This is so only in their consistent violation of laws upon which the principles of open democracy depend, but also in replacing the edict of rule by consensus with that of rule by a media elicited "majority" (Parenti 1993), which is hardly consensual since it is usually in the fifty percentile range, sometimes less. Adorno writes that liberal democracy violates "the will of the majority that ill uses a minority, and so makes a mockery of democracy while acting in accordance with its principles" (Adorno 1974: 77).

Chapter 4

1   See Held (1980: 64).

2   O'Neill writes: "It is not far fetched to consider Weber an archaeologist of the power man exerts over himself, and thus to see him as a precursor of Foucault's conception of the disciplinary society" (1995: 44).

Chapter 5

1   "War," says Gwynne Dyer, "is a central institution in human civilization, and it has a history as long as [patriarchal] civilization" (cited in Davis and Stasz 1990: 281). Further:

> Dyer observes that war is not in the genes; there is no such thing as war in the Bushmen's world. War emerged with the rise to dominance of the warrior class and women's loss of status. Men became politically pre-eminent, because they were militarily pre-eminent. The warrior role, not the bread-winner role, made men dominant. Even in primitive societies, where hunters are transformed into warriors, warfare

is nor lethal. The few that are killed were mostly young
males; society itself remained intact. (quoted in Davis and
Stasz 1990: 282)

Gilles Deleuze and Felix Guattari (1986) seem to concur with Dyer's claim
that war is as old as civilization. They go as far as to suggest that "the war
machine" as they call it, is an archaic and autonomous institution, one that
exists beyond the state form. They write, "as for the war machine in itself, it
seems to be irreducible to the state apparatus, to be outside its sovereignty and
prior to its law: it comes from elsewhere... It is the invention of the nomads...
The State has no war machine of its own; it can only appropriate one in the
form of a military institution, one that will always cause problems. This
explains the mistrust States have towards their military institutions..." (1986:
2-7, emphasis in original). While it is true that the heads of state inherit the
military as a pre-formed institution, and occasionally the military will take
over political power through a coup d'etat and supplant the existing state, their
interrelation is less arbitrary than Deleuze and Guattari seem to suggest. The
military is the instrument of the state. In the case of the dominant industrialized nation-states the military and the state are virtually inseparable dimensions in the perpetuation of power and order.

2   The "normalization" of war has nothing to do with war being benign
or banal; the normalization process too is a form of coercion, insofar as the
public consent for war must be both ideologically and legally generated.
Protest against war is looked upon with suspicion, sometimes being seen as
tantamount to treason. Even though militaries form part of virtually every state
that calls itself a democracy, there is nothing democratic at all about the military. "Military" and "democracy" are antinomical concepts. And yet "democracies" possess militaries and quite often have their national policies dictated
by military demands. C.W. Mills writes:

> In the military world, debate is no more at a premium than
> persuasion; one obeys and one commands, and matters,
> even unimportant matters, are not to be decided by voting.
> Life in the military world accordingly influences the mili-
> tary mind's outlook on other institutions as well as on its
> own. (Mills 1956: 196)

A true democratic society cannot have a military as one of its most
integral institutions. Military privilege and authority contravenes all
of the edicts of democratic openness. The military is quite likely the
most undemocratic institution in existence. Its authority is by decree,
its society is separate from the rest, and its mode of discipline is
entirely autocratic (Mills 1956).

3   Among the ethical concerns about violence in society is the popular
concern over the effects of violence on children. The issue of the cultural normalization of violence gets deflected this way as a concern about the future
of children rather than as a contemporary problem about the behaviour of
adults, especially adult political leaders. Nevertheless the problem arising out
of the raising of children in the context of war is a significant one, to be sure.
The contemporary situations of civil war in African nations, for example, has
allowed for hundreds of thousands of children to be stolen as young soldiers,
with devastating consequences for them, for those they have maimed and for
their families, many of whom do not want the warrior children back.

4   John Kenneth Galbraith writes: "Increasingly, it will be recognized
that the mature corporation, as it develops, becomes part of the larger administrative complex associated with the state. In time the line between the two
will disappear" (quoted in Melman 1970: 12).

5   The cost of war in human life is not confined to military personnel.
It is a central feature of modern war that civilians are legitimate targets of
battle. In World War II for example, "twice as many civilians were killed in
this war than soldiers. It is the first war in history in which civilian casualties
outnumbered military ones" (Davis and Stasz 1990: 283). Similarly Noam
Chomsky writes, "In the 20th century, civilian populations once again became
a prime target [of war], as in the biblical days, the Frankish wars, and other
unusually bloody eras. The Nazi's broke new ground with industrialized genocide – and recall that this was the world's most advanced industrial and technological power and the cultural center of the West as well" (2000: 162).

6   Derrida lists as one of the plagues he identifies in the plagues of the
new-world disorder, the

> ruthless economic war… between Europe, the United States
> and Japan. This war controls everything, beginning with the
> other wars, because it controls the practical interpretation
> and an inconsistent and unequal application of international
> law. There have been too many examples in the last decade
> or more. (1994: 81)

7   See O'Neill's section "Nightlynews" in the chapter "Cave Culture
and Tele-vision" (in 1991: 15-19.

8   As a "document of history" the Bible is a pre-eminent "document of
barbarism" in the Benjaminian sense. Its antinomical character extends to it
being a handbook for genocide and ethnocide. Michael Parenti, citing ancient
historians investigating these contradictions lists some of them, including,
"Why is it that God gave contradictory laws to Moses and Jesus?… Why

would God so heartlessly deny an opportunity for salvation to the countless generations born before the advent of Jesus? Was it only then, after such a long period, that he remembered to judge the human race?" (1999: 46). Parenti continues:

> The Old Testament, incorporated as part of the Christian Bible, repeatedly condones the taking of slaves in war. In Numbers 31.17-18, after killing all the men of Midian, Moses instructs his men to murder every male child and every mature woman. But "all the women children," the child virgins, "keep alive for yourselves." So through much of the Old Testament: mass murder, pillage, rape, and the enslavement of foreigners are acceptable practices, sometimes mandated by the Almighty himself. (Parenti 1991: 62)

9   "A maxim is a subjective principle of action… For Kant, the categorical imperative is the objective principle of morality" (Reiss 1991: 18). Kant writes: "Act always in such a way as if you were through your maxims a law-making member of the universal kingdom of ends." The prescriptive principles of "duty," "ought," and "rationality" typically infuse Kant's discourse in his *Fundamental Principles of the Metaphysics of Morals* (1988). Nietzsche writes: "ethics has never lost its reek of blood and torture – not even in good old Kant, whose categorical imperative smacks of cruelty" (1956: 197).

10   Pierre Bordieux and Loic Wacquant identify the discursive strategy within contemporary political theory as an effect of empire knowledge, as a "cunning form of imperialist reason" that rationalizes cultural imperialism "with fine positivist diligence" (1999: 48). They see the present "globalization" as a manifestation of American imperialism, which is accompanied by a conceptual discourse that renders the concerns and progressions of global society in the terms of a Euro-American rationalist and imperialist doxa. This "new global vulgate," they write, leads "to a kind of principled depoliticization of social and political problems," and is "thereby stripped of any reference to any kind of domination" (1999: 43). In their essay "On the Cunning of Imperialist Reason," they remark on the pernicious form of cultural imperialism of which academics are at once perpetrators and victims. Through their promotion of a discourse which valorizes the "terms, themes and tropes" (1999: 47) of a new planetary doxa that submerges "the effects of imperialism in cultural ecumenism or economic fatalism and of making transnational relationships of power appear as natural necessity" (1999: 42), a "new global vulgate" (1999: 42) is emerging from the uncontrolled universalization and pre-occupations of American society and academe.

11   See Horkheimer (1972).

Chapter 6

1   Jean Baudrillard uses the term "metastasis," a medical term which refers to the growth of cancer cells and thus is an apt metaphor for the growth of death, in his essay "The Anorexic Ruins," in which he writes: "We are no longer in a state of growth; we are in a state of excess ... Crisis is functional" (1989: 29).

2   From Adam Smith to Milton Friedman and Kenneth Galbraith, economic philosophers in contradiction with capitalists have always maintained that the ideal of capitalism is based on the maintenance of certain freedoms, and that artificial, imposed restrictions, interferences or monopolizations that control the economy translate into the curtailing of personal freedoms. Milton Friedman writes that "economic freedom, in and of itself, is an extremely important part of total freedom... economic freedom is an indispensable means toward the achievement of political freedom... [yet it is] clearly possible to have economic arrangements that are fundamentally capitalist and political arrangements that are not free" (Friedman 1982: 8-10).

Chapter 7

1   See "Socialization, Isolation and Human Existence" (Anderson 1996).

Chapter 8

1   This is a sarcastic reversal of Hegel's notion of the "unhappy consciousness," which in the reification of consciousness is realized as a form of repressive satisfaction.

2   Georg Lukács, who is commonly associated with the identification of reification as a fundamental problem of cultural domination, saw reification as a temporary aberration of pre-revolutionary proletarian consciousness which would dissolve with the rise to communism. Adorno's notion of reification departs substantially from the Marxist limitations inherent in Lukács' conceptualization. For Adorno the potential for reification exists in the "primordial" form of culture and emerges from the unconscious fear of death that predisposes human consciousness to reified reactions against this fear.

3   Horkheimer offers a prescription for the practical applicability of critical theory by offering that "one must have insight into one's own responsibility" (1972: v). The reification of consciousness in this regard works to deny the insight that leads to transcendence through the manipulation of perception and transformative understanding.

4   See Adorno's essay "Free Time" (1991).

5   Adorno further remarks that "Carl Schmidt identified the very essence of politics by the categories of friend and enemy" (1974: 132).

6   The biblical injunction to social division is contained in the New Testament words, "He who is not for me is against me" (see Adorno 1974: 131).

7   See Livy Visano on "The Ideology of Fear and the Culture of Violence" (in Visano 1998).

8   Weber, writing on the doctrine of the Protestant ethic and its relationship to modern disenchantment, stated: "In its extreme inhumanity this doctrine must above all have had one consequence for the life of a generation which surrendered to its magnificent consistency. That was a feeling of unprecedented inner loneliness of the single individual" (Weber 1930: 104).

9   On the history of the break with nature and the thesis of instrumental rationalization as disenchantment, see Berman's *Reenchantment of the World* (1981).

10   "Conspicuous consumption," that bourgeois pastime identified by Thorstein Veblen (1953), is a hallmark example of competitive consumer behaviour. In his book *The Theory of the Leisure Class*, "Veblen dramatized as no one before or since, the spectacle of inequality" (Galbraith 1998: 45). Ironically the ostentatious display of wealth by the elite classes did not produce disdain among the general public but an envy that was culturally realized as a type of competitive-consumptive desire.

It was once the exclusive purview of the wealthy to benefit from the riches that could be gained by the possession of economic power. The poor dreamed about having certain things and enjoying a life of wealth, presumably one free from want. Even in the scenario outlined by Veblen, where the emerging consumer classes were enculturated to envy and emulate the rich, the master/slave dialectic of self-negating mimicry is evident. The sort of popular emulation of the lifestyle of the bourgeois elites that is at the basis of Veblen's concept of conspicuous consumption is an ideology which has passed beyond the meagre realm of necessity that once reminded the poor of their position. Today the hoards of middle-class consumers buy into the lifestyle of consumption not because of the need to overcome material poverty but because of the need to satiate the mental poverty (the lack of meaning) that is produced by the consumer "system of objects" (Baudrillard 1996). Despite the abundance of "goods" the "ecstasy of consumption" is wholly unable to alleviate consumer reification.

11   See O'Neill's *Five Bodies* (1985).

Chapter 9

1   The phrase "consumer-democracy" is a sarcastic one. It reveals a conception of society in which citizens are socialized to make all decisions based on the freedom of choice: The system of democratic self-governance which is based on the choice of freely electing one's leaders is conflated with the freedom of buyers' choices in the world of commodities. As Druckrey writes, "The desirability of democracy is consumption" (1994: 10). The democratic dictum of "people's rule," which is "by and for the people," becomes "for the people to buy." Both ideas reinforce one another to create the ideology that self-determination and the edict of free will are both maintained in "consumer-democracy." Nor should we ignore that the use of the capitalist media by politicians who self promote before electoral campaigns is identical to commodity advertising and celebrity glamour.

2   See aphorism number 64 in Adorno's *Minima Moralia* (1974: 101), where he discusses the conventions of popular understanding. He writes:

> Vague expression permits the hearer to imagine whatever suits him and what he already thinks in any case. Rigorous formulation demands unequivocal comprehension, conceptual effort, to which people are deliberately disencouraged, and imposes upon them in advance of any content a suspension of all received opinions, and thus an isolation, that they violently resist... only the word coined by commerce, and really alienated, touches them as familiar. (1974: 101)

3   One is inclined to think that the appeal of shows such as *Jerry Springer* or *Judge Judy* go beyond the mere despising of the individuals at whose expense the celebration of indignity takes place. There is perhaps also an aesthetic of misery inherent in the allure of such shows for the viewer, one in which the viewer inserts him or herself into the position of the guilty party, of he or she who is being publicly stoned; and thus, the viewer unconsciously fantasizes on the possible reprisals of their own indiscretions.

Bibliography

Abercrombie, Nicholas, Stephen Hill and Bryan S. Turner. 1986. *Sovereign Individuals of Capitalism*. London: Allen and Unwin.

Adorno, Theodor. 1967. *Prisms*. Cambridge, MA: MIT Press.

———. 1973 [1966]. *Negative Dialectics*. New York: Continuum.

———. 1974. *Minima Moralia*. London: Verso Editions.

———. 1991. *The Culture Industry: Selected Essays on Mass Culture*. London: Routledge.

———. 1998. "Education after Auschwitz." In *Critical Models: Interventions and Catchwords*. New York: Columbia University Press.

Adorno, Theodor and Max Horkheimer. 1969 [1947]. *Dialectic of Enlightenment*. New York: Continuum.

Althusser, Louis. 1971. "Ideology and Ideological State Apparatuses." *Lenin and Philosophy and Other Essays*. New York: Monthly Review.

Anderson, Benedict. 1983. *Imagined Communities: Reflections on the Origins and Spread of Nationalism*. London: Verso.

Anderson, Karen. 1996. *Sociology: A Critical Introduction*. Toronto: Nelson Canada.

Arendt, Hannah. 1958. *The Human Condition*. Chicago: University of Chicago Press.

———. 1970. *On Violence*. New York: Harcourt Brace.

Arndt, Michael. 2006. *Little Miss Sunshine*. Dayton, Jonathan and Valarie Faris, dirs. Fox Searchlight. Transcript available: www.moviescriptplace.com/data/Little%20Miss%20Sunshine.pdf.

Aronowitz, Stanley. 1994. "Technology and the Future of Work." In Gretchen Bender and Timothy Druckrey (eds), *Culture on the Brink: Ideologies of Technology*. Seattle: Bay Press.

Atyeo, Don. 1979. *Blood and Guts: Violence in Sports*. New York: Paddington.

Axelrod, Robert. 1984. *The Evolution of Cooperation*. New York: Basic.

Barnet, Richard and John Cavanaugh. 1994. *Global Dreams: Imperial Corporations and the New World Order*. Toronto: Touchstone.

Baudrillard, Jean. 1983. *Simulations*. New York: Semiotext(e).

———. 1989. "The Anorexic Ruins." In *Looking Back at the End of the World*. New York: Semiotext(e).

————. 1996. *The System of Objects.* London: Verso.

————. 1994. *The Illusion of the End.* Stanford, CA: Stanford University Press.

————. 1998. *Paroxysm: Interviews with Philippe Petit.* London: Verso.

Bender, Gretchen and Timothy Druckrey, eds. 1994. *Culture on the Brink: Ideologies of Technology.* Seattle: Bay Press.

Benjamin, Jessica. 1988. *The Bonds of Love: Psychoanalysis, Feminism, and the Problem of Domination.* New York: Pantheon.

Benjamin, Walter. 1969. "The Work of Art in the Age of Mechanical Reproduction." In *Illuminations.* New York: Schocken.

————. 1978. "Critique of Violence." In *Reflections.* New York: Schocken.

Berger, John. 1972. *Ways of Seeing.* London: Penguin.

Berman, Morris. 1981. *The Reenchantment of the World.* London: Cornell University Press.

Bernstein, J.M. 1991. "Introduction." In Theodor Adorno, *The Culture Industry: Selected Essays on Mass Culture.* London: Routledge.

Bhabha, Homi K. 1994. *The Location of Culture.* London: Routledge.

Bloom, Harold. 1982. *Agon: Towards a Theory of Revisionism.* New York: Oxford.

Boggs, Carl. 2005. *Imperial Delusions: American Militarism and Endess War.* New York: Rowman and Littlefield.

Bohman, James and Matthias Lutz-Bachman. 1997. *Perpetual Peace: Essays on Kant's Cosmopolitical Ideal.* Cambridge, MA: MIT Press.

Boorstin, Daniel. 1961. "From Hero to Celebrity: The Human Pseudo Event." In Gary Gumpert and Robert Cathcart, eds. *Inter/Media.* New York: Oxford University Press.

Bourdieu, Pierre. 1998. *Acts of Resistance.* New York: New Press.

Bourdieu, Pierre et al. 1999. *The Weight of the World: Social Suffering in Contemporary Society.* Stanford, CA: Stanford University Press.

Bourdieu, Pierre and Loic Wacquant. 1999. "On the Cunning of Imperialist Reason." *Theory Culture and Society* 16(1): 41-58

Bottomore, Tom. eds. 1991. *A Dictionary of Marxist Thought.* 2nd ed. Oxford: Blackwell.

Bourke, Joanna. 1999. *An Intimate History of Killing.* London: Granta.

Brohme, Jean-Marie. 1978. *Sport: A Prison of Measured Time.* London: Ink Links.

Bronner, Stephen Eric and Douglas Kellner, eds. 1989. *Critical Theory and Society: A Reader.* New York: Routledge.

Brown, James. 2000. "Other Means: On the Political Economies of Violence." *Third Text* 51: 91-96.

Burstyn, Varda. 1999. *The Rites of Men: Manhood, Politics and the Culture of Sport.* Toronto: University of Toronto Press.

Busby, Chris, Malak Hamdan and Entesar Ariabi. 2010. "Cancer, Infant Mortality and Birth Sex-Ratio in Fallujah, Iraq 2005–2009." *International Journal of Environmental Research and Public Health* 7: 2828-2837.

Chomsky, Noam.1991. *Necessary Illusions: Thought Control in Democratic Societies.* Toronto: Anansi.

———. 2000. *Rogue States: The Rule of Force in World Affairs.* Cambridge, MA: South End.

Colaguori, Claudio. 2010. "Symbolic Violence and the Violation of Human Rights: Continuing the Critique of Domination." In *International Journal of Criminology and Sociological Theory* 3(2): 388-400.

Colaguori, Claudio and Carlos Torres. 2011. "Policing Terrorism in the Post 9/11 Era: Critical Concerns in an Age of Hypersecurity." In Lorne Tepperman and Angela Kalyta, eds, *Reading Sociology: Canadian Perspectives.* 2nd ed. Toronto: Oxford University Press.

Conner, Steven. 1997. *Postmodern Culture: An Introduction to Theories of the Contemporary.* Cambridge, MA: Blackwell.

Davis, Nannette and Clarice Stasz. 1990. *Social Control of Deviance.* Toronto: McGraw Hill.

Dawkins, Richard. 1976. *The Selfish Gene.* New York: Oxford University Press.

DeBord, Guy. 1995. *The Society of the Spectacle.* New York: Zone.

DeLanda, Manuel. 1991. *War in the Age of Intelligent Machines.* New York: Swerve.

Deleuze, Gilles and Felix Guattari. 1977. *Anti-Oedipus: Capitalism and Schizophrenia.* New York: Viking.

———. 1986. *Nomadology: The War Machine.* New York: Semiotext(e).

———. 1994. *What Is Philosophy?* New York: Columbia University Press.

deVries, Hent and Samuel Weber, eds. 1997. *Violence, Identity and Self Determination.* Stanford, CA: Stanford University Press.

Derrida, Jacques. 1994a. *Specters of Marx.* New York: Routledge.

———. 1994b. *The Gift of Death.* Chicago: University of Chicago Press.

———. 1997. "… And Pomegranates." In Hent deVries and Samuel Weber, eds, *Violence, Identity and Self Determination.* Stanford, CA: Stanford University Press.

———. 1998. *Monolingualism of the Other OR The Prosthesis of Origin.* Stanford, CA: Stanford University Press.

Durant, Will. 1953. *The Story of Philosophy.* New York: Pocket.

Dutton, Dennis. 2009. *The Art Instinct: Beauty, Pleasure and Human Evolution.* New York: Bloomsbury.

Dyer, Gwynne. 1985. *War.* New York: Crown.

Ehrenberg, John. 1999. *Civil Society: The Critical History of an Idea.* New York: New York University Press.

Engels, Friedrich. 1968. "Engels to Franz Mehring." In *Marx-Engels Correspondence 1893.* London: International Publishers

Ewen, Stuart. 1976. *Captains of Consciousness.* Toronto: McGraw-Hill.

———. 1996. *PR! A Social History of Spin.* New York: Basic.

Fanon, Frantz. 1952. *Black Skin, White Masks.* London: MacGibbon and Kee.

Feenberg, Andrew. 1999. *Questioning Technology.* New York: Routledge.

Fekete, John. 1977. *Critical Twilight.* London: Routledge and Kegan Paul.

Fiske, John. 1989. *Understanding Popular Culture.* London: Unwin Hyman.

Fontana, Benedetto. 1993. *Hegemony and Power: On the Relation between Gramsci and Machiavelli.* Minneapolis: University of Minnesota Press.

Foucault, Michel. 1970. *The Order of Things.* London: Tavistock.

———. 1978. *The History of Sexuality Volume 1: An Introduction.* New York: Vintage.

———. 1979. *Discipline and Punish: The Birth of the Prison.* New York: Vintage.

———. 1980. *Power/Knowledge.* New York: Pantheon.

Freud, Sigmund. 1957. "Thoughts for the Times on War and Death." In Ernest Jones (ed.), *The Standard Edition of the Complete Psychological Works*, 14. London: Hogarth.

———. 1961. *Civilization and its Discontents.* London: W.W. Norton.

———. 1986. *The Origins of Religion.* Middlesex: Penguin.

Friedman, George. 1981. *The Political Economy of the Frankfurt School.* London: Cornell University Press.

Friedman, Milton. 1982. *Capitalism and Freedom.* Chicago: University of Chicago Press.

Fromm, Erich. 1973. *The Anatomy of Human Destructiveness.* New York: Holt, Rinehart and Winston.

Fukuyama, Francis. 1992. *The End of History and the Last Man.* New York: Penguin.

Galbraith, John Kenneth. 1998 [1958]. *The Affluent Society.* New York: Mariner.

Gerbner, George. 2002. *Against the Mainstream: The Selected Works of George Gerbner.* Michael Morgan, ed. New York: Peter Lang.

Ghandi, Leela. 1998. *Postcolonial Theory: An Introduction.* New York: Columbia University Press.

Girard, Rene. 1972. *Violence and the Sacred.* Baltimore: Johns Hopkins University Press.

Giroux, Henry. 2005. *Against the New Authoritarianism.* Winnipeg: Arbeiter Ring.

Goldberg, David Theo. 1993. *Racist Culture: Philosophy and the Politics of Meaning.* Cambridge, MA: Blackwell.

Gramsci, Antonio. 1971. *Selections from the Prison Notebooks.* Quinton Hoare, ed. New York: International.

Gray, Chris Hables. 1997. *Postmodern War.* New York: Guilford.

Gray, John. 1996. *Isaiah Berlin.* Princeton, NJ: Princeton University Press.

Habermas, Jürgen. 1971. *Knowledge and Human Interests.* Boston: Beacon.

———. 1984. *The Theory of Communicative Action, Volume One: Reason and the Rationalization of Society.* Boston: Beacon.

———. 1985. *The Philosophical Discourse of Modernity.* Cambridge, MA: MIT Press.

———. 1987. *The Theory of Communicative Action, Volume Two: Lifeworld and System: A Critique of Functionalist Reason.* Boston: Beacon.

———. 1996. *Between Facts and Norms: Contributions to a Discourse Theory of Law and Democracy.* Cambridge, MA: MIT Press.

Haraway, Donna. 1990. "A Manifesto for Cyborgs." In Linda J. Nicholson (ed.), *Feminism/Postmodernism.* New York: Routledge.

Hardt, Michael and Antonio Negri. 2000. *Empire.* Cambridge, MA: Harvard University Press.

Harris, Marvin. 1977. *Cannibals and Kings: The Origins of Culture.* New York: Vintage.

Hegel, G.W.F. 1967 [1931]. *The Phenomenology of Mind.* New York: Harper Torchbooks.

Held, David. 1980. *Introduction to Critical Theory: Horkheimer to Habermas.* Berkeley and Los Angeles: University of California Press.

———. 1987. *Models of Democracy.* Stanford, CA: Stanford University Press.

Heidegger, Martin. 1977. *The Question Concerning Technology.* New York: Harper and Row.

Heilbroner, Robert. 1995. *Visions of the Future: The Distant Past, Yesterday, Today, and Tomorrow.* New York: Oxford University Press.

Herman, Edward S. and Noam Chomsky. 1988. *Manufacturing Consent: The Political Economy of the Mass Media.* New York: Pantheon.

Horkheimer, Max. 1947. *Eclipse of Reason.* New York: Continuum.

———. 1972. "Traditional and Critical Theory." *Critical Theory.* New York: Continuum.

Huizinga, Johan. 1950. *Homo Ludens: A Study of the Play Element in Culture.* Boston: Beacon.

Huntington, Samuel. 1993. *The Clash of Civilizations and the Remaking of World Order.* New York: Simon and Schuster.

Innis, Harold. 1991. *The Bias of Communication.* Toronto: University of Toronto Press.

Jarvis, Simon. 1998. *Adorno: A Critical Introduction.* New York: Routledge.

Jay, Martin. 1973. *The Dialectical Imagination: A History of the Frankfurt School and the Institute for Social Research.* Berkeley and Los Angeles: University of California Press.

Jameson, Frederic and Masao Miyoshi, eds. 1998. *The Cultures of Globalization.* Durham, NC: Duke University Press.

Jenks, Chris. 1993. *Culture.* London: Routledge.

Joxe, Alain. 2002. *Empire of Disorder.* New York: Semiotext(e).

Katz, Jackson. 2006. *The Macho Paradox: Why Some Men Hurt Women and How All Men Can Help.* Naperville, IL: Sourcebooks.

Kant, Immanuel. 1970. "What Is Enlightenment?" In *Political Writings.* Cambridge: Cambridge University Press.

———. 1988. *Fundamental Principles of the Metaphysics of Morals.* New York: Prometheus.

———. 1991. *Political Writings.* Cambridge: Cambridge University Press.

Keane, John. 1996. *Reflections on Violence.* London: Verso.

Kellner, Douglas and Steven Best. 2001. *The Postmodern Adventure: Science, Technology, and Cultural Studies at the Third Millenium.* New York: Guilford.

Kellner, Douglas and Stephen Eric Bronner, eds. 1989. *Critical Theory and Society: A Reader.* New York: Routledge.

Kohn, Alfie. 1986. *No Contest: The Case Against Competition.* Boston: Houghton.

Kohut, Hienz. 1972. "Thoughts on Narcissism and Narcissistic Rage." In *Psychoanalytic Studies of the Child* 27: 360-400.

Krakauer, Eric L. 1998. *The Disposition of the Subject: Reading Adorno's Dialectic of Technology.* Evanston, IL: Northwestern University Press.

Kroker, Arthur and David Cook. 1986. *The Postmodern Scene: Excremental Culture and Hyper Aesthetics.* Montreal: New World Perspectives.

Kuhn, Thomas. 1962. *The Structure of Scientific Revolutions.* Chicago: University of Chicago Press.

Laing, R.D. 1969. *The Divided Self.* London: Penguin.

Lasch, Christopher. 1979. *The Culture of Narcissism.* New York: Warner.

Lasswell, H.D. 1949. "The Structure and Function of Communication in Society." In W.S. Schramm (ed.), *Mass Communication.* Urbana, IL: University of Illinois Press.

LeBon, Gustave. 1925. *The Crowd: A Study of the Popular Mind.* New York: Unwin.

Lee, Martyn J. 2000. *The Consumer Society Reader.* Malden, MA: Blackwell.

Lee, David and Howard Newby. 1986. *The Problem of Sociology.* London: Hutchinson.

Leiss, William. 1972. *The Domination of Nature.* New York: George Braziller.

Leiss, William, Stephen Kline and Sut Jhally. 1990. *Social Communication in Advertising.* Toronto: Nelson Canada.

Lerner, Gerda. 1986. *The Creation of Patriarchy.* New York: Oxford University Press.

Lippmann, Walter. 1922. *Public Opinion.* London: Allen and Unwin.

Lorenz, Konrad. 1966. *On Aggression.* New York: Harcourt, Brace, Jovanovich.

Lovelock, James. 1979. *Gaia: A New Look at Life on Earth.* Oxford: Oxford University Press.

Lukács, Georg. 1971. *History and Class Consciousness.* Cambridge, MA: MIT Press.

Lyotard, Jean-Francois. 1984. *The Postmodern Condition: A Report on Knowledge.* Minneapolis: University of Minnesota Press.

McLuhan, Marshal. 1964. *Understanding Media: The Extensions of Man.* New York: McGraw Hill.

Macpherson, C.B. 1962. *The Political Theory of Possessive Individualism: From Hobbes to Locke.* Oxford: Clarendon Press.

———. 1984. *Democratic Theory: Essays in Retrieval.* Oxford: Clarendon Press.

Machiavelli, Niccolo. 1952. *The Prince.* New York: New American Library.

Magee, Bryan. 1978. "Marcuse and the Frankfurt School: Dialogue with Herbert Marcuse." In Bryan Magee (ed.), *Men of Ideas.* Oxford: Oxford University Press.

Marcuse, Herbert. 1964. *One-Dimensional Man.* Boston: Beacon.

———. 1968. *Negations.* Boston: Beacon.

Marx, Karl and Frederich Engels. 1964. *The German Ideology.* Moscow: Progress.

Melman, Seymour. 1970. *Pentagon Capitalism: The Political Economy of War.* Toronto: McGraw-Hill.

Miliband, Ralph. 1973. *The State in Capitalist Society: An Analysis of the Western System of Power.* New York: Quartet.

Mills, C. Wright. 1956. *The Power Elite.* New York: Oxford University Press.

———. 1959. *The Sociological Imagination.* London: Oxford University Press.

Morin, Edgar. 1989. "Approaches to Nothingness." In Dietmar Kamper and Christof Wulf, eds., *Looking Back at the End of the World.* New York: Semiotext(e).

Morris, Desmond. 1967. *The Naked Ape.* New York: McGraw Hill.

Naiman, Joanne. 2008. *How Societies Work: Class, Power and Change in a Canadian Context.* 4th ed. Halifax: Fernwood.

Nandy, Ashis, ed. 1988. *Science, Hegemony and Violence: A Requiem for Modernity.* Delhi: Oxford University Press.

———.1995. *The Savage Freud and Other Essays on Possible and Retrievable Selves.* Princeton: Princeton University Press.

Nelson, Joyce. 1987. *The Perfect Machine: Television in the Nuclear Age.* Toronto: Between the Lines.

————. 1989. *The Sultans of Sleaze.* Toronto: Between the Lines.

Nietzsche, Friedrich. 1956. *The Birth of Tragedy and the Genealogy of Morals.* Francis Golffing, trans. Garden City, NY: Doubleday.

————. 1957. *The Use and Abuse of History.* London: Collier Macmillan.

O'Neill, John. 1972. *Sociology as a Skin Trade.* London: Heinemann.

————. 1985. *Five Bodies: The Human Shape of Modern Society.* Ithaca: Cornell University Press.

————. 1991. *Plato's Cave: Desire, Power and the Specular Functions of the Media.* Norwood, NJ: Ablex.

————. 1995. *The Poverty of Postmodernism.* New York: Routledge.

O'Neill, John, ed. 1996. *Hegel's Dialectic of Desire and Recognition.* Albany: State University of New York Press.

Ong, Walter J. 1981. *Fighting for Life: Contest, Sexuality, and Consciousness.* Amherst, MA: University of Massachusetts Press.

Orwell, George. 1954. *Nineteen Eighty-Four.* London: Penguin.

Parenti, Michael. 1993. *Inventing Reality: The Politics of the News Media.* New York: St. Martin's.

————.1995. *Against Empire.* San Francisco: City Lights.

————. 1999. *History as Mystery.* San Francisco: City Lights.

Pollock, Frederick. 1989. "State Capitalism: Its Possibilities and Limitations." In Stephen Eric Bronner and Douglas Kellner, eds, *Critical Theory and Society: A Reader.* New York: Routledge.

Popper, Karl. 1986. *The Poverty of Historicism.* London: Arc.

Reiss, Hans, ed. 1991. *Kant: Political Writings.* Cambridge: Cambridge University Press.

Romanyshyn, Robert D. 1989. *Technology as Symptom and Dream.* New York: Routledge.

Rose, Gillian. 1978. *The Melancholy Science: An Introduction to the Thought of Theodor W. Adorno.* London: Macmillan.

Rose, Steven, Leon J. Kamin and Richard C. Lewontin. 1984. *Not in Our Genes: Biology, Ideology and Human Nature.* Toronto: Penguin.

Rosen, Stephen Peter. 2005. *War and Human Nature.* Princeton, NJ: Princeton University Press.

Ruben, Harvey L. 1981. *Competing.* New York: Pinnacle.

Saad, Gad. 2007. *The Evolutionary Basis of Consumption.* Mahwah, NJ: Lawrence Erlbaum/Psychology Press.

————. 2011. *The Consuming Instinct: What Juicy Burgers, Ferraris, Pornography, and Gift Giving Reveal About Human Nature.* New York: Prometheus.

Sachs, Wolfgang. 1992. "One World." In Wolfgang Sachs (ed.), *The Development Dictionary.* Atlantic Highlands, NJ: Zed Books.

Schroyer, Trent. 1973. *The Critique of Domination: The Origins and Development of Critical Theory.* New York: George Braziller.

Schmitt, Carl. 2007. *The Concept of the Political.* Chicago: University of Chicago Press.

Schumpeter, Joseph. 1975 [1942]. *Capitalism, Socialism and Democracy.* Hew York: Harper.

Scott, Alan, ed. 1997. *The Limits of Globalization.* London: Routledge.

Shiva, Vandana. 1988. "Reductionist Science as Epistemological Violence." In Ashis Nandy, ed., *Science, Hegemony and Violence.* Delhi: Oxford University Press.

Simons, John. 1995. *Foucault and the Political.* New York: Routledge.

Surber, Jere Paul. 1998. *Culture and Critique: An Introduction to the Critical Discourses of Cultural Studies.* Boulder, CO: Westview.

Suzuki, David and Holly Dressel. 1999. *From Naked Ape to Super-Species: A Personal Perspective on Humanity and the Global Eco-Crisis.* Toronto: Stoddart.

Taylor, Ian. 1999. *Crime in Context.* Boulder, CO: Westview.

Thompson, E.P. 1967. "Time, Work-Discipline and Industrial Capitalism." In *Past and Present* 38(1): 56-97.

Unger, Roberto Mangabeira. 1998. *Democracy Realized: The Progressive Alternative.* London: Verso.

Van Reijen, Willem. 1992. *Adorno: An Introduction.* Philadelphia: Pennbridge.

Veblen, Thorstein. 1953. *The Theory of the Leisure Class.* New York: Mentor.

Villa, Dana, R. 1999. *Politics, Philosophy, Terror: Essays on the Thought of Hannah Arendt.* Princeton, NJ: Princeton University Press.

Visano, Livy A. 1998. *Crime and Culture.* Toronto: Canadian Scholars' Press.

von Clausewitz, Carl. 1997. *On War.* London: Wordsworth.

Wallerstein, Immanuel. 1974. *The Modern World System.* New York: Academic.

Walzer, Michael. 1977. *Just and Unjust Wars.* N.p.: Basic.

Weber, Max. 1946. *From Max Weber: Essays in Sociology.* H.H. Gerth and C. Wright Mills (eds.), New York: Oxford University Press.

———. 1968. *Economy and Society.* Berkeley and Los Angeles: University of California Press.

Weber, Samuel and Hent deVries, eds. 1997. *Violence, Identity and Self-Determination.* Standford, CA: Stanford University Press.

Wiggerhaus, Rolf. 1995. *The Frankfurt School: Its History, Theories and Political Significance.* Cambridge, MA: MIT Press.

Wilson, E.O. 1975. *Sociobiology: The New Synthesis.* Cambridge, MA: Harvard University Press.

Williams, Raymond. 1976. *Television: Technology and Cultural Form.* New York: Schocken.

———. 1981. *Culture.* London: Fontana.

Williamson, Judith. 1978. *Decoding Advertisements: Ideology and Meaning in Advertising.* London: Marion Boyars.

Wolf, Eric. 1982. *Europe and the People without History.* Berkeley and Los Angeles: University of California Press.

Wolff, Robert Paul. 1969. "On Violence." *Journal of Philosophy* 66(19): 601-616.

Zinn, Howard. 1997. *The Zinn Reader: Writings on Disobedience and Democracy.* New York: Seven Stories.

Subject Index

A

Absolute integration 181, 182, 183, 184, 219

Adversatives 41, 42

Affirmation 7, 21, 30, 31, 51, 96, 129, 149, 179, 183, 187, 203, 206, 207, 211, 213, 224, 236, 247, 250

Agon culture vii, viii, xi, xiii, xiv, xv, 1, 2, 4, 6-12, 18, 20, 21, 23-30, 31, 33, 34, 35, 37, 39, 40, 44-48, 55, 59, 60, 64, 65, 66, 74, 75, 79, 86, 89, 100, 101, 102, 106-109, 119, 120, 121, 127, 128, 131, 132, 139, 150, 151, 173, 176, 179, 181, 182, 183, 185, 187, 188, 190, 191, 192, 194, 198, 200, 201, 203, 204, 218, 219, 220, 222-233, 236, 245, 247, 249

Agon culture, seventeen theses on, 23-30

Agonal discourse xiii, 219, 220, 223, 251

Agonal model of analysis, ix-xi

Agonal rationality 107, 224, 247

Agonal subjectivity 180, 189, 200

Agonism v-ix, xi, xiii, xiv, 2, 4, 5, 8, 10, 11, 23-27, 29, 31-40, 42-45, 47, 48, 49, 52, 53, 64, 68, 69, 74, 75, 98, 102, 104, 105, 106, 108, 113, 117, 127, 129, 130, 131, 135, 147, 153, 189, 193, 199, 200, 202, 204, 211, 212, 217, 219, 221, 223, 225, 226, 228, 231, 233, 235, 236, 241, 242, 247, 248, 249, 251

Agonistic consumerism 65, 82, 214

Agonistic rationality xii, 27, 29, 36, 52, 53, 56, 69, 75, 77, 92, 131, 247

Agonistic values 8, 212, 215, 229

Asymmetrical warfare 12

Authoritarianism 12, 218, 243, 271

B

Biology of selfishness 42

C

Capitalism vi, xi, xii, xv, 9, 11, 15, 18, 19, 34, 39, 44, 53, 55, 58, 61, 65, 67, 70, 71, 77, 81, 83, 84, 88, 89, 92, 98, 105, 133, 134, 140, 143, 152, 155, 156, 170, 171, 179, 185, 188, 207, 222, 224, 230, 235, 239, 242, 249, 255, 257, 258, 263, 267, 269, 271, 274, 275, 276

Commodification 14, 101, 179, 187, 207, 208, 209, 213, 214, 255

Communicative order of control 15, 65

Competition v-xi, xiii, xiv, xv, 1, 2, 4-9, 11, 12, 24, 25, 28, 30-35, 37-41, 43, 45, 69, 74, 78, 80, 84, 105, 108, 118, 122, 157, 163, 167, 168, 171, 172, 173, 176, 188, 189, 191, 192, 200, 211, 212, 215, 216, 218-222, 224, 226-231, 239, 245, 250, 256, 273

Competition, as ideology of neo-liberal capitalism xv

Competitive culture 81, 161, 175

Consciousness vi, viii, x, xiv, xv, xvi, 2, 4, 11-16, 21, 23, 28, 31, 35, 40, 42, 43, 47, 53, 54, 55, 59, 74, 79, 80, 83, 85-88, 94, 100, 101, 102, 110, 113, 120, 129, 139, 142, 144, 147, 148, 150, 175-203, 206, 214, 219, 221, 222, 227, 247, 248, 250, 254, 263, 270, 274, 275

Consumerism 9, 18, 21, 27, 35, 65, 67, 75, 78, 81, 82, 85, 101, 102, 137, 177, 180, 202, 209, 210, 212, 213, 214

Consumption vii, 13, 21, 82, 101, 159, 207, 208, 211, 213, 214, 216, 219, 257, 264, 265, 276

Crisis management 152, 153

Critical theory v, x-xv, 10, 16, 71, 83, 89, 90, 91, 94-97, 109, 135, 185, 195, 253, 263, 268, 272, 273, 275, 276

Cultural domination 10, 18, 21, 23, 36, 51, 65, 79, 102, 178-181, 183, 187, 190, 196, 219, 263

Cultural mimesis (see also mimesis) 39, 193

Cultural products 13, 52

Cultural subjectivity 200, 207

Culture v-xvi, 1, 2, 4-35, 37, 39, 40, 43-48, 51, 55, 57, 59, 60, 64, 65, 66, 70, 74, 75, 79, 81, 85, 86, 87, 89, 91, 92, 93, 95, 100, 101, 102, 105-109

Culture as preservation xv

Culture industry 10-15, 47, 81, 177, 183, 184, 185, 207, 209, 226, 230, 238, 239, 254, 267, 268

D

Darwinian evolutionary theory 172, 176

Dialectic of domination 23, 102, 195, 199, 207, 256

Dialectic of recognition 193, 197

Dialectical method 148

Dialectics 34, 95, 137, 147, 149, 151, 267

Disciplinary order 99, 104

Discourse, defined, 220

Disfiguration of perception 190

E

Eclipse of reason 66, 272

Enlightenment viii, xiv, 11-14, 25, 38, 47-56, 61, 66-74, 75, 83, 86, 91, 92, 97, 105, 114, 123, 137, 143, 164, 183, 208, 248, 256, 257, 267, 272

Ethics 73, 87, 88, 89, 110, 113, 248, 262

Extremification ix, 12, 227

F

Frankfurt School v, xii, 27, 71, 134, 185, 218, 270, 272, 274, 277

G

Global culture 7

Global village 17, 18

Globalization xii, xv, 7, 12, 17, 18, 24, 34, 48, 73, 82, 86, 101, 133, 134, 137, 144, 155, 204, 249, 250, 254, 262, 272, 276

Globalization of exploitation 18

H

Hegelian historicism 147

Hegemonic culture 10, 178

Hegemonized 15, 20, 22

Hegemony vii, 10, 12, 15, 18-22, 48, 97, 98, 99, 102, 226, 254, 270, 274, 276

History of domination 138, 145

Human nature xiv, 28, 37, 43, 108, 157, 158, 159, 161-167, 170, 171, 172, 198, 275, 276

Humanity 51, 53, 60, 62, 72, 79, 85, 87, 105, 122, 152, 154, 161, 276

I

Identity thinking 194

Ideological state apparatus 99, 242

Ideologies of conflict 34

Ignorance 49, 93, 150, 177, 183, 184

Individualism 1, 5, 50, 52, 66, 67, 72, 74, 82, 199, 201, 203, 207, 211, 257, 274

Instinct 157-163, 167-170, 172, 270, 276

L

Lament 64, 91, 93, 94, 95, 121

Liberalism ix, 9, 35, 36, 72, 73, 77, 156, 250

M

Machiavellianism 6

Marxism 20, 134, 143

Mass deception 11, 13, 15, 23, 95

Mass society 15, 16, 17, 21, 53, 181, 183

McCarthyism 204

Media vii, viii, xi, 10, 11, 12, 14-18,

23, 24, 26, 29, 47, 64, 65, 72, 99, 105, 108, 119, 120, 121, 126, 128, 163, 184, 210, 218, 222, 225-231, 236, 238, 239, 243, 244, 254, 259, 265, 268, 272, 274, 275

Mediagon 11, 12, 26, 48, 80, 106, 108, 121, 128, 189, 217, 219, 226-229, 235, 236, 248

Mental production 15, 179

Militarism 9, 32, 48, 61, 119, 128, 218, 224, 236, 268

Military metaphor 225

Mimesis 39, 112, 114, 187, 193, 194, 196, 256

Mythology vi, vii, viii, xv, 27, 35, 38, 42-48, 54, 70, 130, 138, 147, 164, 228, 248

N

Normalization 8, 18, 33, 34, 48, 71, 81, 86, 102, 104, 107, 108, 109, 119, 120, 122, 138, 140, 198, 244, 260, 261

Normalization of war 48, 86, 107, 108, 119, 120

O

Objectification 100, 187, 202, 224

Ontological insecurity 129, 156, 198, 214

P

Patriotism 21, 22, 202, 203, 206, 218, 245

Political subjectivity 66, 200, 202, 203

Popular ideology 165, 219

Positivism 28, 43, 47, 94, 134, 138, 143, 148

Postmodern theory 155

Power of ideology 15

Programming 90, 164, 228

Prosthesis of identity 85

R

Rationalization ix, 29, 74, 86, 101-104, 179, 191, 264, 271

Rationalization of society 101, 271

Reification v, vi, viii, x, xii, xiii, xvi, 7, 9, 25, 27-30, 46, 68, 100, 113, 122, 129, 131, 146, 150, 175-194, 199, 200, 202, 203, 206, 211, 214, 215, 223, 231, 234, 235, 236, 243, 247, 256, 263, 264

Repressive progress 85

Repressive satisfaction 25, 178, 186, 263

Resistance to reification, 190-193

S

Self as enemy 212, 215

Self preservation 28, 122, 175, 176, 189

Self-fetishization 82, 127

Self-interest 21, 50, 66-69, 89, 105, 187, 200, 201, 202, 207, 223, 257

Simulacrum 38

Social control xiii, 11, 16, 44, 72, 101, 102, 110, 134, 152, 153, 170, 173, 185, 207, 269

Social power 37

Social regulation 99, 103, 165, 181, 200, 203, 212

Social technology 14, 65

Sovereign individual 66, 205, 210

Sovereignty 49, 62, 67, 68, 69, 72, 74, 81, 112, 202, 203, 205, 257, 260

Sport vi, vii, ix, xi, xii, 3, 4, 11, 25, 28, 29, 61, 217, 218, 222, 224, 227, 233, 234, 235, 237, 239-245, 248, 268, 269

Subjugation xi, 5, 8, 51, 55, 110, 207

Survival xiii, 33, 38, 39, 42, 54, 55, 56, 92, 101, 114, 115, 167, 173, 180, 181, 193, 199, 215, 221, 227, 231-235, 253

T

Technological control 53, 55

Technological rationality 56, 57

Technological revolutions 61

Technology 14, 17, 50, 52, 55-65, 91, 92, 102, 105, 115, 121, 126, 130,

226, 227, 254, 267, 268, 270, 272,
273, 275, 277

Traditional theory 90

Transcendence v, vi, xiv, 8, 9, 11, 26,
28, 29, 32, 33, 35, 49, 51, 52, 56, 68,
94, 139, 144, 146, 189, 191, 192,
199, 219, 239, 248, 251, 263

U

Utilitarianism 68, 143, 202

V

Violence vi, vii, ix, xv, 3, 4, 5, 8, 9, 24,
25, 33, 35, 36, 37, 40, 43-47, 54, 62,
64, 74, 79, 86, 99, 102, 104, 107,
109-114, 117-120, 128-135, 138,
140, 154, 157-163, 165, 166

W

War, biblical, 123-130

War, justification of, 117-122

Warfare state 109, 111, 118

Western civilization 49, 82, 83, 141,
170

Name Index

A

Abercrombie, N. 67, 199, 205, 257, 267

Adorno, T. v, ix, xi, xii-xv, 1-4, 6, 7, 11-17, 22, 23, 26-32, 38, 46, 47, 49, 50-53, 55, 56, 57, 67, 70, 71, 73, 74, 78, 81, 83, 86, 90, 91, 93, 94, 95, 97, 98, 100, 103, 104, 106, 112, 119, 137, 138, 140, 141, 145-148, 150, 152, 154, 155, 167, 170, 175-181, 185-194, 198, 201, 203, 204, 205, 211, 219, 221-226, 230, 234, 236, 237, 242, 253, 254, 256, 259, 263, 264, 265, 267, 268, 272, 273, 275, 276

Agamben, G. v

Althusser, L. 99, 102, 111, 184, 245, 267

Anderson, B. 254, 267

Anderson, K. 127, 263, 267

Arendt, H. 36, 104, 132, 144, 145, 157, 165, 166, 267, 276

Ariabi, E. 125, 269

Arndt, M. 217, 267

Aronowitz, S. 57, 267

Atyeo, D. 243, 244, 267

Axelrod, R. 164, 267

B

Barnet, R. 134, 267

Baudrillard, J. 24, 65, 150, 155, 156, 207, 208, 210, 235, 263, 264, 267

Bender, G. 57, 127, 267, 268

Benjamin, J. 103, 139, 195, 196, 268

Benjamin, W. 15, 44, 105, 111, 131, 145, 256, 268

Berger, J. 209, 210, 211, 268

Berman, M. 53, 54, 264, 268

Bernstein, J.M. 47, 175, 187, 268

Bhabha, H. 197, 198, 268

Bloom, H. 129, 228, 268

Bohman, J. 258, 268

Boorstin, D. 238, 241, 268

Bottomore, T. 20, 139, 180, 268

Bourdieu, P. 85, 133, 250, 268

Bourke, J. 117, 121, 122, 234, 268

Brohme, J-M. 268

Bronner, S. 268, 273, 275

Brown, J. 105, 111, 130, 131, 135, 269

Burstyn, V. 240, 269

Busby, C. 125, 269

C

Cavanaugh, J. 267

Chomsky, N. 99, 117, 123, 124, 125, 127, 254, 261, 269, 272

Colaguori, C. xvi, 110, 114, 269

Conner, S. 85, 269

Cook, D. 85, 273

D

Davis, N. 108, 109, 259, 261, 269

Dawkins, R. 41, 42, 269

DeBord, G. 65, 208, 211 269

DeLanda, M. 63, 117, 269

Deleuze, G. xii, 61, 81, 99, 111, 155, 260, 269

Derrida, J. 10, 11, 60, 64, 77 79, 85, 90, 112, 118, 126, 130, 133, 140, 151, 156, 254, 259, 261, 269

deVries, H. 130, 269

Dressel, H. 156, 276

Druckrey, T. 57, 59, 65, 127, 265, 267, 268

Durant, W. 139, 270

Dutton, D. 159, 270

Dyer, G. 111, 259, 270

E

Ehrenberg, J. 133, 270

Engels, F. 102, 190, 270

Ewen, S. 209, 254, 270

F

Fanon, F. 85, 132, 197, 258, 270

Feenberg, A. 59 270

Fekete, J. 254, 270
Fiske, J. 185, 270
Fontana, B. 254, 270
Foucault, M. 47, 99, 104, 114, 115, 134, 148, 154, 178, 204, 220, 255, 259, 270
Freud, S. 101, 168, 242, 256, 270
Friedman, G. 71, 105, 263, 270
Fromm, E. 160, 271
Fukuyama, F. 77, 149, 271

G

Galbraith, J. 210, 261, 263, 264, 271
Gerbner, G. 184, 231, 271
Ghandi, L. 154, 271
Girard, R. 256, 271
Giroux, H. 218, 271
Goldberg, D. 51, 73, 258, 271
Gramsci, A. 18, 270
Gray, C., 63, 118, 271
Gray, J., 32, 36, 104, 271
Guattari, F. 61, 81, 99, 111, 155, 260, 269

H

Habermas, J. 66, 94, 185, 191, 208, 271
Hamdan, M. 125, 269
Haraway, D. 61, 271
Hardt, M. 254, 271
Harris, M. 61, 111, 157, 161, 162, 167, 256, 271
Hegel, G. 23, 26, 41, 68, 138, 139, 141, 143, 144, 146, 148, 155, 164, 194, 196, 207, 263, 272
Heidegger, M. 59, 272
Heilbroner, R. 62, 85, 272
Held, D. 44, 50, 68, 71, 100, 104, 133, 149, 158, 160, 167, 169, 184, 185, 192, 194, 227, 257, 259, 272
Herman, E. 99, 254, 272
Hill, S. 199, 205, 257, 267
Horkheimer, M. ix, xiii-xvi, 11, 13, 23, 27, 46, 49, 50, 51, 53, 55, 66, 69, 70, 73, 83, 86, 89, 91-93, 94, 95, 97,
152, 177, 180, 181, 187, 188, 191, 192, 194, 203, 211, 219, 223, 225, 230, 254, 256, 262, 263, 267
Huizinga, J. 32, 172, 272
Huntington, S. 116, 272

I

Innis, H. 17, 58, 272

J

Jameson, F. 7, 86, 134, 254, 272
Jarvis, S. 45, 94, 138, 187, 194, 272
Jay, M. 71, 185, 272
Jenks, C. 165, 272
Joxe, A. 109, 272

K

Kamin, L. 275
Kant, I. 73, 123, 183, 258, 262, 268
Katz, J. 240, 272
Keane, J. 131, 273
Kellner, D. 34, 63, 70, 118, 256, 268, 273, 275
Kohn, A. 157, 172, 273
Kohut, H. 193, 273
Krakauer, E. 53, 91, 186, 273
Kroker, A. 85, 273
Kuhn, T. 148, 273

L

Laing, R. 214, 273
Lasch, C. 192, 273
Lasswell, H. 16, 273
LeBon, G. 182, 227, 273
Lee, D. 19, 273
Lee, M. 208, 273
Leiss, W. 55, 213, 273
Lerner, G. 32, 169, 273
Lewontin, C. 275
Lippmann, W. 17, 273
Lorenz, K. 164, 273
Lovelock, J. 56, 274
Lukács, G. 100, 175, 179, 180, 191, 263, 274
Lutz-Bachman, M. 258, 268
Lyotard, J-F. 90, 155, 274

M

Machiavelli, N. 19, 270, 274
Macpherson, C. 67, 199, 201, 274
Magee, B. 83, 84, 211, 257, 259, 274
Marcuse, H. xii, xiii, 15, 25, 52, 56, 57, 71, 72, 83, 84, 90, 103, 118, 141, 178, 199, 207, 210, 211, 218, 235, 253, 257, 258, 259, 274
Marx, K. 14, 15, 19, 20, 67, 70, 77, 93, 102, 119, 138, 140, 141, 142, 143, 151, 152, 155, 179, 190, 207, 257, 269, 270, 274
McLuhan, M. 17, 254, 274
Melman, S. 63, 100, 261, 274
Miliband, R. 22, 98, 274
Mills, C. 16, 84, 109, 116, 123, 182, 260, 274, 276
Miyoshi, M. 7, 86, 134, 254, 272
Morin, E. 87, 274
Morris, D. 53, 164, 165, 268, 274

N

Naiman, J. 159, 274
Nandy, A. 53, 73, 124, 274, 276
Negri, A. 254, 271
Nelson, J. 53, 58, 61, 63, 64, 65, 118, 124, 125, 208, 267, 273, 274
Newby, H. 19, 273
Nietzsche, F. 9, 139, 147, 149, 150, 170, 262, 275

O

O'Neill, J. 15, 18, 61, 63, 65, 68, 82, 89, 90, 98, 101, 102, 104, 127, 128, 134, 138, 140, 143, 192, 196, 204, 205, 208, 210, 215, 254, 256, 259, 261, 264, 275
Ong, W. 40, 41, 43, 256, 275
Orwell, G. xiii, 119, 182, 275

P

Parenti, M. 99, 145, 148, 153, 254, 259, 261, 262, 275
Pollock, F. 71, 257, 275
Popper, K. 137, 275

R

Reiss, H. 262, 275
Romanyshyn, R. 62, 85, 275
Rose, G. 15, 140, 185, 257, 275
Rose, S. 275
Rosen, S. 159, 275
Ruben, H. 172, 275

S

Saad, G. 159, 275
Sachs, W. 259, 276
Schmitt, C. 204, 276
Schroyer, T. 94, 276
Schumpeter, J. 105, 276
Scott, A. 134, 276
Shiva, V. 62, 276
Simons, J. 36, 276
Stasz, C. 108, 109, 259, 261, 269
Surber, J. 19, 20, 49, 50, 51, 163, 184, 276
Suzuki, D. 156, 276

T

Taylor, I. 1, 229, 276
Thompson, E. 58, 208, 276
Torres, C. 110, 114, 269
Turner, B.S. 199, 205, 257, 267

U

Unger, R. 133, 276

V

Van Reijen, W. 106, 276
Veblen, T. 213, 264, 276
Villa, D. 36, 104, 276
Visano, L. 127, 224, 264, 276
von Clausewitz, C. viii, 254, 276

W

Wacquant, L. 262, 268
Wallerstein, I 151, 276
Walzer, M. 121, 276
Weber, S. 2, 52, 72, 98, 103, 105, 111, 112, 130, 133, 209, 257, 259, 264, 269
Wiggerhaus, R. 71, 277
Williams, R. 7, 14, 17, 210, 277
Williamson, J. 184, 213, 277

Wilson, E. 43, 164, 277
Wolf, E. 148, 160, 277
Wolff, R. 111, 277
Z
Zinn, H. 148, 161, 168, 169, 277

CPSIA information can be obtained at www.ICGtesting.com
Printed in the USA
LVOW04s1923270515

440149LV00006B/21/P